WE SHALL NEVER PASS THIS WAY AGAIN

Stories from Oshkosh's Historic Past

By
Randy R. Domer

First published by Dog Ear Publishing
4011 Vincennes Road
Indianapolis, IN 46268
www.dogearpublishing.net

ISBN: 978-145756-472-7

This book is printed on acid-free paper.
Printed in the United States of America

Product and Brand Trademarks and Copyrights implied with
font italicization, capitalization and parentheses

Riding the White Mule: Oshkosh During Prohibition © Lee Reiherzer
A Child Disappears © Patti Yana

Photo Cover Credits:
Asylum - Julaine Farrow Museum
Garcia - Ed Tiedje
Brewery - Lee Reiherzer
Turkeys - Stanley Schuster
Author - Lee Fenendael

Dedication

To Clarence "Inky" Jungwirth - A man whom I admire,
that dedicated himself to telling "the story"
for the benefit of future generations.
May his wonderful memories and stories carry us forward

Here's to the songs we used to sing...
And here's to the times we used to know...
It's hard to hold them in our arms again, but...
Hard to let them go

—Neil Diamond (If You Know What I Mean)

TABLE OF CONTENTS

INTRODUCTION

Much has changed in my lifetime…I'm sure you can say the same. Memories of those days gone by seem like they happened only yesterday.

As I look back, I'd like to begin with a few things you may be able to relate to…

I remember once exclaiming emphatically, "That will be the day when I _PAY_ to watch my television. There is a perfectly good antenna on the roof that gets _ALL_ the Green Bay stations. And if you don't mind a little fuzz, on a clear day you sometimes even get Milwaukee! And it's _ALL FREE!_" Well, we all know how that worked out.

I remember the first time I saw bottled water being sold. I had a big laugh with that one, "Who in their right mind would _BUY_ water? Water is _FREE!_" Today, at most entertainment venues, a bottle of water sells for between two and three bucks!

Then, to top it all off, something happened to me recently.

I noticed one of my vehicle tires was low on air. I knew that because a warning light came on in my vehicle alerting me that I had a tire pressure problem. That wasn't enough information for me, so I went to the diagnostic buttons located on my dash and hit INFO, TIRE PRESSURE, and there, on the LED screen on my dash, it told me my rear right tire had only 28 PSI, well below standard operating levels. Actually, I could have avoided all this had I just gone home and turned on my laptop. There, I would find an email from the car manufacturer, sparing me no detail, that they received an alert from my vehicle, what the problem was, how to fix it, what would happen if I did _NOT_ fix it, and who to call if I needed help. (I don't recall giving my vehicle permission to talk directly to its birth mother) Well, all this is fine and good. But let me get back to the purpose of this story.

When I arrived at the gas station, I scanned the property to locate the air hose so I could inflate my tire and be on my way. I located it and pulled up alongside. I grabbed the hose, removed the valve stem cap from the tire, attached the air hose…nothing. I tried again…thinking perhaps I wasn't holding the hose nozzle on just right. Nothing again. Feeling a little inept, I went over to the air station and did something most of us men hate to do. I read the directions on the pump. It seems I missed one important detail…insert four quarters. A BUCK for air! My thoughts raced. "WAIT! Isn't air free?" Just like water and TV…I was wrong.

Thinking back on the way things were earlier in my life makes one wonder what the next twenty or thirty years will bring. What we sometimes take for granted today, will undoubtedly make us smile tomorrow.

People ask each time one of my books is published, "Are you going to do another one?" My answer, unequivocally, is always the same, "I will, if I find enough interesting material." For good reason, that has not been a problem. Truth be told, there is a vast amount of "new stories" if one looks hard enough.

We Shall Never Pass This Way Again is another collection of stories I found to be both interesting and educational. The "anchor chapter" for this book is titled '*Four Miles North*'. What started out as a story about the two cemeteries created by the county and state asylums, quickly turned into so much more. It pulled me down a path where I felt I could not find the end. This chapter could easily be a book within itself, evidenced by a couple of books written by others before me. Personal insights by current and retired staff members of both the state and county institutions helped me assemble details on life on the inside…four miles north.

As stories came to light for this book, I found myself, on occasion, wandering out to the edge of town and sometimes into nearby communities just a stone's throw away. They may be considered outside the Oshkosh city limits, but in our minds the entire areas surrounding our great city was considered "home".

In some chapters, you will meet people whose names might be unrecognizable, but find their accomplishments astonishing.

I enjoyed my face-to-face interviews with folks who had interesting stories to share. Sitting with Al Repp at the end of the bar, listening to him spin tale after tale about his life in his family's neighborhood tavern. The Bradley family so proudly shared with me memories of their egg farm business. Richard and Robert Miller reminisced about their family farm and the days when they made their living growing and selling horseradish. I enjoyed listening to members of my family recalling their memories of growing up on the Schuster Turkey Farm.

You will delight to learn about the pole sitter perched high above the Raulf Hotel and the day Gene Autry, the singing cowboy, rode into town.

I also invited a few guest authors and fellow historians to contribute a story of their choice. Patti Yana, Dan Radig, Dan Butkiewicz, Kevin Lisowe and Lee Reiherzer, graciously agreed and have unearthed some very interesting pieces of local history that I know you will enjoy.

Please join me now, on another journey through time.

GROWING UP IN THE 50S AND 60S

In my first book, *Yesterday In Oshkosh…My Hometown*, I wrote about what life was like in my neighborhood as a kid in the fifties and sixties. Where we lived was still considered rural with field and farms surrounding what would someday be a vibrant neighborhood of new homes, a new high school and a neighborhood supermarket.

I guess you could say we lived out in the "pickers".

In my next book, *Oshkosh: Land of Lakeflies, Bubblers and Squeaky Cheese*, my trip down memory lane included a broader view of happenings from both a local and national landscape. Events like war, presidential assassinations, the space race, etc. were events that shaped our adolescent lives during those turbulent years.

Here we are today, a few years later, a few more grey hairs, and fading in the distance are those memories that seem like they happened only yesterday. Our Medicare card is tucked firmly into our wallet. One look in the mirror reminds us of our mortality, and those days gone by seem ever so dear and precious as we wrestle to hold on to them. As we pause and look around, we have lost two Beatles, two Bee Gees, one Everly Brother and countless others who were a big part of our coming of age. We now subscribe to the local newspaper, not necessarily looking for newsworthy items, but to check the obituaries.

The "fire in my belly" urges me to keep writing about Oshkosh's historic past…it is what keeps me going. There is a rich and wonderful offering of stories that we must leave behind for the next generations who will follow in our footsteps, forging a new local history of their own. My grandchildren will never understand the feeling of life without computers, digital games, and cell phones. My youngest grandson at only 14 months old already knows how a cell phone and TV remote control works!

One thing I have learned from writing these stories is that the people of Oshkosh love to reminisce. Whether I'm at the Oshkosh Saturday Farmers Market, or presenting a book talk, scores of people will approach me and want to share their stories and memories. We all love to recall those days when we were young and life seemed so much simpler. Fellow local authors like Clarence "Inky" Jungwirth and Ron LaPoint have forged the way with local history and their books continue to be very popular. I'm sad to say that we lost our friend Clarence Jungwirth in January of 2018. He left behind so many wonderful stories and writings for us to learn from and enjoy. He will be dearly missed by this community.

I like to tell folks, with a wink and a smile, that my definition of *irony* is this: In high school, US History was my least favorite subject. I barely passed the class, and I struggled to even stay awake during those arduous 55 minutes. Today, I am President of the Winnebago County Historical & Archaeological Society and I am on the board of directors for the Butte des Morts Historical Preservation Society and the Oshkosh Public Museum. It seems that it's later in life before many of us learn to appreciate the past.

So here is another look back at a few more of my favorite memories growing up in Oshkosh during the 1950s and 60s.

One of my dad's favorite pastimes was fishing. He bought a boat from Hergert's Sport Center around 1961. On the weekend we would head out, but not without first stopping to pick up some bait. Occasionally we would stop at the Beer Depot on Oshkosh Ave that also sold bait, but this day we would visit von Hoff's bait shop. Albert von Hoff owned a bait shop in a marshy area near the edge of the Fox River at the very end of Taft Avenue and along Campbell Road where the area was still pretty much undeveloped. As a kid I would have never expected it, but von Hoff, as it turns out, was an interesting man in his own right. His obituary in 1983 stated that Albert was a professional fighter named "Tommy Lane" in the 1920s.

Dad would park his car with boat and trailer along the side of Campbell Road. He would grab his metal minnow bucket and walk toward the ramshackle building meant to be a bait shop. We balanced our way precariously across old 2"x10" planks that allowed us to cross the swampy ground that led to the shack. Inside was a dimly lit bulb and a metal tank with an aeration pump that hummed as it churned the water, feeding oxygen to the mass of minnows. "Gimme a dozen shiners and some crawlers," my Dad would call out. Without saying a word, von Hoff grabbed the well-worn dip net and took a healthy scoop into the tank – carefully placing the swirling mass of wiggling minnows into dad's bucket. If one or two would miss the pail and fall to the floor, von Hoff would kick at them with his boot toward one of the cracks in floor where the minnow would find freedom in the water below. He then turned to his old, rusty, refrigerator and grabbed a carton of night crawlers. During this time, Dad would try to ply von Hoff with some key questions on "where they were biting and what were they biting on?" von Hoff mumbled a few things that I figured with my ten-year old mind were probably made up, because we all know fish do not bite in the same place every day. Dad thanked him for the fishing tips that were sure to pay big dividends, paid what was due and we were on our way.

Down to Rainbow Park we drove. Typically, this time of year, the launching docks were full and parking spots were scarce, and this day did not fail to fulfill our expectations. Dad would grumble a few words but eventually find a spot to park the car and trailer. Soon we jumped in the boat and off we went to our favorite fishing holes.

Fishing took other forms for me when dad worked during the day, as youngsters we were pretty much on our own. One could always find one of the neighborhood kids who wanted to go fishing. We'd ride our bicycles down to the far north end of Lark Street to Sawyer Creek. (It was always pronounced *crik*, not Creek). We would throw out a line baited with a big juicy nightcrawler and a bobber, put the rod between some rocks and wait. To pass the time we would walk along the shore line, balancing on the rocks. An occasional slip would usually find you with a "soaker", but it didn't seem to matter much as it did not deter us from continuing…that is until the bobber went down! Our efforts were usually rewarded with a catfish or bullhead, and the occasional giant carp would really add some excitement to our day. One day while feeling adventurous, I started casting with a red and white daredevil. After several casts I was surprised when a huge northern pike hit my bait and the fight was on! After about five minutes I landed that beauty, added it to my stringer, and jumped on my bike and headed home. I couldn't wait to show off my trophy catch!

Sawyer Creek, and the woods in which it meandered westward, always provided some sort of adventure. We liked to follow the creek as it wound its way from the Fox River to the west, through the "Big Woods" as we called it. It continued on through the grassy fields toward highway 41 where it would pass underneath the highway. There was no Kmart or even Pollock Pool back then. By the time the creek reached that point it narrowed considerably. Being enterprising young boys, we concocted the idea to use rocks to damn the creek, narrowing the passageway, realizing that any fish trying to navigate its way west would have to pass through our "trap". We found some sticks and used a jack knife to sharpen a point, making it one heck of a fish spear! The only thing that came along was a few suckers, but nonetheless, we were entertained and managed to spear a few. That fun lasted until one day a game warden approached us. He had been driving by on highway 41 and saw us. "You boys know whatcher doin' is illegal dontcha?" We were too scared to even answer. He was big and with the uniform and all…my thoughts immediately turned to how mad my dad was going to be when he came to bail us out of jail! After a sound lecture and good scolding, the warden was convinced we learned our lesson and let us go on our way. Needless to say, that was the last time we tried that.

Our other fishing excursions would take us to South Park. Armed only with a few scraps of liver and a casting rod, our goal was to land the elusive crayfish. The end goal here was not to get enough for a meal, but just enjoy the challenge of getting those little critters to shore. After examining them and testing the strength of their claws, we would release them back into the lagoon.

Christmas always was, and is, my most favorite time of the year. Each year, our parents would enroll us in the Christmas Club. Christmas Clubs were organized by savings institutions to encourage one to save money for Christmas shopping. In the early years it was at the First National Bank on Main Street, later with the Oshkosh Savings and Loan. We would deposit 25¢ a week and around the first of November we'd receive our check for around $13. That would be more than enough to buy something for mom, dad, and my sister Debbie (my brother Corey was not yet born). After I was married we continued the same tradition with our children. The Savings and Loan would give a free acrylic Christmas ornament for each account opened. We still hang those ornaments on our Christmas tree today.

Christmas was always an exciting time of year. My parents would both go "all out" with decorating our house for the holidays. Mom had dozens of "knick-knacks" that were displayed in the living room and kitchen. Glass wax and stencils were used to decorate the windows. Our kitchen counter always had a large wooden bowl full of assorted nuts, still in the shell. A nutcracker and pick were on hand to accommodate the shelling process. A lazy-susan was located on the kitchen counter that held the holiday cheer. Bottles of brandy, whiskey, and of course the quart size bottles of *Penguin* soda and sour were available for serving guests. Add a jigger, an ice bucket, some cherries, olives and cocktail napkins complete with funny sayings, a good supply of *Peoples* beer in the "fridge", and our holiday bar was ready. It was common back then for "company" to visit, especially during the holidays. Family and friends would come, mom would serve some food, dad would mix drinks and then all would gather around the living room and Christmas tree while mom showed all the gifts.

My dad, who was quite talented as an artist and sign painter, would rise to the occasion every Christmas. I must admit, he had a little "Clark Griswold" in him as he was determined to go to any extreme to collect the prize money awarded by the City of Oshkosh each year for the best outdoor Christmas display. It varied from year-to-year, but it always was spectacular. Santa and his sleigh being pulled by eight reindeer spanned the entire peak of our roof, full-sized carolers were painted with water colors on our front bay window. One year a giant red and white striped stocking bulging with gifts went from the ground to 8 feet over the roof's edge. Christmas music was piped outside adding to the festivities.

Every year when the new school year started, we really looked forward to getting new clothes and school supplies. The best thing was getting new tennis shoes for gym class. High-top *Converse* were the brand and style everyone wanted, and they were available in black or white. There really was not a large variety of shoe brands and styles available like there is today. Back then a good pair of "tennies" cost less than five bucks. When you took them to school, you'd tie the shoes together by the laces and hang them around the post on your desk seat. When it was time for gym class, you would change into your "tennies", then back into your street shoes after returning to your classroom. Street shoes were *never* allowed in the Roosevelt gymnasium.

Dress codes were firmly adhered to at school. Blue jeans were not allowed and the girls had to wear skirts or dresses. Blue jeans, or overalls as we called them, were meant for play, not school. You wore them until you had holes in the knees, then mom would cover the holes with patches and we continued to wear them until the patches wore out. Usually by then, you grew out of them.

Another school memory I fondly recall is when the teacher would select a student to take the blackboard erasers down the Boiler Room where the janitors work area would be. You would exchange them for clean ones and return to class.

A *least* favorite memory of mine was when they added square dancing to the "gym class" curriculum. Adolescent boys were not into "swing your partner", "promenades", and "dosey-does". However, "murder ball" was an absolute favorite.

Each school day, our mornings would start with the Pledge of Allegiance to the Flag. Every classroom had an American flag standing in the corner. When signaled by our teacher, we would rise, stand next to our desk, face the flag with our right hand over our heart. *I pledge allegiance to the Flag of the United States of America, and to the republic for which it stands, one nation under God, indivisible, with liberty and justice for all.* I always felt it was a reminder of what a great country we are so fortunate in which to be living. As children our respect went a lot further than it does today. We respected our teachers, the policeman, our parents, and adults in general. We obeyed the law and rules that governed right from wrong.

Another of our favorite family pastimes was "hickory nutting". We would take a Sunday afternoon drive in the country each fall and find a small country cemetery where the fence lines were full of shag bark hickory nut trees. It was a tradition that carried on into our married life with our children as well...Grandma and Grandpa Steinert included. The grandparents would pack a picnic lunch and off we would go. Grandpa Steinert grew up in the rural areas of the county so he knew all the best places. Once we arrived, we found a good spot to layout a couple of blankets and eat our picnic lunch that Grandma Steinert had prepared. Once our picnic was finished, everyone was handed an old five-quart ice cream pail and the search for hickory nuts would begin. We'd spread out over the cemetery and the pickings were usually very easy. After an hour or so, we'd gather together and empty our pails into a large box Grandpa had in the trunk of his car.

At home is where the "real" work would begin. Grandpa would take the nuts out to his shop behind the garage and gently tap each one with a hammer, breaking the heavy, hard outside shell. Then he and Grandma would sit in the evenings, while watching television, with a bowl on their lap and nut cracker and pick in hand, carefully shelling out the delicious nut meats held tightly inside. It would take hours of work to get a small jar of cleaned hickory nut meats. Grandma Steinert used them in banana nut bread, on top of frosted cakes and even in her fresh fruit salad. They were delicious!

As kids, we had no electronic games or devices to keep us occupied all day. We were always looking to find new ways to play and entertain ourselves. One of things I enjoyed was bowling. I learned to bowl at an early age. My good friend Eddie Buttke and I, would catch the city bus every Saturday morning on Sawyer Street, one block south of Roosevelt School. The bus route only came that far south on Sawyer Street, so we had to walk the seven blocks to the bus stop. The bus took us downtown and we would walk the short distance to the Eagles Club which featured a bowling alley in the basement. It was the Junior Bowling League where we honed our skills and learned from some of the best future bowlers in the city. Larry Miller managed the Eagles Lanes and his three sons, Brian, Mike, and Tom bowled with us. I had enough money for the bus (round trip), three games of bowling, a Slim Jim and a Royal Crown Cola. I would go on to enjoy bowling into my adulthood. When the new Shoreview Lanes opened on Murdock Street, Larry Miller left the Eagles and went to Shoreview Lanes where he would manage that business until he retired. His son, Mike, or "Butch" as he is known, would take over after his dad retired.

Other pastimes we enjoyed were stamp and coin collecting and building models. Sometimes on Saturday, while we were downtown for our bowling league, Eddie and I would saunter over to a little stamp and coin shop on Main Street. We'd spend hours sorting through boxes of old postage stamps, trying to fill in those missing slots in our stamp album.

Model building took on a whole different approach for me. I liked building model cars alright, and occasionally I'd challenge myself to do an airplane or battleship, but my true interest was in assembling model birds. On special occasions, like a birthday or Christmas, my mom would take me to Mary's Toy and Tog Shop on Oshkosh Avenue, next door to the Mueller Potter drugstore. Over time, I collected every bird available. Each one was carefully painted and when finished, proudly hung on the wall of my bedroom.

Our family insurance man was Urban Blank. Urban was employed by Metropolitan Life, the company that held our family's life insurance policies. Urban would stop by periodically, usually in the evening when my dad was home from work. Urban Blank, always the consummate professional, wore a nice suit and carried an impressive leather briefcase. He and my parents would sit at the kitchen table and discuss matters that had no interest to me whatsoever. In later years, when Karen and I married, Urban became our "insurance man" too. We were very young, only nineteen years old when we got married. Urban sat down with us and taught us how to budget our money. "How much a month is your rent?" he asked. "Eighty dollars," we replied. He took a white envelope and wrote $20 on it, put it aside and continued. He then asked about our phone bill, monthly utilities, gas, groceries, etc. and did the same, writing a number on each envelope. "This is how much every week you have to put in each envelope to ensure you have enough money to pay your bills at the end of the month," he explained. If we had an extra $5 left after filling the envelopes, we would treat ourselves to a pizza from West End. It was a great and simple system that taught us a valuable lesson early in life on how to live within our means.

There were no charge cards then. You saved until you had enough money to purchase what you wanted. Larger items, like appliances and furniture, could be purchased by financing it with a short-term loan offered by the retailer or local bank or loan company. Department stores offered layaway plans. You took the item of choice to the checkout counter, put a small amount of money down and the store would put the item away and hold it for you. Then, every week or so you would stop in and make a payment toward it. Once the item was paid for in full, you could take it home. Much different than today's attitudes of instant gratification…"gotta have it NOW" and indifference to running up extraordinary credit card debt with huge interest charges on the balance.

Along with the onset of "Supermarkets", came the modern invention of automatic door openers. Like many around town, the Sawyer Street Super Valu store where I worked had them. As you approached the entry door you stepped onto a rubber mat. This mat held a sensing device that when weight was realized, it sent an electronic signal to open the door. This was especially helpful on the exit doors as one usually had an armful of groceries.

Going to the show as kids was a lot of fun. In the late 50s we could purchase Saturday Matinee tickets through our school. Movies cost only a dime and featured an assortment of serial, movie shorts and, of course, cartoons. One series I remember featured *Francis, The Talking Mule*. Each week a different episode would be run...*Francis Goes to the Races, Francis Goes to West Point, Francis in the Navy,* etc. Before the main feature would begin, we'd be thrilled to watch *The Three Stooges* and when *Woody Woodpecker* or *Tom and Jerry* came on, the theater would explode with cheers. Watching westerns was also a favorite of many. My heroes included Roy Rogers and Hopalong Cassidy. Good always prevailed over evil and at the end of the movie the kids would applaud and cheer as their hero rode into the sunset.

Those sure were fun times.

THE OSHKOSH GIANTS OF BASEBALL

E very spring the "Boys of Summer" take the field with crisp new uniforms, well-oiled leather gloves and metal cleats just aching to dig into the turf. Every boy in our neighborhood would come in an instant if we hollered, "Let's go play ball!" I remember those evenings watching the lights glow over at the Sawyer Street Ball Field located only two blocks away from my home on North Lark Street. The muffled sound of the loudspeaker as each player was introduced, the crack of the *Louisville Slugger*® on the old horsehide, and the roar of the crowd on a big hit or key strikeout are some of my favorite childhood memories.

Baseball…It's the American past time!

Baseball in Oshkosh has a long-standing tradition that goes all the way back to 1865-1872 with the Oshkosh Everetts.[3] The amateur team was organized by Col. Henry B. Harshaw, a one-armed retired soldier who named the team after the local high school principal, Arthur Everett. They played local teams from Green Bay to Fond du Lac.[1] Col. Harshaw was a Civil War veteran who was wounded at the Battle of Laurel Hill, Virginia on May 8, 1864 and had his left arm amputated at the shoulder. Discharged a month later, he returned to the Oshkosh area where he had worked as a teacher prior to his service to the Union.[2] Despite his hardship, Harshaw played the game well. Using his only arm, Harshaw used a short, light bat and replaced force with sharp playing skills, placing the ball skillfully out of reach of opposing fielders. His batting average was just that…average at best. His skills as a pitcher matched those of most other hurlers of the day.

The rules of the game during those early years were quite different than today. The pitcher pitched underhand, and foul balls that were not caught did not count as anything (not a strike). Foul balls were an out if caught in the air or on the first bounce. Also, the balls were larger with a rubber core and the fielders didn't wear gloves.

In 1874, a new team was organized by Sam Hay, Jr. The Amateurs played from 1874 to 1885 and was a dominant squad around the entire state the first two years in existence. From 1877 to 1885, the Amateurs never lost a game.[4] They played many of their games at the old fairgrounds located just off Jackson between Murdock and Annex Ave.[1]

1886 was the year that professional baseball came to Oshkosh. The Oshkosh Baseball Club along with Milwaukee, Minneapolis, Duluth, St. Paul and Des Moines organized the Northwestern League. They would be known as the Oshkosh Amateurs. Edgar Sawyer was a big sports fan and became President of this new club. He, along with other Oshkosh prominent citizens Joseph Porter, S.W. Hollister and Leander Choate were determined to field a championship team.

The first part of the season didn't go well for the Amateurs. One day, Edgar Sawyer brought his father, Philetus, to a game. Philetus was a former US Senator and lumber magnate here and didn't really approve of his son spending money "on something as frivolous as a baseball team." Noticing the ineptness of his son's outfielders to catch flyballs, the senior Sawyer turned to his son and said, "If you're going to spend your money this way, why be penny-wise and pound-foolish? Hire some better men and put them in the outfield to catch those balls." Sound fatherly advice!

Edgar did just that. He went out and signed better players from out east. The results were staggering. Oshkosh finished strong and would face Milwaukee for the League Championship.

It was here that a legend was made. A young man named William Ellsworth Hoy had been hanging around the team all season, begging for a chance to play. He was assigned the nickname "Dummy" as he could not speak or hear. All he wanted to do was have a chance to play baseball.

It was in this championship game that Hoy would get his shot. When the game was ready to begin, Oshkosh realized they were short a center fielder. So "Dummy" got the nod and took his place on the field of dreams. At 5'6" and 160 lbs., and no playing time under his belt, Hoy was hardly considered a big presence on the field. But that day it was his size and quickness that would gain him attention.

It is said that the score was tied in the ninth when a Milwaukee slugger drove a ball into deep center field. Hoy took off after it, running through and around the horses and buggies parked in the outfield area. The story says "Dummy" took one last look back at the incoming flyball, jumped on a horse and made the catch!

Oshkosh went on to win the game, and the championship, in ten innings. Some of the facts here may be a bit distorted, but it makes a good story nonetheless. Records show "Dummy" Hoy played 116 games for Oshkosh in 1887. He batted .367 and stole 67 bases.

The following year Oshkosh was dropped from the Northwestern League because Milwaukee objected to Oshkosh's Edgar Sawyer's use of money to win a title. "Dummy" Hoy went on to a successful career in the major leagues where he played fourteen seasons mostly with Washington and Cincinnati. Today he is enshrined in the Cincinnati Reds Hall of Fame. It is also said that, due to his handicap, he was the reason for

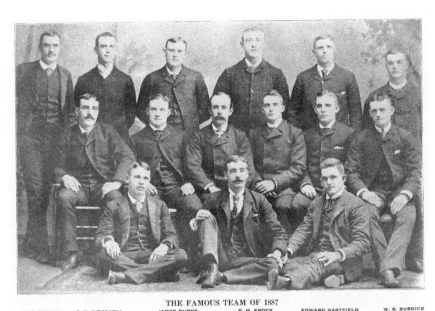

THE FAMOUS TEAM OF 1887

JOHN DORAN	P. H. O'CONNELL	JAMES BURNS	G. H. KROCK	EDWARD GASTFIELD	W. R. BURDICK
THIRD BASE	FIRST BASE	LEFT FIELD	PITCHER	CATCHER	PITCHER
	JOE WILSON	THOS. LOVETT	FRANK G. SEELE	TOM McCARTHY	TAYLOR SHAFER	DAN SHANNON
	CATCHER	PITCHER	MANAGER	RIGHT FIELD	SECOND BASE	CAPTAIN AND S. S.
		W. E. HOY		"CON" MURPHY		JAMES COONEY
		CENTER FIELDER		PITCHER		SHORT STOP

The famous team of 1887

Photo courtesy *Oshkosh in Baseball.* (Oshkosh, Wis.: Oshkosh Base Ball Club, 1913);

umpires using hand signals to call balls and strikes.[1] Hoy's greatest weapon was his speed. As a rookie, he led the National League in stolen bases (82) on his way to a career total of 594. In his Major League career, he scored 1,426 runs in 1,796 games with 1,004 bases on balls. Because of his speed on the base paths, most of his 40 career home runs were inside the park. He possessed a powerful and accurate throwing arm and threw out three runners at home plate on June 19, 1888. In 1896 with the Reds, he tied for the team's home-run lead with four. His career totals read: 1,796 games, 2,044 hits, 726 RBIs and a .287 batting average. On Oct. 7, 1961, the 99-year old Hoy threw out the first ball before Game 6 of the World Series. He died the following December.

From 1891 to 1914, Oshkosh fielded a couple different teams. Then in 1915, professional baseball took a twenty-seven-year hiatus. Amateur and semi-pro teams would come and go as the fever for baseball in Oshkosh failed to diminish. Sunday baseball was very popular in the late 1920s, offering games played in Menominee Park. Teams from that league included The Paines, The McMillans, The West Side Dodgers, Herb Lind's Teelas and the South Side Merchants. Some games, it is reported, drew as many as 2,000 fans on a Sunday afternoon.

On August 30, 1934, an exhibition game between the Chicago Cubs and St. Louis Cardinals was played at the fairgrounds. A crowd of 12,000 people showed up to watch, making it the single largest sports event in Oshkosh's history. Cardinal pitcher Dizzy Dean called the action over the loudspeaker. Leo "The Lip" Durocher played for the Cardinals that day as the Cubs breezed to a 12-5 victory over the "Gas House Gang" who would go on to win the World Series that same year.

By 1940, Oshkosh was ready for the return of professional baseball. The Wisconsin State League was formed and Oshkosh was accepted for the 1941 season. The Class D team would be known as the Oshkosh Braves, led by player/manager Fred Schulte. Schulte was known as the "Belvidere Beaut" during his eleven-year (1927-1937) stint in the majors. His nickname came from his hometown of Belvidere, Illinois. Team owners felt they could save money by hiring one person who could both play and manage the team.

To accommodate this new team, the city provided a piece of land to build a ball diamond. Actually, the land was nothing more than a marsh and the city really had no other use for the property. The site was developed and named Municipal Athletic Field. But because of its location, local folks always referred to it as the Sawyer Ave Ball Park. Consideration was given for the team to play at the fairgrounds like previous Oshkosh teams had done. But local residents were eager to have a new ball park for their new professional team, even if it meant paying more taxes. Everyone pitched in to ensure the site would be ready for the 1941 season. The city used their equipment for excavating and even people from various walks of life pitched in. The Boy Scouts, teachers, local residents all lent a hand. Even Mayor George Oaks slipped on a pair of "overalls" and helped alongside.[1]

Being ready in time for the new season brought a sense of urgency to the project. According to Mayor Oaks, "We didn't bother with legal channels. For the watering, we found a fire hydrant close to the park, laid a culvert under the road and furnished the field with city water." On May 27, 1941, the day of the home opener, the final piece of sod was placed and things were now ready. Mayor Oaks even quipped, "Mudhens were still laying eggs on first base – that's how close it was!"[1]

The Braves lineup for the season opener included Brutchak (3b); Rudnicke (cf); Putnam (lf); Schulte (1b); Bauer (1b); Calhoun (2b); Hembrook (rf); Johnson (ss); Ailworth (c), Zuber (p).

Author's Note: First baseman Bauer was, yes, the one and only Hank Bauer. I'll tell you more about him a little later.

The first game of the season was a catastrophe. A rain delay forced the game, scheduled to be played in La Crosse, to be moved from May 15 to May 17. Defending champion La Crosse handed the Braves an embarrassing 22-2 defeat. They played again the next day and lost again 17-3.

The Braves were 3-5 at the end of their first road trip and were happy to return to Oshkosh for their home opener scheduled at 8:15pm on May 27. The Sawyer Ave Ball Park was ready and their opponents would be the Sheboygan Indians. Radio station WHBY in Appleton was on hand to broadcast the game with Ben Laird doing the commentary. Wally Bronson was the on-field announcer for introductions.

The pre-game ceremonies included an introduction of the Directors of the Civic Recreation Association and a decorated cake was presented to manager Fred Schulte by a local baker named Roger Goodfellow.

Music was provided by four marching bands including The Kimberly Clark Band of Neenah, the Eagles band, the Oshkosh High School band, and the Oshkosh Teachers College band. The bands marched in parade formation from nearby Roosevelt School under the leadership of Curtis O. Drake who carried a lighted baton. The bands performed the *National Anthem* and *God Bless America*.

Eighty-six-year-old George Nevitt, former curve ball hurler for the Oshkosh Amateurs, threw out the first pitch. Then the umpire yelled, "PLAY BALL!"

The game saw the Braves outhit the Indians 13-6 and went into extra innings. Finally, in the 12th inning with an Oshkosh error, two walks, and a sacrifice fly, Sheboygan scored and won the game 4-3.[1]

A young, brawny kid from East St. Louis named Hank Bauer began his baseball career here in 1941. After high school, Bauer worked as a union pipe-fitter in a beer bottling plant. He was only 18 years old, six-feet tall, weighed 200 lbs. and could hit the ball a mile. Hank's brother Herman was playing in the Chicago White Sox system and arranged for Hank to get a tryout. Fred Schulte had seen young Bauer at the baseball tryout camp and discovered he had already signed with a team in Grand Forks, ND. Schulte bought out his contract for $5 and brought him to Oshkosh with high hopes.

Unlike the other players on the team, Bauer didn't want to reside at the Athearn Hotel during the season. He preferred to stay with his manager Fred Schulte and teammate Del Johnson at a cottage on Lake Butte des Morts.

A man I knew in business during my working years, Vernon "Swede" Erickson, played for the '41 Oshkosh Braves and remembered Hank Bauer. Built to be an outfielder, Hank was sometimes used as a pitcher, and let's just say that wasn't his strongest position. He was a bit wild and threw hard, which made batters afraid to stand too close to the plate. "Hank was strong, fast, and had good power...but I never thought of him as a major leaguer," "Swede" recalled.

During his first season in Oshkosh, Bauer played in 108 games and batted .262 with 10 home runs. But his debut career here would be short-lived.

As the 1941 season drew to a close, decisions had to be made regarding which players would remain for the next season. On September 11, Les Stevenson wrote a letter to Bauer saying the team was not willing to pay his $100 signing bonus next season (his salary was about $75 a month) and gave him his release…a decision he would someday regret.

In January 1942, Hank joined the Marines in response to the Japanese attack on Pearl Harbor. He spent the next three years in the Pacific where he suffered 24 attacks of Malaria and received eleven campaign ribbons, two bronze stars and two purple hearts.

After his military service, Hank returned to his job as a pipe-fitter until one day he was approached by a scout from the New York Yankees who remembered him and signed him. Bauer was assigned to the Yankee's minor league system in Quincy, Illinois and was called up to the Yankees in 1946. He was now 26 years old.

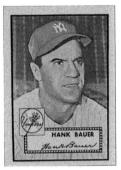

Hank Bauer, New York Yankees, 1952 Topps Baseball Card #215

Bauer went on to a career in the big leagues as a player until 1961, then as a manager through the 1969 season. Eleven of those years as a player, he played for the New York Yankees. In the 1951 World Series, Bauer almost single-handedly won the sixth and final game by hitting a bases-loaded triple and making a game-saving diving catch for the final out with the tying run on base to give the Yankees the championship over the New York Giants. In the '58 World Series against the Milwaukee Braves, Bauer hit four home runs and batted .323 as the Yankees clinched the Series four games to three. Those four home runs were the second highest total hit in a World Series after Reggie Jackson's five in 1977. During his career, Bauer was named to the American League All Star Team three times and had a lifetime batting average of .277 with 164 home runs, 57 triples, 229 doubles and 705 RBI's.[8]

The Oshkosh Braves finished in last place in 1941, but the crowds came out. Attendance that year at the Sawyer Ave Ball Park was 48,162, leading the league in attendance.[1]

It was late in the 1941 season when Fred Schulte used his connections to contact Bill Terry, manager of the New York Giants who played in the National League. Schulte was seeking an affiliation with the senior club, and in 1942 Terry had become in charge of affiliations in his new role as General Manager. Being affiliated meant two things to Oshkosh…better players and more money. Players would come from the Giants farm club system, and the New York Giants gave the Oshkosh team $1,600 for operations.[1]

So, in 1942 the Oshkosh Braves became the Oshkosh Giants.

"Swede" Erickson was still trying to find his path into the major leagues. "I decided to go to this baseball school in Florida because I wanted to get into organized ball. It only cost $120 and two of our instructors were Babe Ruth and Bob Feller". Erickson had heard that Oshkosh was looking for ball players and he had just been cut from the roster in Appleton. So "Swede" went to the Athearn Hotel and met with Schulte. He was in the lineup that night for the Braves as a shortstop against LaCrosse. He only was paid $65 a month but money wasn't the important thing...he was playing baseball. He stayed at the Athearn for $15 a month.

Author's Note: The apple never fell far from the tree in the Erickson household. "Swede's" son Bruce, coached baseball for Appleton West and Appleton North high schools for 28 years. Bruce's son, Matt, is manager for the Milwaukee Brewers Class A affiliate, the Wisconsin Timber Rattlers.

The "honeymoon" season for the Giants was pretty much as expected for a new team. They finished in sixth place with a record of 48 wins and 59 losses. Attendance was still strong as baseball fans in Oshkosh turned out in good numbers. Once again, they led the league in attendance with 44,162.

The 1942 Oshkosh Giants roster looked like this: Del Johnson (3B); Bob Koller (LF); George Bennington (CF); Dick Bixby (SS); Roscoe Slatton (RF); Dan Schneider (1B); Jim McGreal (Util); "Swede" Erickson (Util); Jim Martin (2B); Nello Del Par (C); R. Phil Oates(P); George Kunz (P); Lloyd Schabow (P); Ike Bloohm (P).

Players and umpires both dressed at nearby Roosevelt School. Oshkosh's Bud Lowell was an umpire and after one game, a crowd of fans, angry over questionable calls against the home team, were waiting for him outside Roosevelt School. Lowell was urged to wait them out inside the locker room until the crowds finally gave up and went home.

In 1942 the Giants had a new manager in Ray Lucas. But that season would find itself embroiled in many changes with the beginning of WWII. The Wisconsin State League ceased operations until 1946. During that time, the Sawyer Ave Ball Park was used by local amateur teams. When the league reopened, the Oshkosh team attempted to get an affiliation with the Chicago Cubs, but that club had already committed to Janesville, so Oshkosh remained as a New York Giant affiliate.

Ray Lucas was a former big-league pitcher with the Giants and Brooklyn Dodgers. The '46 Oshkosh Giant's return to baseball was a successful one. By midseason, they led the Wisconsin State League and surpassed 40,000 in attendance. Oshkosh fans were hungry for baseball! The war was over and the country was anxious to return to a normal life.

Tom Gotto was one of the team's top pitchers. The tall, skinny, left hander was known to drink a fifth of booze each night before he pitched. He was wild and threw with reckless abandon. He returned home to Armonk, NY after the '46 season and was tragically killed in a car accident.

Because the Giants were leading the league on July 4th of '46, they received the honor to host the All-Star game. The Giants would play the best players of the other teams in the Wisconsin State League. The All-Stars beat the Oshkosh Giants 8-2. The Giants ended up finishing in second place for the season. Their attendance was huge (83,201) and they were second in the league to Fond du Lac (83,560).

In 1947 the Giants improved their record to 60-59 and finished in third place. The roster that year included Bob Roth, Len Heinbigner, John Wesolich, Stan Jok, Bob Neumer, Ken Hill, Butch Konetzke, Harry Curtis, Skippy Schumacher, Bill Goff, Pete Brozovich, Sam Brewer, Frank Frezza, Harry Parker, and Flip Lucas, nephew of manager Ray Lucas. Flip Lucas led the team in batting (.354), Stan Jok was a big third baseman who pounded 19 home runs, 105 RBI's and batted .335. Sam Brewer was a native Cherokee and a pitcher. He was also a big man. He signed with the team without the team knowing he was coming here from prison where he did time for auto theft. Brewer carried himself well here and posted a 14-11 record and led the league in strikeouts (256).

The following season the Giants fell upon some hard times. Their record slipped to 51-74 and they ended the season in sixth place. Attendance in 1948 dropped to 65,580 and financially the team ended up in the "red". Heinbigner led the team that year in batting (.333). Other team members of the '48 Giants included Carson Bill Proctor, Fred Weber, John Kropf, Charles Fowler, Jim Klappa, John Battaglia,

Oshkosh Giants Player/ Manager Dave Garcia

Photo courtesy Ed Tiedje

Hank Zierer, Dick Fern, Art Smith, Ron Neff, Bill Frey, John Wesolich, Herb Boetto, and Tom Acker.

Manager Ray Lucas left after the '48 season and went on to become a scout for the New York Giants. At a team meeting in December of that year, it was decided the NY Giants wanted a player/manager to replace Lucas in Oshkosh. So they went into their farm system and tapped into a 29-year old second baseman named Dave Garcia.[1]

Garcia arrived in Oshkosh from his East St. Louis home in January 1949. He had never been further north than Chicago in his entire life. "I knew it was up north," he quipped, "but I didn't realize it got that cold. I thought it was going to be like playing at the North Pole." Garcia was well-liked and very popular with fans and players alike.

Garcia's presence made an immediate difference. The Giants won back-to-back championships in 1949 and 1950. Attendance soared to 115,936 in 1949. During this time admission to a Giants game at the Sawyer Ave Ball Park was 65¢ for booster seats, 46¢ for bleacher seats, 25¢ for students and 10¢ for kids. After the 1947 deficit, the Giants showed a remarkable turnaround in '48 with a net profit of $13,305. The '49 team finished with the best record in Giant history at 72-49. Players like Garcia, Rudy Yandoli, Bob Myers, Tom Acker, Jennings Norman, Ed Monahan, Bill Spinks, Bob Purcell, Jim Boyd, Joe Rovner, Carl Springer, Leon Clark, Charles Weidenbach, Frank Neil, Paul Moylan, Ronnie Neff and Wilburn Jenkins gave the fans what they had long waited for – a championship team.

Carl Springer was fan favorite as he hailed from nearby Menasha. He came to the Giants as a second baseman but was put on notice by player/skipper Garcia that he wasn't about to give up his position at second base, so Springer moved to third base. It was said that Springer cost the team a lot of money. He was known to have good contact at the plate and would foul off numerous balls at each "at bat". Neighborhood kids waiting outside the park would chase after the foul balls and head for the hills! Bob Myers was "the Iron Man" named so because he played every single inning that season. He was short in stature and played first base. Yandoli was the star of the team earning MVP honors in '49. Hailing from Brooklyn New York, Yandoli was a pitcher who not only compiled an impressive 15-5 record that year, but also belted 14 home runs.

Because the Giants were leading the league on July 4th of 1949, they were once again awarded to host the All-Star game. The game was scheduled to begin at 8:15 pm on Monday, July 18. The 3,900 reserved seats had all been sold, and additional bleachers were set up to accommodate the heavy demand for tickets. One thousand general admission tickets would go on sale starting at 6:30 pm. Early that evening, the skies opened up and it poured rain, casting doubts on whether the game would be played. But the loyal fans hung in there and found shelter under the stands and near the concession box operated by Harold Schumerth. According to Schumerth, they ran out of food before the game even started.

Soon, the rain subsided bringing Frank Sphatt and his grounds crew to life, removing the tarps and getting things ready after only a 25-minute game delay.

All-Star manager Fred Collins of Fond du Lac decided to start his own pitcher, 19-year old Ivan Abromowitz in front of the fan favorite and top vote getter Bill Allen of Sheboygan.

A memorable moment occurred in the second inning with the score tied at 0-0. The Giants teed off on Abromowitz, spraying the ball all over the place, and before long, had four runs on the board. Collins left Abromowitz in, maybe to save face that he was sticking with his decision to start him when Dave Garcia came to the plate. Garcia was a seasoned veteran compared to the nervous teenage hurler about to face him on the mound. Garcia was an excellent hitter and also was known for his temper. The first pitch from Abromowitz was thrown behind Garcia's back. Anyone who knows anything about baseball understands that is a blatant act of defiance and disrespect. Garcia hit the dirt, then picked himself up, brushed off his uniform and stepped back into the batter's box. The next pitch connected solidly with Garcia's bat as Abromowitz watched the ball easily clear the center field fence-a three run homer. As Garcia rounded the bases he yelled a few words to Abromowitz regarding his misplaced fastball. The Giants

Oshkosh Giants Team Photo 1950. L to R Back Row: Hoffman, King, Butts, Fournier, Fleming, Lovell, Diaz; L to R Front Row: Burpoe, Lettieri, Tomter, Rievere, Little, Hunter, Scollard, Karn, Bonneville, Schultz, Corder, Jones, Wondra, Griffen, Mgr Garcia

Photo courtesy Dan Radig

scored seven runs in the second inning and went on to defeat the All-Stars 7-4.[1]

The Giants repeated their championship form in 1950 with a 74-49 record. They went on to set a number of team records that year with most home runs in one game (5), most AB's in one game (49), highest team batting average (.267), most hits (1,120), most total bases (1,633), most doubles (221), most RBI's (685), best fielding average (.954).

Oshkosh fans celebrated this accomplishment by organizing "Dave Garcia Night" on September 6, 1950. In addition to the recognition received for the championships, Garcia was awarded a television from a local business and a new suit given to him by the players.

As stated earlier, the Giants repeated their championship run again in 1950, but for some unexplained reason there was a significant decline in attendance. Only 69,643 fans turned out that year, about 46,000 less than the previous season. That decline caused the Giants to suffer a financial loss of $8,049.[1]

In 1951 attendance dropped even further to 40,566 even though the team finished strong in second place. The '52 season saw no real increase in attendance and the financial woes started to build while the team endured another $11,000 deficit.

It was the beginning of the end in 1953. The Braves moved from Boston to Milwaukee, and the Wisconsin State League faced stiff competition from the big-league franchise. Attendance at Giants games in '53 dropped to 26,118 while the Giants played to a fifth-place finish.

Many games were played in inclement weather conditions or cancelled due to rain. Also during the early fifties, racial tensions were high across our country. It was no different here in Oshkosh. Another reason, it's been reported, for the decline in attendance was the entrance of Black and Hispanic players in Oshkosh. Spoken only in whispers, it was rumored that local residents were not pleased that some of these players were dating white girls in Oshkosh.[1] But largely the draw to see the new Milwaukee Braves certainly had a dramatic effect.

On September 9, 1953, the New York Giants withdrew their affiliation rights to the Oshkosh team due to the financial burden of the past few seasons. Then in early November that year, a league meeting was held at Oshkosh's Athearn Hotel. It was decided that the Wisconsin

State League would suspend their operations for one season. They planned to resume play in 1955…but that was not going to happen.

Efforts were made to try to save the organization. Team President Art Gruenwald even went to Milwaukee to meet with the Milwaukee Braves. There he plead his case for assistance and support from the franchise, who Gruenwald said was the main reason for the decline in Oshkosh attendance. The Braves assured Gruenwald that "they would do something." A few weeks later they received a check in the mail for $100. Gruenwald sent it back.

The 1953 season would be the curtain call for the Oshkosh Giants of Baseball. Dave Garcia would go on to a successful career in the major leagues, managing the Anaheim Angels (1977–78) and the Cleveland Indians (1979–82).

* * *

In 1971, Jack Schneider brought amateur baseball back to Oshkosh with a new Oshkosh Giants organization to play in the Wisconsin State League. Today, the Giants play at EJ Schneider Field located at Oshkosh North High School.

In 1980, the team re-organized into the Oshkosh Giants, Inc. A Board of Directors was formed and President Don Erickson assumed the role of manager that first season. The following year, Don was joined by Oshkosh native Dave Tyriver and they worked together as co-managers. Tyriver had some major league experience playing a brief time for the Cleveland Indians. Then in 1982, Tyriver took over the managerial responsibilities alone. In 1983, former Giant and UW-O standout Tom Lechnir took over the reins of the Giants as manager and led the team for four seasons. During his tenure, Lechnir led the team as AABC State Champions in 1984 and runners up in 1983 and 1986. They also finished in the top three places in the Wisconsin State League three of the four years. His successors at the helm were as follows:

Tony Gerharz	1987–1988
Kevin Reichardt/Ray Neveau	1989
Pat MacDonald	1990
John Skolaski	1991
Bill Gogolewski	1992–1993

Jim Paulick	1994–1998
Tony Gerharz	1999
Kevin Schamens	2000
Mike Flanigan, Cory Ruhl, Matt Lisbeth	2001
Eric Cruise	2002–2003
Lucas Lechnir	2004
Bryan Burgert/Bryan Schwebke	2005
Phil Glinske	2006–2007
Brian Gerl	2008
Brad Demmin	2009–2010
Luke Westphal	2011–2012
Trey Demler	2013–2014
Alex Brewer	2015
Luke Gajewski	2016–2017

From 1978 through the 2016 season, 44 Giant players have signed major league contracts.

Today, the Oshkosh Giants, Inc, is a non-profit organization which depends entirely on revenue earned through ads in the program books, gate receipts, and donations. Neither the players, coaches, nor the board members are paid for their service.

The Giant Organization is always looking for new members who feel that amateur baseball is a plus for the community and are willing to volunteer their services.

Extra Innings

Having been born in 1951, I have the wonderful opportunity to remember the Sawyer Ave Ball Park. By the late 50s, the Giants were no longer here. As a young boy, I remember hearing stories of Hank Bauer and Dave Garcia and those wonderful Oshkosh Giant teams. The ballpark was our playground. It was used by the Oshkosh High School team and the American Legion squad mostly and by the neighborhood gang more often. Locals like Billy Hoeft, Dutch Rennert, and Bill Gogolewski played here.

Billy Hoeft was an Oshkosh boy with an incredible career in the 'Bigs'. He didn't play for the Oshkosh Giants, but was a standout on both the Oshkosh High School Team and the Oshkosh American Legion club. The wily southpaw gained attention from the Majors by putting together a 34-game win streak in 1948-49. He lost the last game of the '49 season 2-1 with an unearned run. His streak included three no-hitters and the fewest number of strikeouts in any one game was 18. On April 29, 1950, eighteen days shy of his 18th birthday, Billy threw a perfect game…a true perfect game in the sense that he struck out all 27 batters he faced! Hoeft went on to play 15 seasons in the majors from 1952 to 1966.

Getting in the Sawyer Ave Ball Park was easy. If the gates were locked (and they usually were), we'd just throw our bats, gloves, and balls over the chain link fence and climb over. We used second base as our home plate with hopes from there we might be able to hit one over the fence. The outfield fence was made of wood and painted with advertisements of local businesses like People's Beer and Wertsch Motors. This fence was painted forest green and held a scoreboard in right-center field. To get to the scoreboard, you walked through a narrow passageway to get behind the fence. Then you would climb a metal scaffold-like structure that held the scoreboard in place. Long, sturdy planks allowed the scorers to stand and watch the action over the top of the fence and place the needed information on the scoreboard. Plaques with names and numbers were used to identify the team name and the scores. Pegs from 1 through 9 represented the innings and held the numbers that were put up manually.

I remember running the bases and sitting in the dugout pretending we were big league ball players. It was fun to see things from that perspective, imagining having the same view as the players had during a game.

North of the ball field was a large gravel parking lot. The wire-laced backstop caught many of the foul balls that were hit backward… but not all of them. During the night games, we would sit across the street in the driveway of the Standard Station on the corner of Porter Ave and Sawyer Street. If a ball cleared the backstop, it would take one bounce in the middle of Sawyer only to be grabbed by one of us, then the race was on. We'd jump on our bikes and take off before one of the bigger kids would grab us and take the ball away. Sometimes we would return the ball to WOSH Radio Sports Announcer Herb Willis who would pay a quarter for each ball returned. That is, unless we needed one ourselves, of course. We'd use those baseballs until the cover came off, and even then, we would wrap it back together with black electrical tape so we could continue playing.

The site where the ballpark sat was mostly open field and marsh, located between Sawyer and Josslyn Streets. Behind the center field fence was the best patch of wild strawberries in which we would always find time to take pleasure.

Through the years, I watched the ball field decline with age and lack of use. Eventually it was torn down and the property sold to a local church.

Although I was quite young, I couldn't help but think of all those good old days when baseball was in its glory...stands full of people cheering for the home team and the thrill of watching young players fighting against the odds of making it to the big leagues.

Some did.

Today, Zion Lutheran Church stands on what we all remember as our "Field of Dreams".

Sources: (1) *Oshkosh Northwestern,* "The Giants of Oshkosh Baseball" by Myles Strasser; (2) http://www.oshkoshmuseum.org/Virtual/exhibit3/e30045a.htm; (3) http://protoball. org/*Everetts_Club_of_Oshkosh;* (4) *Oshkosh in Base Ball,* written and published by Oshkosh Base Ball Club, 1913; (5) mlb.com/player/116238/dummy-hoy; (6) www.oshkosh giants.org;   (7) http://cincinnati.reds.mlb.com/cin/hof/hof/directory.jsp?hof_id=116238; (8) https://www.nytimes.com/2007/02/10/sports/baseball/10bauer.html

BUCKSTAFF BOOGIES

E very time we lose another historic building in our community, it precipitates angst and handwringing. We feel as though we've lost a piece of ourselves…our past.

I discovered an interesting story that should lighten the hearts of those who mourn the passing of those historical pieces of Oshkosh's past.

Fender Musical Instruments Corporation, commonly known as Fender, is an industry leader and has been known for high quality musical instruments, mainly guitars since 1946.

In 2017, Fender introduced a Limited Edition Exotic Collection of guitars. Mike Born, Fender's director of wood technology assembled a plan that introduced wood for use in guitar construction. The idea was to search for exotic woods to give the "purists" a slightly different experience with tone quality.

Born searched the globe and selected wood that included rescued Mahogany from Honduras and ebony colored wood from an island in Indonesia.

But locals may be interested to know that Born wanted a "special" pine to build his *Jazzmaster*, *Stratocaster* and *Telecaster* models. He found what he wanted right here in Oshkosh.

The Buckstaff company, once the makers of fine furniture and caskets, was located on Oshkosh's South Main Street. After the business closed in 2011, its fate was sealed and the site was abandoned. Eventually it became blighted and an eyesore to the community. Finally reaching the end of its life and usefulness, the site was razed in 2016 to make room for a new arena with plans to host sporting events and entertainment venues. The salvage company moved in and piece by piece the old Buckstaff Company came down. Rescued pine boards were selected in the process and shipped to Fender who repurposed the wood into usable material.

From their website:

The 2017 Limited Edition American Professional Pine Telecaster contains body wood that began its functional life over 100 years ago as part of the Buckstaff Furniture Company's facility in Oshkosh, Wis. before it was reclaimed, cooked and fashioned into an instrument. The new limited-edition model also features a single American Vintage '64 Gray-bottom single-coil Tele pickup, a Lollar Charlie Christian single-coil neck pickup, 22 narrow-tall frets and a 9.5" radius maple fingerboard.

"We thermally treated it to reduce the weight and that also gives it an aged guitar sound and darkens the color a little", Born said. "We don't have to add stain to it. It's natural. And all the defects like the knots in the wood and old bolt holes are all included."

So, next time you hear one of your favorite musical performers, you'll have to wonder if that sound is the history of Oshkosh's lumber industry coming through.

Source: https://www.fender.com/articles/namm-2017/see-the-new-2017-limited-edition -exotic-collection

THE MURDER OF THOMAS R. MORGAN

I f you are from Oshkosh, then you are well aware of the Morgan Company. The Morgan Company was one of the largest manufacturers of wood products including lumber, shingles, sashes, doors, blinds, and more. It was one of the last remaining lumber companies to do business in Oshkosh during its long history of manufacturing.

The Morgan Family was of Welsh descent, having moved here around 1868. Young Thomas Morgan was only twelve years old when he arrived here with his parents Thomas and Jane, and his 3 brothers and 2 sisters. While Thomas' father worked as a farmer, young Thomas found work doing various "odd jobs" around the city to earn some extra money. He attended school and it was said he was a good student and enjoyed studying business. At 18 he became employed as a bookkeeper by Morgan Brothers which was run by his uncles Richard T. Morgan and John R. Morgan.

After about five years, Thomas left Morgan Brothers and took the same position with another local wood manufacturer, Foster & Jones. Upon Mr. Jones retirement, Thomas Morgan bought into the business by purchasing a fourth interest in Foster & Jones, making him part owner of the company.

This arrangement lasted several years until Foster was purchased by Morgan Brothers, bringing Thomas Morgan back into the family fold.

The time came for the torch to be passed when Richard T. and John R. Morgan decided to retire, handing the company over to the next generation of Morgan businessmen. Thomas, along with his cousins Albert T. and John Earl Morgan were now the owners, each having an equal one third share. Upon the death of Albert in 1899, his shares were purchased equally by Thomas and John Earl.

The new company became known as the Morgan Company. John Earl assumed the business communications for the company while Thomas administered the daily operations in manufacturing.

Thomas Morgan's responsibility was working directly with the production side of the business and the employees that worked at the plant, located on Sixth and Oregon Streets. There were approximately 350 workers employed there at the turn of the century. Thomas was respected and well-liked by his employees. He ran his company with a sense of fairness and a keen business mind. It has been said he spoke kindly to them and always offered encouragement. Some would say that he knew each man personally and would show interest in their well-being.

He was also very community minded and served as Alderman in the Seventh ward. As Alderman, he had a reputation for being assertive and at times aggressive when needed to make his position known on civic issues…always having the best interests of the city at heart.

It was a typical summer day on Tuesday, August 18, 1903. Thomas Morgan was making rounds through the plant and in the yard, stopping to speak with employees along the way. This was his style, as he enjoyed meeting and talking with his employees face-to-face.

Just a short distance away, Frederik Hampel was hanging out at a local saloon at 44 Minnesota Street. Fred Hampel was employed at the Morgan Company but was accustomed to miss work due to his heavy drinking. It was quite early in the morning, only eight o'clock, and Hampel was already "three sheets to the wind". He had a reputation for being a heavy drinker and had been kicked out of other local saloons due to his unsavory disposition and quarrelling with patrons. He had been thrown out of Ernst Lang's bar located across the street to the Morgan Company for his bad conduct. Lang explained Hampel would become argumentive when drinking and used a lot of bad language. When drunk, he was known to throw beer glasses or anything handy at someone he was fighting with.

That morning, while in the saloon, Hampel was drunk and grumbling about things like he always did. Hampel was always grumbling when drinking and was accustomed to telling everyone of his troubles. On one occasion, he mentioned the names of Thomas and

John Morgan in one of his drunken stupors and was reported to have said that he "would fix those two fellows".

Hampel returned home shortly after leaving the saloon. His wife told him he should eat something, that it would help his drunkenness. Later, Hampel's wife would reveal she was scared of her husband, especially when he was drinking, as he usually became abusive and threatened her. Hampel refused any food and went to lie down. Mrs. Hampel left the house and went to the store to pick up some meat to make soup for his dinner. When she returned, Hampel was gone. A short time later, Hampel showed up on the grounds of the Morgan Company and talked with Michael Bork, a scaler who was working in the yard. Bork noticed Hampel was intoxicated and advised him to stop drinking and go to work. Hampel danced around in a jovial mood flashing a couple of dollars and commented that he didn't have to work as he still had enough money to buy a cigar or two.

Around ten o'clock that Tuesday morning, Thomas Morgan was walking through one of the company yards with one of his employees, John Rowlands. Like Morgan, Rowlands was of Welsh decent and worked at the Morgan Company as a "slasher". Rowlands had just returned from visiting the Campbell-Cameron mill and was walking along the railroad tracks on Fifth Street when he met Mr. Morgan in the yards. They stopped and chatted briefly about business matters. As they talked, Fred Hampel approached them. It was quite obvious that he was very intoxicated. Morgan knew that Hampel had been away from work and was drunk. Morgan turned to Hampel and said, "Fred, I have no time to talk to you this morning."

Thomas Morgan and John Rowlands turned away from Hampel and started to walk toward Oregon Street. Rowlands said he heard Hampel reply, "Well, I will talk to you later".

Just then, Rowlands said, a shot rang out right near his ear. Thomas Morgan cried out, throwing his arms in the air and staggered to his left. Two more shots rang out, both missing their target, as Rowlands seized Hampel by his gun hand and the other at his throat. Hampel, who was reported to be a large and powerful man, wrestled Rowlands to the ground. Rowlands then let go of his hand on Hampel's throat and used both hands to try to wrestle the gun from the assailant. Witnessing the terrible assault brought employees working nearby to aid Rowlands in subduing the attacker. John Morgan, a yard foreman, arrived first and pulled Hampel off Rowlands. Hampel took a swing at John Morgan but missed. Morgan responded with a solid punch to Hampel's left temple. The gun was wrestled away from Hampel, and as others arrived, they held the assassin on the ground. By this time, a local Police officer named Meyer was on the scene and cuffed Fred Hampel.

Thomas Morgan, mortally wounded and bleeding badly, ran to a nearby office and exclaimed, "Call a doctor, quick! I've been shot in the back by old Fred Hampel". An ambulance was summoned while Morgan was seated in a chair. When the ambulance arrived, the police officers on the ambulance reported that Mr. Morgan did not speak and was experiencing labored breath, groaning and bleeding from the mouth. Morgan was immediately placed in the ambulance, which then took off at a high speed for St. Mary's Hospital. The route took the ambulance over the Light Street bridge to Pearl St., where it turned right toward Main Street.

Thomas R. Morgan never made it to the hospital alive. He died before the ambulance reached Main Street, approximately 15 minutes after he was shot. Thomas R. Morgan was 47 years of age.

Morgan, his wife Lydia, and their two daughters, Enid and Marion, lived at 32 Franklin Street. Per their usual tradition, they were spending the summer at their cottage on Stony Beach, just south of Oshkosh. The Morgans enjoyed spending their summers there, as the cool breezes of the lake brought welcome relief to the hot summer days and nights.

That morning, Mrs. Morgan was in the city doing some shopping. She was at the Main Street store of Charles Radford, looking at wallpaper when suddenly an ambulance went dashing by. Lydia walked over to the door to see which direction the ambulance was heading and commented that it must be on the way to the hospital with an injured person. Another customer in the store, Mr. Ralph Burtis, had just walked across the street to E.S. Wilson's music store when he learned the details of what just happened. Word of the shooting was spreading quickly all over town. Burtis returned to Radford's store to deliver the news to Mrs. Morgan. By the time he arrived there, Mrs. Morgan had already heard another passerby comment that there had been a shooting. It is said that Mrs. Morgan saw by the look on Mr. Burtis' face that something was dreadfully wrong. Burtis then quietly asked Mrs. Morgan to accompany him to St. Mary's Hospital. Mrs. Morgan asked if something had happened to Mr. Morgan, and Burtis replied only that he had been hurt. Although Mrs. Morgan did not know the details, her intuitive feelings told her it was serious and she fainted. She was then taken to the home of her mother, Mrs. E.E. Jones, who lived across the street from their Franklin Street home. The shock of the news caused Mrs. Morgan to become very ill as she remained unconscious for about two hours. There, she remained under the care of her physician due to her condition of having a weak heart.

Back at the plant, chaos ensued. Officer Meyer worked to contain his prisoner, while Morgan employees that heard the news quickly gathered around Hampel and Officer Meyer. Shouts of rage came from the angry mob which began to cry out about lynching the perpetrator. Officer Meyer quickly took charge of the situation and ordered the crowd back. Meyer then loaded Hampel onto a nearby wagon belonging the McMillan Company. Hampel was shackled to the wagon, Meyer climbed aboard and instructed the driver to hurry to the police station.

Once the ambulance delivered Mr. Morgan's body to St. Mary's hospital, Justice of the Peace F.A. Kaerwer was notified. A jury was assembled that viewed the remains and then adjourned, agreeing to meet at the Justice's office the next morning. Doctors C.W. Oviatt, J.C. Noyes, George Noyes, G.M. Steele and C.M. Richards were at the hospital and examined the remains as well. The post-mortem examination showed that Morgan was wounded by only one shot, even though there were reports that three shots were fired by Hampel's .32 caliber Smith & Wesson handgun. The evening newspaper reported "the bullet entered through the back, passing through the spine and through the left auricles of the heart, then through the lower border of the upper lobe of the left lung. The cause of death was internal hemorrhage and the pericardium and chest were full of blood".

When Hampel arrived at the jail, he was searched, leaving him with only his handkerchief. He was relieved of a watch, knife, pocket book and a pipe. The assailant was placed in a cell normally used to hold state prison convicts under triple locks. The cell was located on the south end of the jail which was quite dark due to the lack of lighting. Shortly before noon, District Attorney Carl D. Jackson and police officer Fitzpatrick went to the cell where Hampel was placed to talk with the man. Hampel was sitting on the floor with his back against the bars of the door cell. The DA spoke to Hampel but Hampel did not answer. Officer Fitzpatrick put his hand on Hampel's head and

Jackson instructed the officer to leave him alone, thinking Hampel was sleeping off his drunken state. A few minutes later, officers Fitzpatrick and McCusker returned, lit a match, and upon further investigation discovered Hampel was dead. He had committed suicide by removing his suspenders, wrapping them around the bars, then his neck. Physicians were called in and made attempts to revive him but those attempts failed. It was determined Hampel died of strangulation around 11:30 am.

Justice of the Peace Kaerwer was notified and again a jury was empaneled to view the body. The jury was composed of George Overton, D.E. McDonald, J.C. Voss, L.K. Bronson, Mayor J.V. Mulva and Oscar Spalding.

Talks of lynching continued throughout the day. Morgan employees discussed organizing a group, storming the jail and taking Hampel to be hung. Once word reached the street that Hampel had committed suicide, the angry group refused to believe it, thinking that authorities were lying to prevent the lynching. After the body was taken to the undertaker, it was viewed by a great number of persons that afternoon and evening. It was only after this that people then believed Hampel was really dead.

As the details of the heinous act continued to unfold, the *Oshkosh Daily Northwestern* learned that Hampel had previously committed two other murders and was a fugitive all the time he had lived in Oshkosh. The report came from a former employer of Hampel, J.D. Ruddy of Nekimi. Ruddy said that he heard it directly from Hampel himself. According to the story, Hampel killed a man in Germany and fled the country. After arriving in the US, Hampel moved to Hurley Wisconsin, where he lived for eight years. There he killed another man, then fled Hurley by hiring a man to drive him to the railroad station. He came to this part of the state and found work as a farmhand about six miles from Oshkosh until "the matter had blown over". Ruddy said that Hampel was known then as "Big Fred" and all the farmers in the area were afraid of him. He then shared that on one occasion, Hampel went after his (Ruddy) brother with a pitchfork.

The funeral for Thomas Morgan was held on Friday, August 21 at the Thomas Morgan home located at 32 Franklin Street and was reported to be one of largest funerals Oshkosh had ever witnessed. Members of the societies in which Mr. Morgan belonged and friends

Thomas Morgan Family, Front: Mrs. Lydia E. (Jones) Morgan, Thomas R. Morgan; Back: Daughters (Lydia) Enid on the left and Marion on the right

Photo Courtesy of the Winnebago County Historical & Archaeological Society

of the family were received into the home to view the body. Hundreds lined the sidewalk and street outside the home for a block long in both directions. Over 300 persons entered the home to view the body and pay their respects. "The visitors were of all classes and ages and everyone who gazed upon the features of the dead turned away with sorrowful looks and tears in their eyes, bearing mute testimony of the esteem and respect in which he was held by the residents of Oshkosh."

The funeral cortege to the cemetery was headed by platoons of the police and fire departments including Chiefs Dowling and Brauer. A large number of city officials followed next. Then came the employees of the Morgan Company including fourteen office workers and 288 laborers of the plant, a tearful illustration of the affection and respect the workers had for their employer. The Morgan Company employees marched together that morning from the plant located at Sixth and Oregon Streets to the Morgan residence on Franklin Street.

Following the Morgan employees were the fraternal organizations of which Mr. Morgan was a member. Ninety-five Masons and twenty-three Odd Fellows led the forty-eight carriages that followed the procession to Riverside Cemetery, where Thomas R. Morgan was laid to rest in the Masonic Plot.

Morgan daughter Enid married Henry H. Kimberly (1883-1949) of Neenah who joined the Morgan Company and served as President before his retirement.

Daughter Marion married Oshkosh industrialist Rufus K. Schriber (1882-1959)

Lydia Jones Morgan continued to live in her home on Franklin Street until her death in 1940. In her later years, Mrs. Morgan was very generous with the community. She provided funding for the Morgan Memorial Library which opened in 1927 at Carroll College (now Carroll University, Waukesha). Various other charitable interests that Mrs. Morgan gave generous gifts to include the First Presbyterian Church in Oshkosh, the YMCA's Camp Hiawela and various other youth organizations. According to Lydia's great granddaughter, Elizabeth "Dede" Schriber Cummings, Mrs. Morgan was very generous with educational institutions and youth organizations. Elizabeth is married to Oshkosh Mayor Steve Cummings. They, along with their son Adam and grandson Oliver, represent three generations of Thomas Morgan descendants that still live in this area.

Sources: *Oshkosh Daily Northwestern,* August 18, pp 1,4; August 19, pp 3,4,6; August 20, p 3; August 21, pp 1,3; August 22, p 8;

THE SCHUSTER TURKEY FARM

Frank Michael Schuster was a farmer.

His family emigrated here from Germany in 1891 and Frank was born on American soil two months after they arrived. He was the eldest son of Frank and Theresa Schuster. He liked to say "The best things are made in Germany," a tongue-in-cheek reference to his own self.

Frank lived with his parents in Oshkosh on 19th St. until he married Elsie Ott, my grandfather Clarence Ott's sister, on October 1, 1914. He was employed by the Paine Lumber Company, same as many of the laborers who emigrated here in the late 19th century. Because of the rapid growth of this city and the entire Fox River Valley, demand for building materials was strong. The lumber business was booming in Oshkosh and work in the numerous lumber mills was easily obtained. Many immigrants carried their skills and trades here from their home countries, but ample opportunities to learn new skills on the job were numerous.

Frank Schuster with wife Elsie (R) and Elsie's sister Edna Ott Volz (L)

Photo courtesy Bob Volz

By 1916, Frank had changed jobs and was working for the Foster-Lotheman Mills, a door and sash manufacturer located on Minnesota Street.

But soon Frank realized mill work wasn't his cup of tea.

Frank and Elsie purchased a two-acre plot of land from Joseph Weber in the Peoples subdivision on 9th Street Road on April 23, 1917[2] for the low price of just one dollar! It was here Frank became a milkman[3], starting his own business known as the *Twin Elm Dairy*. Today the house at 1719 West Ninth

Street Road is still standing. Together there they raised six children. The eldest was Robert (b.1915), then Florence (b.1916), Marion (b.1918), Jane (b.1919), Gladys (b.1921), and John (b.1922). During this time, Ninth Street was very rural once you traveled west of Knapp Street and what we know today as Interstate 41 was nothing more than a country road.

Twin Elm Dairy, the Schuster children L to R: Marion, Jane, Gladys, John, Robert, Florence

Photo courtesy Carol Miller

In 1927, Frank decided to expand his interests in owning a dairy farm. He purchased a small, 60 acre farm on Fourth Street Road (County E today) about two-and-one-half miles west of the city limits. It was arranged through a land contract with James Mather. By 1943 the land contract was satisfied to one Hazel Todd and the land now belonged to Frank. With only 16 head of Guernsey cows, Frank named his small dairy operation *Fern Hollow Farms.*[1] He used the land to grow grain and corn to subsidize his livestock feed needs.

Frank was content being a dairy farmer.

That is until one day in 1932, when his youngest son John brought home some young turkey poults from his 4H meeting. Ten-year old John raised the birds to maturity, sold a couple and kept a few. The experience gave his father the idea that maybe there was something to be had in raising turkeys. So, a few more were added, then a few more, and before he knew it, it was 1934 and Frank Schuster was in the turkey business.

To write this story I knew I would need some help. What I wanted to know could not be found in a book at the library and the internet offered few details. So I contacted some family members on the Schuster side and asked them to share their memories with me.

Neil Starke was married to Frank's daughter Gladys. I called Neil and asked him if I could visit and "talk turkey". Neil agreed, so during the early morning on December 1, 2016, I drove the 50-mile stretch of snow covered, country roads to the tiny town of Wild Rose, Wisconsin where Neil lived. Neil was 96 years old, but his memories of the early days on the turkey farm were as clear as if it were yesterday. *(Author's Note: Sadly, Neil passed away shortly after this interview on Wednesday, January 25, 2017)*

"I was still in high school in the late 1930s. I was looking for work to earn some money so I agreed to work on the turkey farm," Neil said with a smile. Neil and Gladys eventually married in 1944 while Neil was home on leave from his duty with the U.S. Coast Guard. As Neil reflected back on the work at the turkey farm, he said with a grin, "It was one of the worst jobs you could ever have. There was nothing glamorous about the work." His least favorite job was the processing of the birds. He described from start to finish what was done. Most of what he described I was familiar with having worked in the meat business nearly my entire life. He described how a knife was inserted into the brainstem or medulla. That action helped release the feathers which made dressing the birds easier. While the heart was still beating, an incision was made on the neck to bleed the bird out. "Frank did most of the gutting. Elsie would help with de-feathering and then wrap each bird to be ready for sale. Everybody helped out, it was quite a production," he recalled. The remains from processing were sold to Gilbert Rhyner who owned the D & R Mink Ranch located at 1513 South Park Avenue. (old address system previous to 1958)

Sometimes the turkeys were sold as 'round dressed'. Neil explained further. "That meant they were de-feathered and cleaned but still had the entrails inside. When a customer bought the bird, it was weighed, dressed and wrapped." Many folks back then still clung to old traditions and used the heart, gizzard, liver, etc. as part of the meal preparation.

Neil went on to describe the farm located on Fourth Street Road. "It was a dairy farm and Frank had a few head of cows that he kept for milking. The birds were held in a large pen with wire fencing, creating a 'free range' environment. There were a few farm buildings used for milking and one small shed used for killing and processing." He added that Frank was new at this and really didn't quite know what he was doing initially, but he learned quickly as he gained experience from trial and error.

Raising turkeys was truly a family business and everyone was involved. In the fall, the processing would begin in preparation for Thanksgiving. They processed birds all year long according to demand but preparing for Thanksgiving was the busiest time of year. "John and

Processing turkeys, L to R: Clarence Hill, Elsie Schuster, Unknown, John Schuster

Photo courtesy Stanley Schuster

Bobby would help catch the birds, Jane and Gladys delivered turkeys to local customers, and Elsie did many jobs from accounting to helping process." Neil remembers even extended family members helping out on the farm.

Neil's daughter, Ellen Mueller, remembered visiting her grandfather's farm. "Grandpa used to say 'Don't ever buy just parts of a turkey or chicken. Chances are they came from a bird that was bruised or defective in some way'."

Frank's brother-in-law Carl helped out, and so did Uncle 'Pruney'. I asked Neil about Uncle Pruney and why the strange name? He explained he was one of Frank's brothers and his real name was Rupert. "They called him 'Pruney' because he was stewed all the time," Neil said with a chuckle.

Turkeys are strange birds. "They are not very smart!" Neil stated in a rather *matter of fact* manner. Curious by nature, turkeys are attracted to things of interest like bright colors or even one's shoestrings. But caution prevails around children. Although not mean tempered, the strange birds have been known to peck at the eyes of small children. When excited or struck by cupid's arrow, the male gobblers will fan their tail in a display and fluff up their feathers to attract a hen. He will also perform this ritual if irritated or angered. This act makes the tom look larger and uses this tactic to intimidate and ward off other suitors. It also serves to impress the "ladies" as well.

Each spring, day-old chicks were purchased from a hatchery in Tennessee and placed in a brooding pen for about 12 weeks. At this point they were mature enough to be moved out into the open-air pens. The beaks were clipped to prevent the birds from pecking and injuring each other.

While still very young, one wing was clipped to prevent the birds from taking flight. The birds were kept in a penned in area where they would spend the next 3-4 months eating and growing. At about six months of age, they were at the ideal size and weight for slaughter. Hens generally run smaller, about 10-16 pounds dressed weight, while the Toms would get much larger, sometimes reaching 25-30 pounds dressed weight.

Foxes, coyotes, and even packs of local dogs would come sniffing around after dark. Being in the open with only a wire fence for containment, the opportunity for predators was a problem for the Schuster's. Smudge pots were lit and set around as a deterrent. Robert was the oldest son and was relied upon to do almost everything on the farm. That included occasionally sleeping in a make-shift shed, located inside the pen among the turkeys. Armed with a shotgun to ward off any unwelcome guests, his presence there was also for another reason. By nature, turkeys spook easily if they sense a predator or an incoming thunderstorm. They can panic and will trample one another to death seeking safety. Robert's presence among them provided a sense of security as they were familiar with him through daily contact, feeding, etc.

Other issues, like disease, could threaten the flock and had to be monitored on a regular basis. Severe cases of sinusitis could cause widespread death if not immediately detected and treated. A "turkey hospital" was located on the grounds. This "turkey triage" was the location where sick birds would go for treatment and isolation.

The breed of turkey grown by Schuster was the Northwestern Broad Breasted Bronze variety.

The Bronze has been the most popular turkey variety for most of American history. It originated from crosses between the domestic turkeys brought by European colonists to the Americas and the eastern wild turkeys they found upon their arrival. The hybrid vigor of this cross resulted in turkey stocks that were larger and more vigorous than the European birds, and they were also much tamer than wild turkeys. The coppery-bronze colored metallic sheen, which gives the variety its name, was part of the inheritance from its wild ancestors.

In the early 1900s, a broader breasted Bronze turkey was introduced from England into Canada, and then into the northwestern United States. These were crossed with larger, faster growing US stocks and the resulting bird, the Broad Breasted Bronze, became the commercial variety of choice.

Beginning in the 1960s the Broad Breasted Bronze was replaced by the Broad Breasted White turkey. Processors favored the white-feathered variety because it produced a cleaner looking carcass. Today, the Broad Breasted Bronze is no longer used by the turkey industry, but it is promoted for seasonal, small-scale production.
Source: The Livestock Conservancy

In the later years of the turkey business, Frank also switched over to the Broad Breasted White variety as well.[4]

By 1948, Frank decided he wanted a bigger farm. He sold his parcel on Fourth Street Road on June 29; twenty acres to Leonard Pollack and forty acres to Paul Hildebrand. He purchased a dairy farm on June 7 of that same year from Crescentia Merk further south of town on State Highway 44 at County Road X. This new farm featured 160 acres of land, more than double the size of his Fourth Street location, with plenty of room to raise turkeys and operate a dairy farm. Here he installed a freezer to keep pace with the growing demand for turkeys. It also allowed him to build inventory going into the busy holiday seasons of Thanksgiving and Christmas.

Aerial view of the Schuster Farm on Highway 44
Photo courtesy Stan Schuster/Carol Miller

The next stop of my search for information brought me in touch with other family members. My third-generation cousin, Carol Miller, granddaughter of Frank and Elsie and daughter of Marion, was eager to talk with me as she has been researching the Schuster family business for some time now. Carol recalled the times she would visit her grandfather's farm and vividly remembered many of the details of those early days. I also arranged a meeting with Stanley Schuster, son of John Schuster and grandson of Frank and Elsie. Stanley's family lived next door to Frank and Elsie on Highway 44 and County Road X and has fond memories of growing up on his grandfather's farm. Pulling out all the stops, I then placed a phone call to another distant cousin, Bob Volz, who lives in Arizona now. Bob is the son of Edna Ott Volz, Elsie Schuster's sister.

Carol and Stanley shared some wonderful photos of the turkey farm, some of which are included in this story. All three shared something even more valuable – their memories of what life was like on the Schuster farm.

Carol Miller and her uncle 'Bobby' Schuster surrounded by turkeys. Circa 1952

Photo courtesy Sally Hill Clark

Frank Schuster sold his turkeys for sixty cents per pound. One year he sold a load of turkeys to the Piggly Wiggly warehouse, and the Piggly Wiggly stores sold them to the public for 39 cents per pound. "That made Frank very angry" Neil Starke remembers. "The stores were under-cutting his price." What most upset Frank was the fact he had to try to explain to customers why the grocery store prices were so much lower than his.

In addition to raising turkeys, the farm included a herd of cows and a dairy production. "I still remember Elsie sitting on a wooden stool milking cows," Bob Volz remembers. "She tied a bicycle tire over the tail to keep it from swishing in her face." Elsie worked hard as the matriarch of her family. She was an excellent seamstress and even made aprons and rugs from used feed sacks. Carol Miller remembers her grandmother sitting at an old oak "Mission Style" desk taking turkey orders over the phone. That desk and some of those hand-made aprons remain in the family today. All this was in addition to keeping house, cooking meals and looking after six children.

The Schuster family – L to R: Marion, Robert, Elsie, Jane, Frank, John, Florence, Gladys

Photo courtesy Stan Schuster

Bob Volz recalled spending the night with Robert out in the old shed among the flock of turkeys. "Some nights it was so cold. There was no heat in the shed and when we went to sleep we'd take our boots off only to find them frozen to the floor the next morning."

Volz related a memory he had as a boy spending time on the Schuster farm. "We'd get up early and milk the cows. Chores always came first. When the milking was done, we'd go back to the farmhouse where Elsie had prepared a breakfast you wouldn't believe. Eggs, pancakes, bacon, sausages, potatoes, hot coffee and toast. You had to eat well as you worked hard all day and needed the energy". Carol Miller then added, "She also served a large meal at noon, then leftovers in the evening. My grandmother was in the kitchen much of the day and she saw to it nothing went to waste." When she wasn't inside cooking and doing housework, laundry, and looking after the children, she was out in the yard working alongside Frank - mostly during the busy time of year when the processing of the turkeys began.

Oshkosh Daily Northwestern, November 5, 1969

In 1969, Frank Schuster turned the key for the last time on the turkey business. Frank was getting up there in years and his oldest son Robert began experiencing health problems. In addition, low market prices made it very difficult to turn a decent profit. An ad was run in the *Oshkosh Daily Northwestern* on November 5 of that year, informing patrons and the public that the Schuster Turkey Farm was no longer in business, graciously thanking all their customers for so many years of loyal patronage.

An auction was held to sell off the machinery and livestock.

Frank and Elsie continued to live in the farmhouse until early 1975.

Robert Schuster died at the young age of 55 years in 1970.

On January 31, 1975, Frank Schuster passed away and Elsie moved into the Simeanna Apartments on Oshkosh's west side. Elsie died on November 12, 1990 at the age of 97.

Sources: Personal interviews with Schuster family members; (1) *Oshkosh Daily Northwestern* 5/11/1939; (2) *Oshkosh Daily Northwestern* April 23, 1917; (3) 1920 Census; The Livestock Conservancy; Winnebago County D.H.I.A. No. 2 Report for October 1939 as published in the *Oshkosh Daily Northwestern* 11/16/1939; (4) *Oshkosh Daily Northwestern* 10/18/1968, p 23;

THE AMAZING JOE POTTER

By Kevin Lisowe
(Introduction by Randy Domer)

It was a late fall day in 2017 and I was sitting at my desk working on stories for this book, when I received an email through the phone message system we have setup at the Winnebago County Historical Society. As President of the Society, all messages that are left on our answering system there get forwarded to me.

The message was from someone in the Neenah area who was doing research about a man who once lived in Oshkosh.

The person leaving the message was Kevin Lisowe.

As I listened to his message, I had no idea who the person was in which he was seeking information. I responded we had nothing on the subject, then provided my contact information should he have any further questions.

A few days later he emailed me back with an apology saying he had given me the wrong name.

The person he was seeking was named Joe Potter. William E. Joseph Potter to be exact.

Well, I was still stumped having never heard of this person. My first thoughts were that perhaps this was a relative from the Potter family of the Mueller Potter Drug Store fame here in Oshkosh.

It turns out that THIS Joe Potter was more than that. Kevin and I exchanged more communications and as I learned more about his quest, I became very intrigued. Kevin quickly filled me in and I immediately invited him to write his story for this book.

He agreed.

As I usually like to do with "guest authors", here is a little bio on Kevin Lisowe.

First, Kevin is not a writer or author by trade. He and his wife Melissa own The Great Harvest Bread Company in Neenah, a business they've owned since 2005. One of Kevin's favorite pastimes is listening to podcasts while he's walking the family dog, driving, doing the grocery shopping or cooking tonight's dinner.

One evening, he was listening to a program on the early history of Disney World in Florida and they were talking about a man named General Joe Potter. Kevin quickly hit the rewind button because he was interested and wanted to hear the podcast in its entirety. He then heard the host say that Potter hailed from Oshkosh, Wisconsin.

That peaked Kevin's interest and sent him flying into action, wanting to know more. He began searching the internet and even contacted one Jim Korkis, a Disney historian. With Jim's help and countless hours pouring through on-line newspapers, Kevin assembled a story about a man who accomplished more in his lifetime than anyone could in three lifetimes.

Many people in the Disney fan community are familiar with the name, but few people know who he was. Hopefully, more people locally will come to appreciate Joe Potter and his association with Oshkosh, Wisconsin, for what he accomplished in his lifetime had an impact all around the globe.

Here is Kevin's story.

"Without a Joe Potter, there would be no Disney World today"
These were the words of Dick Nunis, former President of Walt Disney World Attractions, given in an interview with the Orlando Sentinel in 1988. Walt Disney World would not exist, as we know it today, without Joe Potter's ingenuity and dedication. He was hired by Walt Disney to oversee the early construction of 27,000 acres in Florida that would eventually become Walt Disney World.

That is just one rung in the ladder of accomplishments of an Oshkosh native who helped make a difference in places all around this world.

William (Joe) E Potter was born in Oshkosh, Wisconsin on July 17, 1905. He was the son of William B. and Arlie Potter. Joe's father worked in Oshkosh as a photographer and later as a ticket agent for the railroad.

The family moved often throughout the city in Joe's early grade school years. At the time of his birth, the Potter family lived at 45 Baldwin Street (today's address is 114 Baldwin Ave). According to census records and Oshkosh City Directories, the Potters were living at 151 Beach Street in 1908, then by 1910 their address was listed as 321 Jefferson Street (after the 1957 address change the new address was 817 Jefferson Street – today that location is a church parking lot). The 1912 and 1914 City Directories report the Potters resided at 505 Mt. Vernon Ave. (today 1221 Mt. Vernon Ave). By 1918 the family moved away from Oshkosh.

Home on Baldwin Street where Joe Potter was born in 1905

Photo courtesy Randy Domer

During the first World War, young Joe and his family moved to Beloit, Wisconsin where his father worked for a time as an assembler in an automobile factory. Later the Potter family moved to Toledo, Ohio where Joe would graduate from Scott High School. In 1923 he would head out on his own and attend the United States Military Academy at West Point, the Massachusetts Institute of Technology (MIT) and the National War College in Washington DC.

During World War Il, Potter directed logistical planning for the invasion of northern France with an operation known as "Red Ball Express". This was the name of a trucking supply route designed to constantly supply the Allied front lines and their ever-advancing march across France. After the invasion of Normandy, the railways in France were bombed to cut off resupply routes for the German forces and to limit their abilities to obtain reinforcements. A high-speed truck delivery system was designed to bring a constant supply of food, fuel and ammunition to Patton's Army. There were around 6000 trucks used in the operation.

After the war he served as Assistant Chief of Engineers for Civic Works and Special Projects. He worked on flood control in Kansas City, a large dam construction on the Missouri River and worked on St. Lawrence Seaway projects.

In 1956 President Dwight D. Eisenhower appointed Potter as Governor of the Panama Canal Zone. The role of Panama Canal Zone Governor was to watch over and maintain the daily operations of the canal zone. This would include the workers medical, safety, and education. Potter would serve there for four years. In 1994 the American Society of Civil Engineers recognized the canal as one of the seven wonders of the modern world.

Joe Potter retired from public service after 38 years as Army Major General in 1960 at the age of 55. In his military career he was decorated with a Distinguished Service medal, Bronze Star, Legion of Merit, and the French Croix de Guerre (awarded to individuals or groups for feats of bravery during the two World Wars).

After leaving the military, Joe Potter served as Executive Vice President of the 1964-65 World's Fair under Robert Moses in Queens, New York. His responsibilities included the handling of construction of federal and attractions from the participating states.

This is where he would come to meet Walt Disney.

The Disney company was building four attractions for the fair. Walt was so impressed with Potter that he recruited him to oversee the construction of the yet un-announced Walt Disney World in Florida.

Potter officially joined Disney in September 1965, ten years after the opening of Disneyland in California. At this time, Walt Disney was pursuing a much larger project in Florida known as Project X or Disneyland East. This was to become a prototype city of tomorrow with a Disney theme park as a portion of it. It became publicly known as EPCOT in 1966. Disneyland in California was built on a 300-acre sandy orange grove. The land purchased for the "Florida Project" was over 27,258 acres (47 square miles) of Cyprus trees and swamp land.

A development of this size would require millions of dollars and years of work just to prepare the site for the construction phase.

Joe Potter's job at the EPCOT site (Walt Disney World in Florida) was to ready this newly acquired swamp land for construction. In the end, this included creating 55 miles of natural looking canals to drain the water and control flooding, and miles of roadway had to be constructed at the same time, creating usable land to build upon. He also was in charge of the development of underground utilities, sewer, power, and water treatment plants on the property. High voltage electrical power had to be brought in from 15 miles away. Everything about this project was done on a grand scale.

Potter introduced new techniques which were considered revolutionary at the time. Because of Florida's famous sink holes, the entire site had to be drill tested and compacting had to be done on the areas where building was to take place to determine if construction was feasible.

In 1967 the Florida State legislature, working with Walt Disney World Company, created a special taxing district – called the Reedy Creek Improvement District – that would act with the same authority and responsibility as a county government. General Potter sat on the Reedy Creek Improvement District board, allowing Disney to exercise control over its large property. This would come to serve Disney well early on as it would expedite things typically governed by a building inspector's office. His brilliant strategy of having Disney's own people oversee the planning and building process would help eliminate red tape and expedite things. This efficiency was not designed to cut corners as most of what was being built was so advanced it exceeded the expertise of the Orange County inspectors at the time. They just had not come across plans on this scale before. When the plans became too complicated for the Reedy Creek people, the new arrangement allowed them to bring in outside specialists to assist on a short-term basis.

One of the most important responsibilities Joe Potter had to the people of the Orlando area, was to serve as the middle-man between them and the Disney corporation. Potter was the one answering questions locally, and was often seen giving tours to help ease community concerns during the transition. He was looked upon as "Walt Disney" to the locals.

There are three places in Walt Disney World that pay tribute to Joe Potter for his work.

The first is a façade window inside the Magic Kingdom. The windows inside the park show the names of the people who have made significant contributions to the Walt Disney World project. It reads, "General Joe's Building Permits Licensed in Florida, Gen. Joe Potter - Raconteur." His window is located above the Confectionery on Main Street USA.

There is an un-official tribute crisscrossing the property in the waterway canals. They have been referred to as "Joe's ditches."

The final location is found on a large ferry boat that transports people from the ticket and transportation center to the entrance to the Magic Kingdom and back. The white, two-level ferry boat has two black smoke stacks set one in front of another. It is decorated in blue trim and has a sign reading "General Joe Potter" boldly printed across the front of its bow. There is also a plaque onboard that reads as follows:

General Joe Potter
Major General William E. "Joe" Potter had already spent 38 years with the U.S. Army and served as Panama Zone governor when Walt Disney hired him in 1965 to direct the construction of the infrastructure for Walt Disney World. He used techniques that were considered at that time revolutionary. Following the opening of Walt Disney World, he became its senior vice president until retiring in 1974. This boat is named in his honor.

Joe Potter died December 5, 1988 in Orlando, Florida. His list of accomplishments can still be felt to this day. He helped bridge a gap for thousands of men in France between their supplies and their fighting locations during World War II. His work connecting the Gulf of Mexico to the Pacific Ocean transformed not only the country of Panama but the entire way shipping is done on this side of the world. Finally, he helped the Orlando, Florida community transform into a world-wide tourist destination all while raising two girls with his wife Ruth.

It's quite remarkable to see the imprint left by one man who grew up in the small city of Oshkosh, Wisconsin.

Sources: *History Net Magazine*, "On the Road to Victory: The Red Ball Express" David P Colley; *Orlando Sentinel*. December 6,1988. "Joe Potter Disney Behind-the-Scenes Man, Dies at 83", Kirsten Gallagher; Encyclopedia com. Panama Canal Zone Article; Mouse Planet.com "The Lost Joe Potter Interview", Jim Korkis, August 13, 2014; "Connecting with Walt" Podcast. Episode 11, "Disney Legends Who Build a World". April 8, 2016; 023 The Official Disney Fan Club website; History.com. Panama Canal Facts and Summary; apps.westpointaog_org. William E Potter 1928; *New York Times*. Dec. 7, 1988. Obituaries. W.E. Potter, 83, Army Engineer; Walt Disney World. Wikipedia; www.rcid.org/about/

THE TWENTIETH CENTURY CLUB

The Twentieth Century Association was a society organized by Mrs. Mary Jewell Sawyer and many other prominent Oshkosh women. The first meeting was held October 31, 1896, at the Congregational Church on Algoma Blvd.

The all-female group was interested in the culture of the day. The club was organized with seven departments, art & music, education, philanthropy, and social. The name was The Twentieth Century Association. Eventually all the departments were discontinued.

The club originally met once a month, but latter that changed to two per month with President's Day, October 12, the opening of the club's season.

The first president was Mrs. R.H. Edwards, but she and her family moved west and that left Mrs. Leander Choate in charge.

Jessie Jack Hooper served as the club's seventh president from 1911-1914.

The home where this group would meet and conduct their social activities was built by lumberman Joel Mead about 1860 and later occupied by his son, Frank Mead and his wife, it is located at the northeast corner of Wisconsin and High Ave. The home was at one time bequeathed to the Oshkosh Benevolent Society and was being considered as a home for elderly women, but they deemed it unfit for their purposes.

The ladies of the Twentieth Century Association purchased the building in 1900 from the Oshkosh Ladies Benevolent Society for $5,000, and an additional $1,000 in improvements. The building was remodeled and a ballroom on the east side of the building was added. The home was known as "The Century" and was first occupied about October 16,1901, with first official use on October31, 1901, by the

Guild of St. Cecelia of Trinity Episcopal Church. The building was rented out to several groups through the years and was also used for wedding dances. It was home to the ladies for 69 years. In 1910 the name of the organization changed its name to the Twentieth Century Club.

The club finally sold the property in 1968, but the ladies met there until January 1969. Then from 1970-1994 the ladies met at the Legion until 1996 when they gathered at the new Senior Center on Campbell Road.

Other early members: Mrs. John Hicks, Mrs. Charles C. Chase, Mrs. Leander Choate, Mrs. B.C. Gudden, Mrs. Luther Davis, Mrs. John Bray and Mrs. L. M. Webster.

Sources: Much of this this transcript was provided by The Twentieth Century Club in April 2017 with written permission by President Ruth Vorpahl to use in print. Source for this information is the Oshkosh Public Library

THE DEATH AND FUNERAL OF
SENATOR PHILETUS SAWYER

EX-SENATOR SAWYER DEAD.
Unexpected End of the Venerable
Statesman and Philanthropist
Occurs This Morning.
OSHKOSH SHOCKED BY NEWS.

This was the glaring headline in the *Oshkosh Daily Northwestern's* five o'clock edition on Thursday, March 29, 1900. The former US Senator from Oshkosh had died unexpectedly. He was 83 years of age.

Perhaps one of most noteworthy and prestigious of Oshkosh's city residents, Philetus Sawyer served in both the House and Senate for twenty-two years. Born Philetus Horace Sawyer (he preferred not to use his middle name or initial in life) in 1816, Sawyer spent his early years living with his parents in the states of Vermont and New York. He began working at a very young age and assisted his father, a blacksmith by trade, in various tasks. By the age of 21, Sawyer focused his labors in the lumber industry.

In 1841 he married Miss Melvina M. Hadley and one year later his first son was born…Edgar P. Sawyer. A few years later a second son was born and Philetus had the urge to move further west in to the frontier where lumber was abundant. His travels took him to St. Louis and up the

Senator Philetus Sawyer

Photo Courtesy Library of Congress - Public Domain

Mississippi River into Wisconsin, ending up in Fond du Lac County. There, in Rosendale, Wisconsin, he built a log cabin on 525 acres of land which he purchased for $1.25 an acre. He returned home to New York, gathered up his family and their belongings and moved them to their new home in Wisconsin in 1847.[6]

"When he came to Wisconsin...Sawyer could scarcely write. But he came with ambition and a fair bit of knowledge about saw mills", according to local historian, James Metz. He had tried his hand at farming in Rosendale but that didn't suit him so he became involved in the lumber industry.[6]

In 1850, Sawyer went to work in a mill owned by D.W. Forman in the Town of Algoma. Three years later, the mill failed and Sawyer purchased it with help from a few other local businessmen. The new mill was known as Brand, Olcott & Company – later to become W.B. Brand & Company. It was during this time the company purchased some prime pine acreage along the Wolf River. Then war broke out. In 1862, Mr. Brand became nervous and wanted to sell his share of the business. Sawyer had a more forward-thinking posture, seeing nothing but opportunity and eagerly bought his partners shares. The impact of the Civil War saw the price of manufactured lumber soar and Philetus Sawyer was well on his way to build his fortune.

In spite of his lack of formal advanced education, Sawyer learned to become an astute businessman and as the result his lumber business grew in leaps and bounds. His business interests were quite diversified including ventures with the Railroad, a Texas Cattle Company and even a local gas company. The *Oshkosh Daily Northwestern* reported in 1882:

> *It is probable that Mr. Sawyer's youthfulness and large-hearted good nature have had much to do with his success. Starting out poor, without the help of education or friends, he finds himself at sixty-five a millionaire and a Senator... We may call it "luck", but it is the luck that attends good management and farseeing.*[8]

Along with his businesses, his aspirations to become a public servant flourished and he was elected to the Wisconsin State Assembly in 1857 and 1861. It was here that Philetus formed a business partnership with his son Edgar, who was 21 years of age at the time. The firm was known as P. Sawyer & Son. He became Oshkosh Mayor from 1863-1864 and left that office only to be elected to the US House of Representatives from 1865-1875. He returned to public office in 1881 as a US Senator and held that office until 1893 when he decided against running for a third term. He was considered a leader of the Republican party.

In 1884, Sawyer purchased over 2,000 acres of land in what then was considered Ashland County (later to be named Sawyer County). He was said to be a generous and kind man. He gifted $25,000 for the building of a new public library in Oshkosh. Construction on the library began in 1899 with the grand opening on September 3, 1900…five months after Mr. Sawyer's death. One of the two concrete lions that adorn the front of the library are named "Sawyer" in his honor.

The Death of Philetus Sawyer

As reported in the *Oshkosh Daily Northwestern* on the evening of March 29, 1900, Sawyer died at 9:16 that morning at the Algoma Boulevard home of his son, Edgar P. Sawyer. He expired in the Northeast Chamber, the room where he stayed each winter while living in his son's home. It was customary for him to live with his son each winter, his nearby residence closed for the season. Sawyer had been ill, but it seemed nothing serious according to an article published in the day's previous edition of the newspaper. The article stated that Sawyer was confined to his bed by Dr. T. P. Russell, but the illness was "not considered serious".

The death was unexpected. Dr. Russell filed the following report on the former Senator's condition in the days leading up to his death.

He was in his usual condition until Sunday. Saturday, he felt a little indisposed, but he did not go to bed. He did not sleep well Saturday night and Sunday spent an uncomfortable day. Sunday, he passed a restless night and on Monday I made an examination of his heart. I found that it was affected and was becoming irregular. The disease of the heart became much worse Monday and Tuesday I examined his kidneys and found them inactive.

This caused him to turn yellow. He became sore and complained he was uncomfortable while riding in his carriage. Tuesday morning he went down town and attended to some duties at the bank. He complained of pain caused apparently from the jolting of the carriage. Tuesday afternoon he went down town again and called at my office. When he returned home at four o'clock he went to bed. Then he gradually grew worse and worse until the end came. It was a general breaking up of his system.[2]

Senator Sawyer had an appointment with Dr. W. A. Gordon on that Thursday morning, but when the physician arrived he found Sawyer had passed away.

Edgar had conversations with his father in the days before his passing and felt the elder statesman sensed the end was near. As they discussed business matters, Philetus often included the phrase "...if anything should happen...", leaving little doubt that he was preparing to die.

The only person in the room with the former Senator at the time of his passing was Caroline, the wife of his grandson, Phil H. Sawyer II. Edgar was in the room moments previous to the end, but stepped out momentarily, unaware the situation was about to take a turn for the worse. His father seemed to be resting comfortably and exhibited no cause for alarm.

As his grandson's wife sat at his bedside, tending to his needs, Sawyer raised his hand over his head, possibly indicating he wanted his pillows adjusted. When the young Mrs. Sawyer asked if his pillows suited his comfort, he indicated that he was comfortable. A few moments later he asked her to remove his shoes and stockings – but had none on. It was his last request.

Sawyer then raised his hands over his head, took a long breath and seemed to fall asleep. At first Mrs. Sawyer thought he was asleep, but soon realized he was gone. She summoned the other family members into the room where they paid their last respects. The only family members in the house at the time were his son Edgar, grandson Phil and his wife. Mrs. Edgar Sawyer was away in Washington.

Philetus Sawyer's next of kin included his son, Edgar, a daughter, Mrs. W. O. Goodman of Chicago, a half-sister, Lydia Sawyer Shaw of Garden Grove, Iowa,[9] several grandchildren and two great-grandchildren. His beloved wife, Melvina, died on May 21, 1888 after a lengthy illness. Philetus and Melvina had two other children that died in infancy. A daughter Ella E. (1849-1851) and a son Earl T. (1845-1848)

Granddaughter Nia (Mrs. Charles Curry Chase) was unable to attend the funeral under the advisement of her physician. She was bereaved and shocked over the recent loss of an infant child and it was feared the strain of travel and attending the funeral would be too much for her. Mr. Chase would travel to New York to meet his wife immediately after the funeral and accompany her home.

Word of Sawyer's death spread quickly throughout the city, state and nation. Here at home, flags were lowered to half-mast. Cablegrams were received from across the world. Oshkosh's Col. John Hicks sent a cablegram from Italy where he was vacationing, expressing his condolences for the loss of his friend and colleague.

Local churches honored the elder statesman in various ways. The First Congregational Church of which Philetus was a member, draped the Sawyer pew in mourning and placed a bouquet of Calla lilies at the entrance. A memorial service was conducted in his honor. Across town, churches dedicated their Sunday service to the qualities of a man who endeared himself highly within the Oshkosh community.

The Funeral

Funeral arrangements were made to take place on Sunday, April 2. The family wanted the service to be simple with "little of display and free of ceremonials".[3] The funeral was originally planned to be held at the West Algoma Street home of his son Edgar Sawyer. On the evening before that plan had changed. Mrs. E.P. Sawyer and Mrs. W.O. Goodman (daughter of the deceased) arrived that evening and after meeting with the family, it was decided the funeral services would be held in the residence of the deceased. The ex-Senator's home had been closed for some time as the Senator preferred to live with his son during the winter months. The family felt the accommodations would be preferable and the family considered it to be the wish of Mr. Sawyer, though unexpressed by him prior to his death. It was agreed the Senator would undoubtedly prefer to be prepared for his burial from his old home where he had spent so many of the last years of his life.

Around eight o'clock that evening, the casket was taken to the second-floor hallway outside the room where "all that was mortal of the former senator reposed". The casket was too big to enter the room so the body was carried from the "death chamber" to the hallway and carefully placed in the casket. Family members and the undertaker then slowly carried the casket down the stairway, out the front entrance and across West Algoma to the deceased senator's residence. The casket was situated in the parlor located in the southeast section of the residence where the family nurse kept vigil over the deposed dignitary through the silence of night.[7] From the time of his death until that evening, the Senator's body remained in the room where he died. The reason for this was that "The temperature of the rooms on the first floor is maintained at a degree that would be detrimental to the appearance of the body…"[3]

One day after his death, it is reported that the attending physician's orders were to delay embalming to allow the remains to remain undisturbed for a brief time. Newspaper accounts reported that Sawyer "looked exceedingly natural, and the grand old man appears to be fast asleep. His features are somewhat drawn, but the saffron hue which came over his countenance Tuesday will have disappeared by the time the remains are exposed to the view".[3]

Public viewing and visitation were held from 10 am to noon and then 1pm until the time of the service at 2 pm. Services at the home and cemetery were conducted by Reverend E. H. Smith of the First Congregational Church.

Before his death, the Senator expressed his desire to have a special casket designed. Undertaker H. P. Soper was contacted to provide a temporary casket until the one specially designed by Sawyer could be constructed. The casket in which Senator Sawyer would lie in state was perhaps one of the finest caskets ever provided to anyone in the State. The exterior of the casket was massive and impressive, trimmed with black broadcloth and gold handles, attached with a solid gold bar and four heavy plates of ebony and gold. An inscribed plate was inserted on the center panel of the lid. The plate had an ebony finish and edged with brandished gold. It was engraved with: **Philetus Sawyer 1816-1900**

The *Oshkosh Daily Northwestern* article in the March 30, 1900 edition went on to say –

The interior of the casket is elegantly trimmed, the satin concealing all but the upper edge of the heavy copper case which fits closely inside the wood and broadcloth outer case. This copper case is fitted with plate glass for one half its length so that the remains of Mr. Sawyer can be viewed. The interior of the casket is trimmed with rich satin honeycomb with tufted edges. At the head is a pillow of embroidered satin.

This casket would be placed in the Sawyer vault until the permanent casket made to the Senator's specifications was ready. The permanent casket was made of Red Cedar, copper lined and hermetically sealed.

As reported earlier, son Edgar had reported he felt his father had sensed the end was near. Another indication of that is supported by the actions taken by the elder statesman just weeks before his death. He commissioned an artist from Madison to paint his portrait. James R. Stewart, who had painted about fifty portraits of men considered prominent in Wisconsin history, was selected to do the work. Sawyer sent Stewart two photographs and a written request that he put his likeness on canvas. The portrait was finished the day before Philetus Sawyer's passing.

Due to the anticipation of heavy crowds attending, the Citizen's Traction Company arranged to have streetcars transport people from Main Street to Riverside Cemetery every fifteen minutes throughout the day. Between the hours of noon and three o'clock the service was

Senator Philetus Sawyer's Home on West Algoma
Photo used with permission of the Wisconsin Historical Society

doubled with cars leaving every seven minutes. Special train schedules were made to accommodate out-of-town mourners who traveled great distances to pay their respects.

Crowds formed outside the Sawyer home - thousands of mourners from all walks of life, waiting to pay their final respects. The wealthy and poor, laborers, farmers, businessmen, politicians, friends young and old all waited with quiet grief, standing in line for hours in a drizzling rain – heads bowed in honor of the man who meant so much to this community. The floral offerings on display were described as "magnificent". Flags continued to wave at half-mast across the city and the National Bank of Oshkosh was draped in festoons of mourning in honor of their former director and chief stockholder.

Mr. Sawyer was dressed in a fine, black, Prince Albert suit that he had tailored just a short time ago. He recently wore the suit on a business trip to Washington DC. His left arm rested across his chest naturally and his shirt bore the same gold stud that Mr. Sawyer was known to have worn regularly.

Floral tributes began like no other this city has ever seen. Palms, lilies of every kind, wreaths of carnations and roses some measuring six-feet across filled the room. On the walls of the parlor were full length portraits of family members. On the wall behind the casket was the portrait of the Senator's deceased daughter, Mrs. Emma White. To one side was the portrait of the Senator and another of his deceased wife, Melvina. Opposite the casket displayed the portrait of the Senator's daughter, Mrs. W.O. Goodman.

A cadre of ushers were assembled to ensure the arrangements were carried out smoothly. Messrs. A. Von Kaas, Louis Schriber, R.P. Finney, Harry Gould, D.B. Curtis, Jr., Harry Birely, H.I. Weed, A.R. Hollister, J. Earl Morgan, William C. Bouck, C.D. Jackson, Charles Freeman, George N. Hoaglin, Edward Hill, Vernon Andrews, John Lloyd, Ed T. Cole, William Wallen, George Finch, William Bigger, Jay Hume, Fred Barkman, Ben C. Reed and James Jenkins held the honor on this most reverent day.

Public visitation began at 10 am and continued until noon, then resumed again at 1:00 pm until the time of the service. It was reported by the *Oshkosh Daily Northwestern* that 2,745 people passed by the casket before the doors to the palatial Sawyer estate finally closed at

2:30. The number of "humble and lowly" far outnumbered those of "high estate". The house was filled as the service began at 2:20pm. Rev. E. H. Smith from the First Congregational Church gave the service which lasted about an hour.

At the conclusion of the service, the casket was carried from the room down the hallway and out the front entryway to the waiting funeral carriage parked there.

The Pallbearers chosen to carry the prominent Senator to his final resting place were all Sawyer family members that included Edgar P. Sawyer, Phil H. Sawyer, C.C. Chase, William O. Goodman, Henry A. Jewell and W.T. Ellsworth. Senator Sawyer was a member of the Masons and Odd Fellow Fraternal Organizations – they were both present to pay their respects but did not formally take part in the ceremony. The Knights Templar, Masons, and Odd Fellows served as honorary escorts.

The carriage pulled away from the Sawyer Mansion and began the slow procession down West Algoma to Riverside Cemetery. The funeral cortege was led by two National Guard units - Company B under the command of E.W. Paine, and Company F under the command of U.G. Carl. Then came the members of the Knights Templar commanded by Thomas Whitely, followed by the Funeral Carriage and carriages of family, common council members and family friends. Both the military and Knights Templar groups marched in full uniform. The streets were lined with thousands of mourners who braved the bad weather for a final glimpse of Senator Philetus Sawyer.

As the funeral procession reached Riverside Cemetery, the scene was described by the *Oshkosh Daily Northwestern*:

> *At Riverside Cemetery it was with great difficulty that the crowd could get within hearing distance of the services. Long before the conclusion of the services at the house people who were anxious to see the casket placed in the crypt in the vault went to the cemetery and waited. The drizzling rain rendered the place exceedingly uncomfortable, yet many people braved the discomforts and remained near the vault. The bare, lifeless trees dripping with wet seemed melancholy and sad.[5]*

The Sawyer mausoleum was built a few years earlier after the death of Philetus' wife Melvina. Sawyer paid $10,000 to have the vault constructed as it was his wish to provide a final resting place of honor and dignity for his family.

A horse drawn carriage arrived first with the floral display that covered the casket at the Sawyer home. The flowers were arranged inside the vault awaiting the arrival of the Sawyer casket. The pathway to the vault was lined with members of the Knights Templar who took their position with swords drawn along with two lines of Policemen. As the funeral carriage pulled near the vault, it was met by the pall bearers who carried the casket into the vault, placing Philetus next to his wife. Only family members, Governor and Mrs. Scofield, and Rev Smith entered the tomb.

A brief prayer service was offered bringing conclusion to the funeral service for Senator Philetus Sawyer.

"Then the sorrowing relatives departed, the doors of the vault were closed, and the dead was left in silence and alone." -Source: *Oshkosh Weekly Times, June 2, 1888, "BORNE TO HER REST – Remains of Mrs. Senator Sawyer Deposited in the Vault At Riverside Cemetery"*

(Author's Notes) One day recently, as I traveled into Oshkosh from my home north of the city, my driving route took me past Riverside Cemetery. As I usually do, I could not help but to gaze into this massive graveyard and marvel at its history – thinking of all the names of those who helped shape Oshkosh's history. I had a little extra time on my hands as I was running a bit early for a meeting at the Oshkosh Public Museum, so I turned into the entrance that led me into the cemetery. Some of the narrow roads within are named to help visitors find their way. As I knew where the Sawyer Mausoleum was located, I decided to visit there first. This old cemetery is nestled on the northeast shore of the Fox River, across from Rainbow Memorial Park. My thoughts drifted back to those early years when loggers navigated their harvest from the northern woods down the Wolf and Fox Rivers, across Lake Butte des Morts, to the numerous sawmills located here. Old wood pilings that were used to keep the thousands of giant floating timbers in check can still be seen along the water's edge near the cemetery, reminding us of those days when Oshkosh grew on the backs and shoulders of the lumber industry boom.

I noticed the lane I had chosen was named Laurel Ave and I followed it until I reached Maple Ave and turned north. Immediately I noticed the Sawyer Mausoleum just a short distance ahead. As I slowly rolled toward it, I was taken aback by the fact that not unlike in life, the Sawyer family's final resting place was among the elite...the most privileged and influential. Some of the greatest family names carved in the legacy of Oshkosh's history surround the family burial tomb. Jewell, Paine, Hay, Nevitt, Rahr, Hardy, and Pollock families, just to name a few, now rest in peace near Philetus and Melvina and their descendants.

Sawyer Family Mausoleum at Oshkosh's Riverside Cemetery

Photo courtesy Randy Domer

Twenty-four souls in all rest in peace here today (2018).

Here is a list of the Sawyer Family members who have been laid to rest in the Sawyer Mausoleum. Some are full burials and some cremation ashes.

Name	Relationship	Born	Died
Sawyer, Philetus		1816	1900
Sawyer, Melvina M.	Wife of Philetus	1825	1888
Sawyer, Edgar P.	Son of Philetus	1842	1927
Sawyer, Mary E. Jewell	Wife of Edgar	1842	1910
Chase, Charles Curry	Husband of Nia Sawyer	1859	1917
Chase, Mary Henrietta	Infant daughter of Charles and Nia Chase	1892	1892
Chase, Prescott Sawyer	Infant son of Charles and Nia Chase	1899	1900
White, Emma Sawyer	Daughter of Philetus and Melvina, wife of Howard G. White	1855	1896
White, Sawyer B.	Young son of Howard and Emma White	1883	1885

Sawyer, Ella E.	Young daughter of Philetus and Melvina	1849	1851
Sawyer, Earl T.	Young son of Philetus and Melvina	1845	1848
Meredith, Jewell Chase	Daughter of CC and Nia Chase, wife of Roy Meredith	1888	1935
Chase, Nia Sawyer	Daughter of Edgar and Mary Jewell Sawyer	1865	1935
Sawyer, Phil H. II	Son of Edgar and Mary Jewell Sawyer	1873	1941
Fatio, Maurice	Husband of Eleanor Chase Fatio	1897	1943
Meredith, John Francis	Young son of Roy and Jewell Meredith	1926	1931
Sawyer, Caroline Upham	Wife of Phil H. Sawyer II	1876	1941
Fatio, Eleanor Chase	Daughter of Charles and Nia Chase; wife of Maurice	1903	1944
Sawyer, Edgar P. II (Ted)	Son of Phil H. Sawyer II	1918	1973
Sawyer, Elizabeth	First wife of Phil H. Sawyer Jr.	1910	1976
Sawyer, Mary Radke	Second wife of Phil H. Sawyer Jr.	1923	1981
Sawyer, Philetus H. Jr.	Son of Phil H. and Caroline Sawyer	1907	1982
Sawyer, Ann Katherine Fish	Wife of EP Sawyer II (Ted)	1920	2007
Von Liphart Sawyer, Barbara (Bobbi)	Daughter of EP Sawyer II and Ann Katherine	1943	2010

Additional Interesting Anecdotes on the Life of Philetus Sawyer

- **Death of Mr. Sawyer's Colored Boy** (*Oshkosh Daily Northwestern*, Aug. 30, 1876, p.4)

The colored boy named Eben Dorsey, who has been in Philetus Sawyer's family for the last 8 years, died very suddenly Monday morning. He had been suffering for some time from consumption which was growing upon him, and, on Monday, while in the yard near the house, suddenly the blood from hemorrhage in his lungs, burst out of his mouth so copiously and in such clotted masses as to strangle him to death before the family could reach him. He was 16 years of age, and a very bright and remarkable boy. Mr. Sawyer took him out of the colored Orphan's Home at Washington eight years ago and has kept him at school ever since. He was very intelligent and a constant reader. The family had become very much attached to him. Mr. Sawyer purchased a lot especially for him in the cemetery and he was buried with much solemnity and ceremony.

The Sawyers brought Eben back to Oshkosh in the late 1860s, and in the 1870 census he is listed in their household as a waiter. The Oshkosh Weekly Northwestern reported in 1873 that Eben went to high school and had perfect attendance. At the end of the 1873 school year he was ranked 95.3 in attendance, deportment and scholarship.

- **Senator Attends Wedding Ceremony**

Social news was much in the forefront in the late 19th century. Articles would appear in the local papers announcing who the Sawyers were entertaining for guests, which social events they were attending and even activities as simple as a card game would make the social pages. On March 2, 1883, the *Oshkosh Daily Northwestern* reported the Senator attended the Washington wedding of fellow Senator Tabor and former Oshkosh socialite, Elizabeth B. McCourt (Baby Doe Tabor). Tabor was billed as "the Millionaire Senator from Colorado". US President Chester A. Arthur was in attendance as well that evening.

- **Mr. Sawyer's Corpulancy**

Physical descriptions of Philetus Sawyer, especially in his later years, are told in quite amusing fashions.

  ○ *...The fattest and the heaviest Senator is Philetus Sawyer, who, though he is short, will pull the beam at 250 (Van Wert [Ohio] Republican, Sept. 23, 1886)*
  ○ *Washington Letter: Philetus Sawyer has a bristling white beard and his big head sits close to his fat, healthy shoulders. His forehead and crown, and side whiskers of silver, shine out over his ears. He has a wisp also at the back of his neck and he looks much like a blacksmith with brains (Oshkosh Daily Northwestern, Jan.10, 1888)*
  ○ *Senator Sawyer used to be so round and fat that some of the boys irreverently called him "Roley-Boley" whenever he walked or waddled across the senate chamber. (Burlington [Iowa] Hawk-Eye, Sept. 7, 1890)*
  ○ *Senator Sawyer has for some years been troubled by his excessive corpulancy. But at last he has found an efficient anti-fat remedy. Eight months ago, he weighed 240 pounds but by means of severe dieting he has at last succeeded in reducing his weight seventy pounds. Sawyer urged his family physician to give him something to help him lose weight, but all he received was some sound advice. Well, he told me to eat nothing for forty days; and, when I protested that it would kill me, he said I might as well be dead as to be so fat and uncomfortable. After a great deal of begging on the part of the portly politician, the doctor agreed to a diet that would only half-starve himself. Basically, he removed potatoes from his diet, leaving the senator feeling satisfied at mealtime. (Oshkosh Daily Northwestern, Sep. 12, 1890, p.4)*

- **Oshkosh's Most Prominent Resident**

  ○ *...ex-Senator Sawyer...the wealthiest man in Oshkosh (Oshkosh Daily Northwestern, Dec.7, 1895, p.1); Ex-Senator Philetus Sawyer has been personally and intimately acquainted with* *every (US) President since the time of Lincoln. (Oshkosh Daily Northwestern, Apr. 2, 1898, p. 5)*

Sources: (1) *Oshkosh Daily Northwestern*, March 28, 1900; (2) March 29, 1900, p. 1; (3) March 30, 1900, p. 1; (4) March 31,1900, pp. 1,3; (5) April 2, 1900, p. 1; (6) James Metz article for WCHAS *County Fare* Q1 2014; (7) April 2, 1900 p. 4; (8) *Oshkosh Daily Northwestern*, March 20, 1882, p. 2; (9) *All About The Sawyers,* V. 1, p. 288, by Ginny Gross and the Oshkosh Public Museum, 2016; *Biographical Directory of the United States Congress, 1774 to Present*, http://bioguide.congress.gov/scripts/biodisplay.pl?index=s000091

RIDING THE WHITE MULE

Oshkosh During Prohibition

by Lee Reiherzer

Lee Reiherzer is a local historian who specializes in the research of the brewing history of Oshkosh and Winnebago County, and more broadly the State of Wisconsin. Lee is locally famous for the depth of his knowledge in the brewing industry. It could be said that brewing and selling beer was probably second only to the lumber industry here in the 19th and 20th centuries. The European immigrants that settled here loved their beer. He publishes a beer blog on social media and has written and shared many stories in recent years, which I always enjoy reading. It is for that reason that I invited Lee to write a chapter on a topic of his choice for this book. After some serious consideration, he said "I'd like to write about Prohibition in Oshkosh." Here is his story...

An Oshkosh Wake

It started with a party. One last blowout. They were going to drink Oshkosh dry. People began early. They gathered anywhere liquor was sold. The Oshkosh Wine and Liquor Company on North Main got cleaned out. All three Oshkosh breweries sold off their stock of bottled beer before sunset. This would not be a typical Monday.

By early evening, the saloons were packed, filled with rowdy patrons whose intent was getting loaded. At some places, they smashed their glasses after each round they downed. "It was more or less of a wild night about town," reported the *Oshkosh Daily Northwestern*. "Jags were numerous and many people got a 'bun' on who have not been intoxicated in a long time."

They were inspired to drink by a new law that would forbid just that. It was the first of many such ironies that epitomized the dry years in Oshkosh.

The big party of June 30, 1919, was in reaction to the Wartime Prohibition Act. As WWI was grinding to an end, Congress passed an agricultural bill aimed at conserving food resources. But the bill also carried a rider banning the sale of alcoholic beverages. It was to become law on July 1, 1919. In another six months, the 18th Amendment and National Prohibition would go into effect. By then, liquor had already been made illegal.

Meanwhile, the Monday night party roared on. At the Oshkosh Elks Club, they wanted to send booze off in style. The Elks held a wake at their lodge on Jefferson Ave. They planned to follow it with a funeral procession down North Main St. But when it came time to parade, the Elks couldn't be persuaded to leave the bar.

At midnight, revelers spilled out of downtown saloons and onto North Main St. They brought with them all the liquor they could carry. The party continued in the street. The cops let it all go. Just four arrests were made. Even those guys were let off after they sobered up.

The Tuesday morning of July 1, 1919, was dry and warm. Many in Oshkosh woke to a hangover. The headaches would pass. The new reality would not. The sale of intoxicating liquor was now illegal. The party was supposed to be over. The party wasn't over. In some ways, it was only just beginning.

The Dry Tide

The impossible dream of James Densmore had come to be. Densmore launched Oshkosh's first newspaper, the *Oshkosh True Democrat*, in 1849. He used his paper to advocate for prohibitory liquor laws. The *True Democrat* was generously spiced with local samples of drunken mayhem.

Densmore was also a realist. It wasn't long before his cautionary booze tales were giving way to advertisements for Oshkosh beer, London porter, brandy, gin, and wine. Oshkosh, after all, was a drinking town. And Densmore had to make a buck. He later admitted, "Necessity compelled us to change our tactics." Densmore left Oshkosh for good in 1853.

A string of temperance boosters took up where Densmore left off. The list was long. Their grand vision surpassed only by their lavish names. The Oshkosh Temple of Honor and Temperance. The Iron Clad Temple of Honor and Temperance. The Royal Templars of Temperance. Their fervor always outpaced their effect.

Brewery owner August Horn was vice-president of Oshkosh's Anti-Prohibition Association. His casual dismissal of the dries was telling. Invoking the patron saint of beer, Horn published a rebuttal to his adversaries in 1886 saying, "Gambrinus is still hale and hearty, and very able to cope with any soda water devotee we ever saw."

The majority in Oshkosh paid little mind to either side of the argument. Perhaps they were too busy drinking. By 1893, Oshkosh was home to four breweries, a distillery and 126 saloons. This with a population of approximately 23,000. There wasn't dry land in sight. But the tide was slowly turning.

In the early 1900s smaller communities surrounding Oshkosh began to vote in dry laws. The restrictions weren't uniform, but the emerging pattern was. Neenah, Omro, the Town of Oshkosh, Winneconne and other townships and villages in Winnebago County went dry to varying degrees. Meanwhile in Oshkosh, try as some might, they couldn't even get the saloons to close on Sunday.

When it came to liquor, Oshkosh maintained a sense of exceptionalism. It had been ingrained over decades. It remained undiminished even after the dawn of National Prohibition in 1920. The city met the dry law with a mix of disbelief and disregard. And went right on drinking.

Crimewave

Initially, there were two paths to remaining in the drink. Those who could afford to, stockpiled. Alcoholic beverages purchased before Prohibition remained legal, though for personal use only. The other option was more commonly employed. Make your own. Moonshiners and homebrewers were suddenly everywhere in Oshkosh.

Their stories became the stuff of local legend: Women pushing baby carriages down city streets, but where the child once lay were now pints of moonshine for sale. Sewers on the south side were clogging again and again with spent mash. Neighborhoods across town made pungent with the unmistakable aroma of hops being boiled into beer.

The sudden interest in ho-made alcohol spawned cottage industries. Beer flats – one-room saloons in private homes – became common. People flocked to them to play cards and drink, just as they had before Prohibition. But now the barroom might also be the neighbor's dining room.

Beer doctors specialized in adding the kick back to near beer. Harry E. Wiese was one such practitioner. He operated from his home on West 12th Ave., near South Park. His specialty was known as "needling". Wiese would inject moonshine into bottles of near beer to make it something nearer to real beer. When he was arrested in 1927, police found enough materials on hand to "cure" 160 cases of non-alcoholic beer.

Wiese was a typical Oshkosh liquor-law offender. The son of German-born parents, he had a clean record before his arrest. He was a WWI Vet and worked a day job in the warehouse at Buckstaff's. In normal times, Wiese would not have been the type to turn to crime. But with the new law, respect for the law went out the window. Never in Oshkosh was criminal activity so commonplace.

A former Oshkosh bootlegger preferring to be known only as "Tom" summed it up best. "It was a bad law," Tom said. "The common man sure wasn't for it. Nobody thought it was wrong to violate it. Everybody drank."

White Mule

What they drank now was quite unlike what they used to drink. Moonshine had never been commonplace in Oshkosh...until Prohibition. Then it was everywhere. It was relatively quick and easy to make. And a little bit went a long way. Some in Oshkosh referred to it as the "white mule." A salute to its devastating kick.

The illicit allure of hard alcohol compounded its popularity. The "flask on the hip" became a symbol of defiance. The young were especially drawn to it. Underage drinking, always an issue in Oshkosh, grew endemic. Dancehalls that once catered to adults now staged youth dances to offset the loss of business that followed the loss of liquor sales.

"Anyone in town, who has goods to dispose of, can rent a hall, hire an orchestra and the dance is on," a letter writer to the *Daily Northwestern* complained. "Young men come with stocked hip pockets, and mere boys of 16 and 17 are drunk, and in the morning the janitors go about and gather up the flasks."

It all came to a head in the summer of 1922. On the night of July 29, a dance was held at Tyriver Hall, a former saloon owned by Louis Tyriver at the intersection of Oshkosh Ave. and Sawyer St. Now that Tyriver couldn't sell liquor, he rented the space out for dances. The July 29 dance was an ugly affair from the start.

Moonshine was being sold from two cars parked near the entrance to the hall. Neighbors reported seeing drunken boys loitering in the street and in front of the hall. It was a scene becoming all too common in Oshkosh. It wasn't enough to keep 19-year-old Marie Repp away. She wanted to dance.

Marie Repp was born in Oshkosh in 1903. Her parents were ethnic Germans born in Russia. They were among a wave of emigres from the Volga Region who came to Oshkosh at the turn of the century. The Volga Germans established a tight-knit, conservative neighborhood on the west side of Oshkosh. In the middle of it was Tyriver Hall. Marie Repp lived a block away.

The booze had already been flowing for a while when Marie Repp entered Tyriver Hall. Inside, she met Carlton Youngwirth. He was 20 and lived with his parents on Prospect Ave. His father was a cop. Prior to meeting Repp, Youngwirth had gotten into a fight outside the hall. He'd been drinking. He asked Repp to dance. She accepted. And about 10 p.m., they left Tyriver Hall together.

They were next seen shortly after midnight. Friends who saw her said Repp's white dress and shoes were muddy. They said Youngwirth appeared disheveled. Marie Repp arrived home shortly after. She was alone.

In the morning, her body was discovered by three young boys. She was partially naked, floating face down in Sawyer Creek. Youngwirth was arrested. Though there was little evidence, he was charged with criminal assault. The uproar on the west side was immediate.

"It is not the young men of West Algoma who are responsible for the disorder at the public dances," said one of the residents. "It is a group of pool hall graduates from the north side and some of the tough youngsters from the south side who come out here with a bottle on the hip and raise trouble."

Marie Repp's death would later be ruled a suicide. In the days that followed, Repp was portrayed as a victim of the moonshine epidemic. Her death a consequence of the lawlessness that had taken hold in the city since the onset of Prohibition.

What began as a lark no longer amused. "Into the jaws of death, into the mouth of hell, ride our sons and daughters, and we grease the wheels," an Oshkosh parent lamented. For the first time, a groundswell of anti-liquor sentiment was forming in Oshkosh. Something had to be done.

The Oshkosh Chief

Oshkosh police wanted nothing to do with it. Prohibition enforcement by city cops was lax in the extreme. Their indifference was hardly surprising. The better part of the 40-man force was drawn from the same working-class neighborhoods where the corner saloon was a fixture of daily life. Police in Oshkosh had little desire to arrest their neighbors for something that had long been part of the cultural fabric.

Federal officials bemoaned the local squad's lack of engagement. As early as 1921, the feds were voicing their displeasure. The complaints fell on deaf ears. The resistance ran from the mayor on down. After a raid by federal agents in 1921, Oshkosh Mayor Arthur C. McHenry made it plain. The feds weren't welcome in his city. McHenry lashed into Prohibition officials. "The City of Oshkosh is not in sympathy with prohibition enforcement," The mayor declared.

Oshkosh Police Chief Arthur Gabbert

Photo courtesy of Lee Reiherzer

A year later, things were different. The belligerence had been tempered by the Repp incident. If ever there was a point Oshkosh would fall into line it was now. And there was a new, tough talking chief of police promising to make that happen.

Arthur Gabbert was a 20-year veteran of the Oshkosh Police. He'd been named its chief a month prior to the Repp tragedy. In its wake, public pressure for a police response mounted. Gabbert responded. He said all the words he was supposed to.

"We intend to clean this city up, if possible, so far as moonshine is concerned," Gabbert told the *Daily Northwestern*. "There has been altogether too much of that sort of thing going on and we are going to put a stop to it."

Gabbert was wading into a morass. By the summer of 1922, the black-market liquor trade in Oshkosh had outstripped the ability of police to stop it. It was estimated that as many as 120 speakeasies operated in the city. Basement distilleries proliferated. Often, they were housed in the residential neighborhood. Some grew large. Frank Penzenstadler's still at 737 West 5th Ave could produce 90 gallons of white mule at a turn.

Art Gabbert was anything but naive. He knew he couldn't stop it. His own son, Art Jr., while living at the family home, had been arrested on a liquor charge in 1921. The chief himself wasn't opposed to alcohol. He made his own wine. All the same, Gabbert had a job to do. It didn't matter that the job was impossible.

Two weeks after the death of Marie Repp, Oshkosh police staged the first in a series of raids on suspected speakeasies. The initial sortie of Saturday August 12, 1922, went about as well as expected. All the targets were tipped off in advance. When the cops showed up the places were dark. If the raids proved anything it was that rank and file Oshkosh cops were more committed to their pals in the speakeasies than they were to the execution of an unpopular law.

Gabbert took matters into his own hands. Later that same evening, he and two officers made another round. This time, there was no forewarning. Gabbert hit six speakeasies. All six were selling liquor. The proprietors were arrested. It was that easy. And it was still impossible.

On Monday, The *Daily Northwestern* ran a laudatory report on Gabbert's raids. The story was placed next to a follow-up article on the death of Marie Repp. The juxtaposition was too striking not to have been intentional. There was more. A few pages over was an editorial lionizing the chief. "Chief Gabbert is entitled to respect and commendation for his patriotic and courageous attitude… The head of the Oshkosh police should be accorded every assistance in his vigorous assault upon one of the worst evils of the current period."

In reality the "vigorous assault" had all the impact of a leaf trying to stop the wind. Gabbert wasn't winning converts, either. The day after the *Northwestern* articles appeared he received an anonymous letter. The author chided Gabbert for the raids advising him to let "the dirty prohibition men do it as that is their work and not yours." The writer told Gabbert that the entire city was talking about him for "…doing such a thing. If you want to be liked, you better stop these raids. Hope you will think this over."

Perhaps Gabbert did. By the fall of 1922, the chief's zeal had waned. His pledge to clean up the city would go unfulfilled. Though Gabbert remained Chief of Police through the entirety of the dry years his early pledge was never renewed. It was a failed promise the public allowed him to forget. The city was coming to accept the fact that some things could not be controlled.

Homebrew

Compared to the white mule, beer was gentle as a pup. And just as familiar. Oshkosh had always been a beer town. It had breweries even before its 1853 incorporation as a city. The lone interruption came with Prohibition.

After 1920, Oshkosh's three breweries – Oshkosh Brewing Company, Peoples Brewing, and Rahr Brewing – did anything they could to scrape by. They made root beer, ginger beer, near beer.

Anything but real beer. But brewing hadn't ended. It went underground. Literally. Home breweries were assembled in basements across the city.

Clarence "Inky" Jungwirth was born in 1919 next door to Steckbauer's saloon in the old Sixth Ward. His birth coincided with Prohibition. It didn't matter. "We were all brought up on beer," he says. Jungwirth remembers well the brewery his grandfather operated in the basement of the family home.

"They'd ferment it in big crock jars," Jungwirth says. "Grandpa had crocks upon crocks of beer down there. They even

People's Xtra Brew Near Beer
Photo courtesy of Lee Reiherzer

Anna Windhauser

Photo courtesy Lee Reiherzer

had their own bottling process. It was good beer. Some of it had a high kick!" For families like the Jungwirths, Prohibition was more nuisance than deterrent. "My grandpa died at the age of 65," Jungwirth says. "I never once saw him take a drink of water. He always had the beer pail by his chair."

The Jungwirth family brewery was typical. Homebrewing in Oshkosh became as common as baking bread. Neighborhood grocery stores carried all the ingredients needed to brew up a batch of beer at home. Malt extract. Hops. Yeast. Add water and off you go.

By 1925, the home craft of beer making had grown so popular in Oshkosh that stores dedicated to it began to appear. The first of them was initiated by the last person you'd expect to do such a thing. Her name was Anna Windhauser.

In 1925, Charles and Anna Windhauser separated. They were living in Green Bay. Before Prohibition, Charles had been a moderate beer drinker. But then the beer dried up. He switched to the more readily available moonshine. It was more than he could handle. "It turned some of the men literally crazy," his daughter Thelma remembered. "My dad never became violent, but he did develop a dependency."

His decline was rapid. By 1924, Charles Windhauser was floundering. "It seemed imminent that his business, along with his health, was certain to go down the drain," Thelma said. "Both parents agreed that my mother would have to assume responsibility for the family. My father then sold his business in order to provide money for mom to start a new life."

Anna Windhauser took her four children and moved to Oshkosh. She rented a storefront at 17 North Main St. She hung a sign that said Rex Malt Products. What she was about to do was legal, but just barely. Anna was going to sell homebrew supplies. The irony of it was inescapable. But her instincts were uncanny. In a place like Oshkosh, it was the sort of business that couldn't help but succeed.

Anna quickly outgrew her Main Street shop. In 1926, she moved the store to 1013 Oregon St. The location was ideal. It put her in the part of town where homebrewing was most intensely pursued. The business continued to grow. By 1928, Rex Malt Products was selling supplies beyond the scope of the typical home brewery. Anna offered malt and hops in bulk. Half-barrel kegs. Bottling equipment. Basically, everything needed by a small production brewery. And there were at least two of those within a half mile of her store.

Butch and the Wildcats

They were called wildcat breweries. The suggestion of something feral was on the mark. They were unregulated, unlicensed and utterly illegal. They thrived in Oshkosh. It's unknown how many such breweries made bootleg beer in the city. Their black-market tactics makes an accurate counting impossible. But certainly, no fewer than seven wildcat breweries operated in Oshkosh during Prohibition. The city hadn't had that many breweries when beer was legal.

Some wildcats were productive in the extreme. When the feds busted a brewery run by Hubert "Hub" Molitor and Fred "Fernie" Heinzl on 20th Ave., they discovered 350 barrels of fermenting beer on hand. Before Prohibition, the typical batch size at the Oshkosh Brewing Company had been 230 barrels.

Another large wildcat crouched at 1325 Oregon St., just three blocks south of Anna Windhauser's brewing supply store. The brewery was in a building owned by speakeasy owner Mary Kollross. When the feds raided the Kollross brewery, they found a fully equipped production and packaging facility with a four-head bottling line.

The wide-open atmosphere had federal officials renewing their complaints about Oshkosh police. A 1929 report by the Bureau of Prohibition exposed a thoroughly "wet" city.

Oshkosh is the center of a large number of wildcat breweries. Federal prohibition forces have seized a number of such establishments there. Soft-drink establishments dispensing hard liquor and beer are also numerous. Local police in Oshkosh are active and efficient with respect to all law violation, except, of course, those connected with the liquor traffic.

-Wickersham Commission, 1931.

Frank 'Butch' Youngwirth

Photo courtesy of Lee Reiherzer

Much of that traffic was at the direction of south side roofer turned bootlegger. His name was Frank Joseph Youngwirth. Everybody called him Butch.

Butch Youngwirth was prototypical Oshkosh. Both his parents had migrated from Bohemia. Frank was their first son, born in Oshkosh in 1892. He grew up on the south side and left school before he'd turned 16. He wound up working as a roofer. A few years of that was enough. He was 28 when Prohibition hit. When he turned 20, he took over a soda parlor at the north east corner of 6th and Ohio. Selling soda was probably the last thing he had in mind.

Youngwirth had barely been at it a year before he was caught selling liquor. His place was targeted by Police Chief Gabbert when the chief made his August 1922 raids. Youngwirth was arrested, fined, and kept right on going.

Youngwirth parlayed his corner speakeasy into a growing empire. It was built around bootleg beer. "Tom", the anonymous bootlegger mentioned earlier, worked as a driver for Butch Youngwirth. "There were two big operations," Tom said. "Butch Youngwirth ran one of them, and he was quite a guy. The finest. He was always out and about drinking and gambling. Geez, he was a *wildman*. Big. About 6-3 and 250 pounds. Everybody knew him."

"Butch had quite a few places in town where he could be back in business in 24 hours if the feds came in and busted things up," Tom said. "He only had one going at a time, but the others were always ready. There was one on Sixth Street, one on Oregon Street; they were all over. Usually in the basements of houses."

By 1928, Youngwirth had abandoned his speakeasy to concentrate on his breweries. When those not in the know asked what he did, he'd say he was a roofer. Or an insurance agent. He was rising fast. Now, he paid others to take the risks.

"He'd pay the guy who owned the land to keep the brewery there, and also take the rap if they got caught," Tom said. "If the guy got sent to the House of Correction in Milwaukee, Butch would pay him well for the time he spent there. I think about a hundred bucks a week."

Youngwirth could afford it. The money was rolling in. "I remember Butch made $38,000 one year and $40,000 the next," Tom said. "That was a lot of money in those days. I remember him and his buddies driving around in their Buicks every Monday to make their collections at the saloons."

Saloons. It was what everybody still called them. Everybody except the city clerk who issued the yearly licenses for the "sale of non-intoxicating liquors." In the eyes of the law, they were soft drink parlors. But when those eyes were averted – and they usually were – the pretense was immediately abandoned.

Speak Easy

In most places, such places were hush hush. Not in Oshkosh. During Prohibition, even the newspaper still regularly identified them as saloons. Others were more creative. Al Steuck, operated a speakeasy named The Annex at 434 North Main. He took to calling his place a "Thirst Parlor." Call them what you will, Prohibition hadn't put a dent in Oshkosh's love for the neighborhood beer joint.

Pep Ad by Oshkosh Brewing Company

Photo courtesy Lee Reiherzer

Wright's Oshkosh City Directory of 1919 listed 96 saloons and no soft drink parlors. The 1922 directory listed 83 soft drink parlors and no saloons. Compare the addresses of the 1919 to saloons to the 1922 soft drink parlors. A pattern immediately emerges. They're the same damned places.

"How many saloons sold alcohol illegally in Oshkosh during Prohibition? Only about 100 percent," said a former bootlegger wanting to be identified only as "Dick". "It was impossible for them to make a go of it during Prohibition if they didn't sell beer. Legally, they had soda pop and Pep, which was a kind of near beer with a lousy taste, but nobody drank that stuff. Everybody wanted something with a wallop."

For most saloon keepers the stark choice presented by the dry law left them with little choice at all. Either go out of business or make money like you never had before. When liquor was made illegal its price immediately spiked. Before Prohibition, a nickel in an Oshkosh bar would buy you a beer. For a dime, you'd get a shot of whiskey. After Prohibition hit, that beer would cost you a quarter. A shot of white mule was also a quarter, sometimes more. For saloon keepers, the premium prices added up quick. But it wasn't all to the good. With the money, came risk.

Witzke's on Oregon Street in 2017

Photo courtesy of Lee Reiherzer

As the 1920s wore on, federal agents began regularly visiting Oshkosh. Unannounced, of course. They made a point of keeping local police in the dark. The feds would arrive by train. A couple automobiles would be waiting for them at the station. They'd head straight for the bars.

The pickings were so easy. They'd walk in, order a drink, and make an arrest. Nothing to it. They could hit five or six spots in a night before word got out. Rarely did they come up dry.

Some places tried to keep it low key. Utecht's Saloon at 413 Ohio St. didn't bother much with beer. Too conspicuous. They sold plenty of moonshine, though. Wenzel Gams worked as a bartender at Utecht's. "They'd keep the bottle hidden in special places," Gams said. "You had to be careful."

Over on Oregon was a guy named Witzke. He wasn't so careful. August Fred Witzke was his given name. But everybody was given a nickname. His was "Fuddy". Born in Oshkosh, 1886. His folks came from Germany. Fuddy was short and stout with blue eyes and sandy-brown hair. He was gruff, but in an agreeable way. His 8th-grade education got him a job in a match factory. After that it was a lumber mill. He was 34 when he discovered his true calling. Witzke was going to be a bartender.

He learned the trade at Louis Clute's old saloon on West 7th near Oregon. After about a year with Clute, Witzke got his break. In 1914, the Oshkosh Brewing Company was looking for a new man to run a bar the brewery owned at 17th and Oregon. Witzke was their man. He got married and moved into the apartment above the bar. People began calling the place Fuddy's. They'd call it that for the next 52 years. The first 10 were probably the hardest.

Fuddy's high visibility was a blessing before Prohibition. The beautiful building on the south-side's main thoroughfare couldn't be missed. When Prohibition began, that advantage turned against him.

Federal Prohibition agents weren't especially creative when it came to picking their targets in Oshkosh. Speakeasies tucked into quiet neighborhoods weren't entirely immune from their harassment. But almost. The feds preferred going after places operating out in the open. Places like Witzke's. Fuddy was among the first to get busted.

Prohibition agents paid their inaugural visit to Witzke's on a Friday night in August, 1921. They walked in to find a tumbler of moonshine like it was waiting there just for them. Witzke was arrested, fined, and undeterred.

They got him again in 1924. This time he wavered. Or pretended to. He walked into court and immediately pled guilty. Witzke told the judge he was getting out of the business. He promised he'd never traffic in illegal booze again. He asked for leniency. The judge made no comment. He let his sentence do the talking. Witzke was hit with 30 days of hard labor at the county jail and fined $300 (about $4,000 in today's money).

While away, Witzke had time to reconsider his pledge. He found it wanting. In early winter, Fuddy got back to town and back behind the bar. And then back to jail. In 1931, the feds staged a massive raid on Oshkosh. Of course, they had to visit their old friend Fuddy. He didn't disappoint. This time he was sent to Milwaukee for a six-month stay in the House of Corrections.

When he returned to Oshkosh in 1932, things were different. Witzke wasn't. He went back to work at the bar. The scene, though, was changing. The onerous grip of Prohibition was faltering. It was on the verge of failing.

April 7, 1933

At midnight, sirens and whistles began to blow. They wound out like a prolonged sigh of relief. Prohibition wasn't over, but a gaping hole had been blown through it. Beer – so long as it wasn't stronger than 4% alcohol by volume – was now legal. The dam was gradually opening. There was no putting it shut after this.

National Prohibition was doomed. The election of 1932 hastened its end. Democrat Franklin D. Roosevelt was elected president. Congressional control also now rested with Democrats. They'd campaigned on a plank promising full repeal. That was coming. In the meantime, Roosevelt signed the Beer Revenue Act. The new law decreed 4% beer to be non-intoxicating and, therefore, not prohibited by the 18th Amendment. Beginning April 7, 1933, August Witzke could legally sell a schooner of beer over his bar again.

The celebration greeting the return of legal beer wasn't nearly so raucous as the party 14-years earlier that bid it farewell. The headline scribe for the *Daily Northwestern* sounded disappointed. "Beer Accorded quiet welcome by Oshkoshians. Although Whistles Scream and German Band Plays, Celebration is Marked By No Disorder." The subdued response was understandable. In Oshkosh, at least, beer had never entirely gone away.

For Oshkosh's three breweries, it was like coming up for air after almost suffocating. Nowhere was the sense of relief so palpable as at the Rahr Brewing Company. The small, family-owned brewery had been decimated by Prohibition. The Rahr's managed to get by selling soda, but each year saw their business decline. This was a moment they needed to make the most of. In the weeks leading up to April 7, the brewery ran full tilt. Blanche Rahr told the *Daily Northwestern*, "We're not saying how much we've got, but we've got all we can legally have stored."

For Matt Sitter it was an equally frantic time. The Sitters had been involved in the beer business in Oshkosh since arriving from Bohemia in 1883. Born in 1901, Matt Sitter's entire life had been spent in the company of beer. During Prohibition, he ran a wildcat brewery out of his home at 1255 Harney Ave. He'd been arrested for that. He was going into the distribution business now that he could legally deal in beer again. Problem was, there wasn't enough beer to go around.

Prior to the April 7 release, Oshkosh's breweries were flooded with orders. The requests were too numerous to accommodate. Matt Sitter got caught short. He finally contracted a Milwaukee brewery to fill the gap. As the delivery truck made its way into Oshkosh, people along North Main St. stopped and cheered the driver on. The reaction was so intense the driver claimed to have been frightened by the response.

There had never been any doubt what people in Oshkosh thought about Prohibition. On April 4, 1933, their sentiments were made explicit. Voters across the state went to the polls to vote whether or not Wisconsin should support repeal of the 18th Amendment. The outcome was no surprise. But the vehemence was. By a 5 to 1 margin, Wisconsin voters supported repeal. In Oshkosh, the resolve ran even stronger. In the largest turn-out the city had seen, almost 90 percent of Oshkosh voters cast their ballot in favor of repeal.

It was over. On December 5, 1933, the 18th Amendment to the Constitution of the United States was repealed. The ignoble experiment was terminated. But its repercussions echoed on.

The Silence

There came a hectic rush to return to something more like normal. Applications for liquor licenses flooded city hall. The clerk couldn't keep up. The Oshkosh Brewing Company couldn't acquire new labels in time. They had to use their old, pre-Prohibition stock. Soft drink parlors across the city hung new signs. They weren't allowed to use the word saloon on them. They were taverns now.

It was all a fine distraction from the economic depression crippling Oshkosh and the nation. *Happy Days Are Here Again* became the theme song of repeal. Some sang it, *Happy Days Are Beer Again*. Not everyone was celebrating. Those who had made the best of the bad situation found the rug pulled from under them.

"Nobody in Oshkosh ever came out of bootlegging with enough money to set themselves up for the rest of their lives," Tom the bootlegger said. "They all came from poor families. They never knew how to make their money work for them."

For Butch Youngwirth that meant going back to work. He was 41 years old. Youngwirth bought a bar on the west side of Wisconsin St. near the river. He named it Butch's Tavern. Butch and his son Harold ran that tavern for the next 30 years.

Anna Windhauser faced the same predicament. Her business was made redundant the moment beer was made legal. At least timing was on her side. Windhauser's children had reached adulthood. She had pulled them all through. She took an apartment and supported herself with part-time work. She began seeing a Madison business owner. They married in 1942.

It was all swept away so quickly. And there seemed little desire for remembering what had occurred. The countless arrests, fines, and jailings were things best not spoken of in most families. The businesses that failed and the loss of livelihood stemming from a detested law were not memories to cherish. It was time to move on.

After it ended, Anna Windhauser didn't talk about selling homebrew supplies. Her grandchildren only heard snippets of her incredible story. "We knew there was some kind of malt shop, but we didn't ever really know what that was all about," said Janet Wissink, a granddaughter. Anna Windhauser died in Oshkosh in 1974.

Butch Youngwirth died in 1973. He was 80 years old. His obituary covered his early life and marriage. It also mentioned that "Mr. Youngwirth had been a tavern operator in Oshkosh for many years." There was nothing about the time when he was Oshkosh's most notorious bootlegger.

Fuddy Witzke died in 1969, three years after retiring. He ran his tavern until he was 79 years old. After that last time, he was never arrested again. His old tavern still has his name on it.

"They're all dead now," said Tom the bootlegger. "And they've got families still living in Oshkosh, still in business here. It wouldn't do them any good. Let's leave 'em dead."

What survives are the sites of resistance. A number of the old speakeasies are still popular gathering places in Oshkosh: Jerry's Bar, Leroy's Bar, The Nickel, Oblio's Lounge, Player's Pub, Repp's Bar, The Reptile Palace, Witzke's Bar... the list goes on.

It hits even closer to home. Some of us live in homes where the dining room once served as a beer flat. Or where the basement was converted into a brewery or distillery. These are places that sheltered secrets. This is a history that surrounds us without our knowing.

© Lee Reiherzer, October, 2017

THE BRADLEY EGG FARM

L eland Bradley was a farmer. His father and grandfather were farmers too.

Born in 1926, Leland was the youngest of three boys of Carl Bradley who owned and operated a dairy farm near Pickett, Wisconsin. The boys all grew up helping with chores around the family farm, learning first-hand how to run a dairy farm from their dad.

Sadly, Leland's mother, Esther, died during his birth. Carl eventually remarried but only six years after losing Esther, he died too. After Carl's death, his second wife sold the Pickett dairy farm.

Leland and two of his brothers, Carlton and Roger, moved in to live with his aunt and uncle, Herman and Lydia Raddatz, who owned a farm on Nekimi Avenue, just off Old Knapp Street Road a few miles south of Oshkosh. He grew up there and when of age, worked as a "hired hand" which mostly included milking cows. Raised by his aunt and uncle, Leland attended grade school and high school in nearby Oshkosh. One evening, at the Eagles Dance Hall on Washington Avenue, he would meet a girl named Harriet Pietz, who worked as secretary at the CR Meyer Company. In the summer months Harriet also worked in the concession stand in Menominee Park's Miller House.

On June 3, 1950 Leland and Harriet were married. Because farming was in his blood and it was what he knew best, his greatest desire was to someday own his own dairy farm. But the likelihood of that coming to fruition was not to be. As he and his wife were newlyweds, they didn't have the financial resources to make that dream a reality. The cost of setting up a dairy farm was high and beyond the young Bradley's means.

A few years later, in 1957, a farm with 206 acres of land on Old Knapp Street Road became available, just a "stone's throw" away from his uncle's farm. It consisted of an old farm house and a few buildings, but it was something Leland could afford ($26,000) and he was anxious to start a farm life of his own. The property was in need of updating and repairs, but the price was right and Leland was willing to do the renovations that were needed. He started with updating and remodeling the farm house, and soon after Leland and Harriet moved in.

In the beginning, Leland worked the land with cash crops, but he yearned to do more. It was in 1960 he "hatched" the idea to try his hand at raising chickens for eggs. The egg business seemed like a lucrative business and he decided to start out small to see how things went. If successful, he decided the business would progress along with it. If not, he would manage his losses to be minimal.

I'm sure you've heard of the age old question… "What came first… the chicken or the egg?" Well, in Bradley's case it was obvious. He started with purchasing 250 day-old "Kimber" chicks from a local farm supply company. (Once the local farm supply closed their doors, Bradley would go to the Wilkes Hatchery in Beaver Dam, Wisconsin to buy new stock). The "Kimber Farm" variety was a snow-white bird, genetically engineered through breeding programs in California conducted by Kimber Farms. This breed was preferred as they were reputable as high egg producers with an average laying hen capable of laying up to 250 eggs per year.[1]

To appreciate this business, you have to understand the cycle of the chicken. The day-old chicks were housed in one of the sheds that was converted into a brooding house. There they will spend the next 16 weeks maturing into laying hens. Once the birds are ready for egg production, they were moved into a large laying house stocked with rows of cages. Their productivity as egg layers lasts about one year. At that point, the bird's cycle of productivity starts to diminish and the eggshells become thinner. The birds are then processed and sold and headed for the stewing pot as fresh chicken.

Once the Bradley Egg Farm reached its peak of production (about 18,000 laying hens on site) the cycle would run every four months…6,000 hens culled out for slaughter, 6,000 day-old chicks brought in as replacements, and so forth.

In early January of 2017, I paid a visit to the Bradley Farm. Their egg business had come to end in 2008, but son Brian Bradley still works the land and runs the farm. His mother Harriet lives in the same house on the farm she and Leland purchased in 1957. As I drove into the drive, I put my vehicle into park and looked around. I imagined the farm looked very much today like it did during its years as an egg farm. All the buildings that shouldered the egg farm business for many years, still stand in excellent condition and are well maintained. Just then, Brian opened the door to his mother's house and walked out to greet me. I was welcomed with a firm handshake and a smiling, friendly face. I mentioned my observation regarding the farm and Brian said, "Everything you see here is just as it was in the days of the egg farm business. Some of the buildings still have cages in them." He offered to take me inside one of the large buildings, but the snow between the driveway and building was too deep.

He then opened the door of a nearby building situated alongside the driveway and said, "This is the first building we used when dad started the egg business." He opened the door and we side-stepped our way through an area now used for maintenance and storage. As we reached the other side of the building, he pointed to a small room, "This was our cooler. As the eggs came through here they were washed, candled and graded. Then they were stored here under refrigeration until it was time to ship." He then took a moment to explain that the term "candling" is used to describe the inspection each egg must go though before it is passed for quality. The egg passes across a special "mercury" light that allows the person inspecting to see opaque images inside the egg. Eggs with cracks, spotting or other defects are removed here and discarded. Before automation and modern lighting systems, a real candle was used to do this...
thus the term "candling".

I looked around the room and spied an old chalkboard hanging on the wall. Undisturbed from the day their business came to an end, it stood there frozen in time, reminding those who pass by of the days when this now silent storage area was the heartbeat of a vibrant and successful business. On it, scratched in chalk, were the egg prices by size for November 30,

The Bradley chalkboard was used to keep track of important information

Photo courtesy Randy Domer

2008. It was the last day of business for the Bradley Egg Farm. Nearby, another chalkboard held a scripture from the bible. Brian explained that his mother liked to write inspirational messages to remind them of greater things in the circle of life.

Brian then invited me inside the farm house to meet his mother Harriet. Greeting me at the door was a very pleasant lady who invited me inside. She asked me to have a seat at the dining room table, where she had prepared a few things for our meeting. Old photos and newspaper clippings were scattered about, waiting to help her tell the story.

We sat down and after some introductory comments Harriet asked me "Where should we begin?"

I said, "Wherever you would like…tell me your story."

She smiled as she began to reminisce. She started by explaining like any other business of this nature, this was a family run business which meant everyone had a job and pitched in.

The Bradley Family, The Early Years - Leland, Harriet, Brian and Cindy Bradley

Photo courtesy Harriet Bradley

The days were long. Most days the alarm was set for 2:30 am. Eggs from the previous day's production had to be graded, candled, washed and placed into "fillers" which was a square, grey cardboard flat that held 30 eggs. The eggs would be packed into cases and loaded into the truck for that day's deliveries. Most of the customers were hotels, restaurants and institutions like hospitals and prisons. It surprised me to learn that no eggs were sold to local grocery stores.

A pretty good "pickup" system developed over the years where locals would drive out to the farm to buy fresh eggs. "It's how we started the business," Harriet told me. "We advertised in the local newspaper and sold eggs off the farm. We even took orders and delivered eggs to people's homes originally," she added. Brian remembers that being the "fun part" of the business, interacting with the local people. "I still hear from people all the time. They tell me how they used to bring their grandmother out here every Saturday to get fresh eggs!" he shared with a grin.

Harriet paused for a moment to share a story and a lesson with me. "People would come to me and complain that the eggs, when boiled, did not peel very easily. I told them that's because it's the nature of fresh eggs. Let them stand a week or so and they will peel much easier."

Being a family owned business meant each of the kids had their own job. Collecting eggs was one of those duties that fell squarely on the shoulders of the five young Bradley children. Darlene, Valinda, Brian, Cindy and Shelly helped gather eggs and move them to the next station for processing. A cart was pushed between the rows of cages as the eggs were collected twice daily, sometimes up to as many as 15,000 eggs each day.

In later years, Brian's wife Laurie (nee Koplitz) found out that marrying into the Bradley Family meant being part of the family business. "Actually, Laurie helped out on the farm when she was still in high school," Brian shared with me. "I would give her my car to drive to school so she could come to the farm right after her last class to help with the eggs."

Brian explained how much of the feed was produced right there on the farm. The chickens were provided a special diet that included 42% corn, ground up oyster shells for calcium and trace amounts of elements and protein. Corn was grown on the Bradley acreage while the oyster shells, trace elements and proteins were purchased locally. Brian estimates about 18 tons of feed was ground and mixed every week. This form of vertical integration within the supply chain provided a cost savings while satisfying a common need. The land must produce and the chickens must be fed.

As their business grew, the need for automation became imperative for production to keep pace with demand. For example, hand feeding the feathery little egg producers was eventually automated to a conveyor belt system controlled by a timing device. The belt would activate every hour for 15 minutes.

The hens were kept in wire cages – three to a cage. Water was provided by a hose into a trough that ran outside the cage. As the chicken laid an egg, it gently rolled through an open slot in the cage floor onto a shelf below where it came to rest. Eggs were collected twice daily. Once collected, the eggs are taken to the room where they were washed, candled and graded. Leland would load the eggs onto the automated machine with a lift that suctioned 30 eggs at a time. The eggs would pass down the line where Harriet would conduct the candling process. The eggs would then pass through the washing stage where nylon brushes cleaned each one. Next the eggs are graded, not by size as one would think, but by weight (jumbo, x-large, large, medium and small). Brian told me most of the 'small grades' were just given away.

Over the years, the Bradleys experimented with different things to try to increase egg production. They found the most effective practice was a good diet and anything to make the chickens more comfortable. Heat would often be a problem, with the birds themselves generating a lot of heat. It was not a problem in the cooler months, but summers offered its share of issues. Exhaust fans were installed to remove the heat and circulate the air which alleviated the problem during the summer months when temperatures could soar.

Another test included playing music in the buildings to increase egg production. It turned out that the music actually relaxed the birds, but production didn't noticeably increase. One day a tube burned out on the radio, and when the music stopped, production nose-dived. It then took about 6 weeks for normal production to resume.

As mentioned earlier, the laying hens had reached their peak production cycle after about one year of laying. That meant the older birds needed to be culled out, butchered and sold as meat.

Leland and Brian did most of the slaughtering. The process was done with a homemade device that consisted of two nails in a board. Brian explained the head of the bird was placed between the nails, then chopped off. He would hold the bird for a minute or two until it stopped flopping around and was bled out. This process was necessary to properly process the bird for eating. The bird was then tossed into a container for further processing.

The rest of the processing cycle involved everyone, including Mrs. Bradley. "It wasn't a lot of fun and the work was long and hard" Harriet recalled.

Other than a few locals who came to the farm to buy fresh chicken, the birds were mostly sold to a company from Minnesota, that processed them for soup. Locals would come and buy fully-cleaned and processed birds for $1 each. Then local laws changed, requiring each bird to be weighed and sold by the pound. "We made enough money selling the meat to pay for the next batch of day-old chicks," Brian explained. But that would change slightly over the years. At one point, the company no longer wanted to pay for the birds, in fact, they wanted to charge the Bradleys to come and "take them off their hands". Of course, this was not acceptable to the Bradleys. Also, the government then announced that an onsite inspector must be present if number of birds processed exceeded 1,000. Brian arranged a deal with a network of Hmong communities located in Wisconsin. They would come every four months and the Bradleys would donate the birds to them. Although they no longer received any monetary payment for the livestock, they no longer had to deal with the labor costs associated with killing and processing. It was money saved on the expense side of the business.

Harriet recalled another situation that arose as the business started to grow in the early years. "Each year on Good Friday it was our family tradition to attend church services. One year we came home from church and the cars were lined up all the way down the street. People wanted eggs for Easter. After that year, we were never able to go to church on Good Friday."

Bradley's eggs were sold for 60 cents a dozen for many years. Then they decided to follow the market up and down. Brian explained. "When egg prices in the grocery stores would fall below 60 cents, our sales would drop. Then when the prices in the stores went over 60 cents, we were very busy." Fluctuating pricing with the changing markets brought more stability to the demand.

In the early 80s, Leland and Brian continued to expand their operation by adding more buildings and grain bins, doing all the work themselves. In 1980, Leland became very ill, diagnosed with ALS. He died on January 3, 1983 at the young age of 56 years. It would be up to Brian and his wife Laurie to take charge and keep the family business running. Brian's sisters, Cindy and Valinda, lived nearby and helped when needed on the farm as well. As Brian and Laurie's children grew up, they also pitched in. Lee (named after his grandfather), Becky, and Justin Bradley became the third generation of Bradleys to work the egg business. The families worked together and Brian, Laurie, and Harriet would keep the business going for another 25 years.

By 2008, it became evident that the business had run its course. After 48 years, time had taken its toll. The cages and equipment were old, and considerations to replace with new had to be made, which would be very costly. Also, continuing new regulations became very restrictive and the Bradleys decided it was time.

The business was not sold; they just put up a sign and gave notice to their customers and the community that November 30, 2008 would be their last day of business. Brian helped his customers locate new sources to purchase eggs as a courtesy and in appreciation for all their years of loyal business.

During the time the Bradley Egg Farm was in operation, the family continued to farm 400 acres of agricultural land, a practice that continues today. Brian, along with his son Justin, still works the farm. Brian lives next door to his mother Harriet, where he can help keep an eye on things.

As you drive south on Old Knapp Street Road, look to your right for the yellow buildings where black silhouettes of chickens adorn the sides.

It is…rather, it was…the Bradley Egg Farm.

Sources: (1) *The Business of Food: Encyclopedia for the Food and Drink* Industries by Gary J. Allen, Ken Albala, pg 305; *Oshkosh Daily Northwestern,* October 27, 1967; personal interviews with Harriet and Brian Bradley

CARL LAEMMLE

T his is a story about a man who came to Oshkosh in search of a dream. Carl Laemmle came to Oshkosh at the age of thirty-years old. His journey became one that started by working in a local business and ended as a mogul in the motion picture industry. Here is his story.

Carl Laemmle was born on January 17, 1867 in Laupheim, Wurtemburg, Germany, the son of Judas and Rebekkah Laemmle. Both parents had the same surname (Laemmle) as they were first cousins. As a young boy, Carl loved to read American dime novels about Indians and Cowboys which led him to leave for America after his mother died in 1883. Carl emigrated to the United States in 1884 at the young age of seventeen years.

He found his way to Chicago, where he worked various jobs while studying to become an accountant, which would prove to serve him well in his future endeavors. In 1898, he moved to Oshkosh to work for Mr. Sam Stern, at the Continental Clothing Store on Main Street. Laemmle accepted the position as a bookkeeper at a wage lower than he was making in Chicago, but determination was on his side and with only a rudimentary education and no formal training, Carl followed his instincts which would prove beneficial in the grand scheme of things.[6]

In 1898, in Oshkosh, he married German-born Recha Stern, niece of Sam Stern, and they lived at 186 Church Street (today's address is 422 Church Avenue), just west of Jackson Street. By 1903, they had moved to 86 Union Street (614 Union after the 1957 address change – Note this block of Union Street is no longer there) and their daughter Rosabelle was born. Later, in 1908, his wife Recha would give birth to their only son and second child, Carl Laemmle, Jr.

It was during these early years that Laemmle's creative juices started flowing. By 1898, he had worked his way up in the Continental business and became manager. In 1905, the Thanksgiving holiday was fast approaching. Carl was anxious to find a way to take advantage of the holiday season and drive sales at the Continental Clothing store, which would surely please his boss. He decided to advertise a promotion that offered patrons a free turkey with any purchase of $10 or more. An event like this had never been seen before in Oshkosh. Unfortunately, not to be outdone, a local competitor, namely L. Stuebing Co., upped the ante by offering a free turkey with the purchase of $9.50.

The turkey war was on!

The price cutting volley continued right up until Thanksgiving. Shortly before the holiday, The Continental's offer was down to $5. Then L. Stuebing went below that. Finally, the Continental announced their store would be open on Thanksgiving Day until noon, and also cut the special offer to any purchase of $3 or more!

The battle gained national notoriety and the promotion was deemed a success. That is, until Laemmle's boss got the bill for the turkeys. The $3,000 invoice put the owner of The Continental over the edge and Carl found himself out of a job. His career as a clothier had come to an abrupt end.

Well, that's one side of the story. On February 19, 1906, the *Oshkosh Daily Northwestern* published an article in which the headline reads, "Mr. Laemmle Resigns". The article went on to say that the reason for the resignation was due to his wife, Recha's poor health. The article quotes Mr. Laemmle as saying,

Yes, you can say goodbye for me to all the friends I have made in this grand old city. It's hard and it hurts, but there is no alternative. Mrs. Laemmle and I have found it has been impossible for her to regain her former good health here, so we decided to go. I will go into business for myself, as I have reached that period in life where a man ought to branch out for himself if he ever expects to go up in the world. Maybe I am making a mistake in giving up all my pleasant relations I have enjoyed with the people of this city, and the boys at the store, but health is more important than money in this world, after all.

Mr. Stern, owner of The Continental, has finally accepted my resignation and I believe he did it with as much regret as I experienced handing it in, for the relations have been unusually fine and of long duration.[3]

Other reports say that Laemmle traveled to Chicago to confront his employer with his displeasure over what he called "unfair wages". The dialogue between Laemmle and Stern rose into a heated discussion and Laemmle was handed his walking papers. Stern, who prided himself running his business with an iron fist and not his heart, felt he could replace Laemmle with a younger, lower paid employee. This move would light the spark that had been burning inside the soon-to-be movie producer.[6]

John Spoo and H. C. Weyerhorst then succeeded Laemmle in management of The Continental.[3]

So, at the age of 39 years old, Carl Laemmle packed his bags and headed to back to Chicago[4] where he opened a five-cent movie house, known as a nickelodean.[2] Being the entrepreneur that he was, Carl soon owned a pair of these five-cent venues. One year later, Laemmle expanded his film interests by organizing a film exchange network he called the *Laemmle Film Service*. In this business, Laemmle rented films to other theaters.

As his interest in the film industry continued to grow, Laemmle founded the Independent Motion Picture Company (IMP) in New York City in 1909. As an original member of the Edison Patents Company, he was required to pay royalties which cut into his profit margin. Forging ahead and ignoring this financial obligation, he continued by producing a few economical films which brought the Edison legal team a calling. Laemmle continued to discard Edison's claims and fought the legal battle over the next three years. In the end, he rose victorious.

In 1912, Carl took a step that would bring him international fame and fortune. He reorganized IMP and called the new company Universal Studios. He produced two more films in 1912, *The Dawn of Netta* and *The Nurse*, before moving this new company to Los Angeles.

In the coming years, Laemmle would produce and work on over 400 films. The list includes a silent film version of Jules Verne's *20,000 Leagues Under The Sea* (1916), *All Quiet On The Western Front* (1930), *Showboat* (1929), and a black and white short film of *Dr. Jekyll and*

Mr. Hyde (1913). Laemmle was hesitant to venture into horror films initially, but through the urging of his son Carl, Jr. who followed in his father's footsteps and produced many of Universal's films as well, Laemmle relented and the result was many of the old time classics such as *The Phantom of the Opera* (1925), *The Hunchback of Notre Dame* with Lon Chaney (1923), *The Black Cat* with Bela Lugosi and Boris Karloff (1934), *Frankenstein* (1931) and *The Bride of Frankenstein* (1935) - both also Karloff thrillers, *Dracula* (1931), *The Invisible Man* with Claude Rains and Gloria Stuart (1933), *The Mummy* (1932), and many more.

But the movie industry was not the only thing that captured Carl Laemmle's attention. World War I had just ended and Laemmle, a German born Jew, was concerned over the ascent of Adolf Hitler. He secured visas for first his relatives, then other families in his hometown of Laupheim, Wurttenberg, Germany. Once the war ended, Laemmle made several trips back to Laupheim and sent food to Jewish villagers. His interest in rescuing them came once he heard that streets in Laupheim originally named after himself had been changed in Hitler's name. It is said that during this time, Laemmle was responsible for the rescue of 250 Jews from Nazi Germany.[5]

As fame and fortune seemed his lot, Carl Laemmle never forgot his former home. In 1912, he sent a film crew to Oshkosh to shoot a short film titled *Oshkosh In Motion*. The *Oshkosh Daily Northwestern* ran several articles in the days prior to the filming, encouraging local residents to gather on Main Street on May 31st. On that day, Director Watterson R. Rothacker arrived with his cameraman, Charles Kaufman, and they began shooting. They filmed that day and the next, then sat idle for two days due to rain. The project was completed on June 5th. The film showed a rare glimpse of what life was like in Oshkosh in 1912. Scenes included some of our private premier residences, business and civic buildings, horse drawn fire wagons, scores of people moving up and down the downtown business district, schoolchildren at play and more. The film had been lost until 1974, when Vance Yost, a local film collector, discovered an original copy and produced a negative from the deteriorating film in which copies were made. Today, the Yost Collection is in the hands of the Oshkosh Public Museum.[2]

In 1935, Laemmle would undertake his final film for Universal Studios with the production of *Showboat*. It was during the Depression and times were hard. Previous films had not produced profitably and the overruns from *Showboat* forced Laemmle to take a $750,000 loan from Standard Capital. This decision caused Laemmle's forced retirement from the film business and Universal Studios was sold to Standard Capital in 1936.

Carl was very popular among his peers and colleagues. He was commonly known as "Uncle Carl" and his son, Carl Laemmle, Jr. was known as "Junior". They were a team producing movies together as father and son. In 1939, only three years after his ouster from Universal Studios, Carl Laemmle died of a heart attack in Los Angeles. He was 72 years old. Forty years later to the day, son Carl Jr. passed away. His wife, Recha, died on January 13, 1919.

Carl, Recha and Carl Jr. are all laid to rest in the Home of Peace Cemetery in East Los Angeles in the family mausoleum.

Author's note: The Home of Peace Cemetery is also the final resting place for other Hollywood notables including Louis B. Mayer (MGM), Shemp and Curly Howard (Three Stooges), Jack, Harry and Sam Warner (Warner Brothers)

Sources: (1) James Metz, WCHAS County Fare, Q4 2013; (2) oshkoshinmotion. uwosh.edu; (3) *Oshkosh Daily Northwestern*, Feb. 19, 1906, "Mr. Laemmle Resigns"; (4) *Oshkosh Daily Northwestern*, Dec. 14, 1906; (5) *Wisconsin Jewish Chronicle*, December 29, 1969; (6) *Oshkosh Daily Northwestern*, July 18, 1931;

THE TRAGIC DEATH OF J. R. LOPER

O ver the years, Oshkosh has seen its share of tragedy, including several major fires that decimated the city on more than one occasion and, as you can imagine, created a number of casualties along the way.

This story is about a local businessman named J.R. Loper. Jarvis Rogers Loper owned a soap factory that was situated near the St. Paul Railroad Depot on the corner of Marion and Market Streets. He was a hardworking man, well known and respected among the Oshkosh business community. Jarvis was one of seven sons of Isaac Loper, who moved his family to Oshkosh from Saratoga Springs, New York in 1862. Isaac started the Loper Soap Works that same year and was forced to rebuild his business three times after each of the great Oshkosh fires. His son Jarvis enlisted in the Union Army that same year and served in Company I, 2nd Infantry Regiment, Rhode Island as a Private. He returned home from service in 1865 and took over the business from his father in 1868. From 1868-1870 the business was known as Jarvis R. Loper & Company and Loper Brothers and Rich. By 1876 the company became J.R. Loper.

The Loper Soap Works was the manufacturer of toilet and laundry soap "…of equal grade to any and much superior to great quantities often put on the market." The 1879 City Directory reported that Loper's capacity equaled about 50,000 pounds of soap per week. Additionally, he manufactured large quantities of "strictly pure" neat's-foot oil, a softening, conditioning and preservation product used to treat leather, and refined cylinder tallow which was used for lubricating purposes in steam engines.

On Wednesday, July 11, 1883, tragedy struck. Mr. Loper perished in an industrial accident that shocked the city. As was the norm during that time, the newspaper account of the accident was very explicit and described the event in vivid and morbid detail.

The *Oshkosh Daily Northwestern* the following day headlined the story as such: **"Awful Accident – Horrible Death of J. R. Loper"**. The sub heading went on to explain: "He Accidentally Falls into a Vat of Boiling Soap – Recovery of the

Loper Soap Works
Photo courtesy Richard Jungwirth

Body with the Flesh Nearly All Eaten from the Bones – One of the Most Terrible Happenings Ever Chronicled in this City".

From this point on, much of what has been written is purely speculation as there were no witnesses to the accident. Local authorities worked to piece things together on what they think happened that tragic day.

The *Oshkosh Northwestern* reporter who wrote the story began with:

It becomes the duty of the chronicler of public events today to describe one of the most horrible accidents that ever occurred in this city. That so prominent of a businessman as J. R. Loper, the soap manufacturer, should fall into his own boiling soap vat and meet not only a horrible death, but should have been cooked and the flesh eaten from his bones in the boiling acids, was a calamity that shocked the entire community beyond telling and produced excitement scarcely less than was occasioned by the loss of life in the burning Beckwith House.

Evidence gathered by investigators pointed to the following sketch of what might have happened:

Mr. Loper was working in his factory adding ingredients into a 16-foot deep, two-story vat of boiling soap when he apparently slipped and fell into the cauldron. As he was working alone at the time, no one was there to witness the accident or say what exactly happened. A young boy named John who worked in the soap factory said Loper sent him home to bring him his supper as he could not leave the boiling soap unfinished or the job left to anyone else. It was Loper's rule that only he could put the finishing touches on the soap. Another younger boy working there, named Peter, remained in the factory with Loper. As Peter left the room with the vat, he recalled hearing Loper breaking up the ingredients to be added to the boiling concoction. Soon after, he noticed the noise being made by Mr. Loper had ceased and it was oddly quiet. Peter returned a few minutes later but could not see or find Mr. Loper. When the older boy John returned with Mr. Loper's supper, they assumed he had left temporarily and both boys went home to supper. They returned about seven o'clock that evening, still finding Mr. Loper absent. It was then they suspected he may have fallen into the vat. They took a long pole and fished around inside the vat, feeling something at the bottom. The boys ran to Loper's house and found he was not there. They told the neighbor, Ed Cole, what they suspected and all three returned to the factory. Additional help was summoned as word quickly spread throughout the community. A long pole with a hook was located and used to bring the body to the surface. According to the *Oshkosh Northwestern* account "When the body was brought to the surface it was seen that most of the flesh had been eaten off and great care had to be taken to prevent the bones from falling apart". The article continued with more graphic and morbid details, too gruesome to recount here.

A dentist named Dr. Drucker was summoned to make a proper identification. Dental records confirmed the remains were that of Jarvis Loper. The body, or what was left of it, was then placed in a metal casket, tightly sealed, and transported to the Loper residence at 37 Church Street.

Loper's tragic death was the talk of the town. Groups gathered on street corners and in saloons, and exaggerated stories of what happened quickly spread. It is perhaps for that reason, one would think, that the *Oshkosh Northwestern* went into so much detail in their account. A week after his death, the newspaper felt compelled to tell its readers more about the vat of soap that claimed the factory owner's life. The newspaper reported, "Had he merely drowned and the body recovered whole, no objection to using the soap could have been valid. But as it was, a large amount of his flesh was boiled off and remained in the soap, (thus) the entire vat of soap has been buried in deep trenches near the factory. The value of the large vat of soap was over $500, and every particle of it has been buried out of sight..."

After Loper's death, the business was sold to William T. Ellsworth and William P. Findeisen. The new business was named Ellsworth & Co. and continued to produce the same products in the same location on the corner of Market and Marion Street.

Jarvis R. Loper was 48 years old at the time of his death. He is buried in Oshkosh's Riverside Cemetery.

Sources: *Oshkosh Daily Northwestern* 7.12.1883,p.4, col 2, also 7.17.1883, p.4, col 2; *Oshkosh Aflame, Traumas and Triumphs of its Sawdust Citizens (A History)* by James I. Metz, p. 135; longislandsurnames.com/Loper; Holland's Oshkosh City Directory, 1879 pp. 62-63; Oshkosh City Directory 1884, p. 135

THE MILLER HORSERADISH FARM

As a young boy growing up in the 1950s, one of my favorite memories is of Sunday drives in the country. Our travels would usually take us into the rural areas of Winnebago County – usually around Omro and Winneconne. On occasion, my dad would stop at one of the local farm stands to buy some tomatoes, cucumbers, apples, or whatever was being offered in season at the time. These farm stands were owned and operated by local rural folks who took gardening to heart. These were not your run of the mill backyard gardens. Living in the country allowed them to use acreage and more industrial type farm equipment to plant acres of orchards, fruits and vegetables.

Just a few miles west of Oshkosh was an apple orchard owned and operated as Rasmussen Apple Acres. It was an annual event for our extended families to gather there and pick apples by the bushel. And the best part was to see how many apples you could consume while picking. There was nothing better than picking an apple off the tree, wiping it on your shirt and taking that first bite. The apples were crisp, juicy and oh so sweet.

Some of these rural gardeners would have fruit and vegetable stands right in the front yards of their homes. Others would load up a pickup truck and slowly drive through the city neighborhoods peddling their produce. A few of the larger ones had accounts with the local supermarkets and would furnish them with fresh, locally grown fruits and vegetables and sometimes eggs.

Such was the case with one special family who "market farmed" for many years on Omro Road, also known as State Highway 21. (Today, Highway 21 is a bypass around Omro Road as you travel west until Leonard's Road). Jacob Miller (1833-1912), started market farming

George Miller

Photo Courtesy Robert Miller

in the late 1800s on a 160 acre farm near Allenville, Wisconsin. In an *Oshkosh Daily Northwestern* article published in 1958, his son George reminisced about working with his dad when he was twelve years old in 1891. George would take the harvest from his dad's fields and transport the produce to Neenah-Menasha by team and wagon or sleigh. Travel could be difficult back then as roads were not of today's standards…usually mud or gravel. Weather conditions also played a role as George had to deal with rainstorms, blizzards and occasionally a "spirited" team of horses.

George's grandsons, Richard and Robert Miller who were the fourth generation of Millers to work the farm, recalled a story they were once told as children by their grandfather. On a return trip from delivering his products to grocery stores in the Neenah area, George drove his team and buckboard along Woodenshoe Alley. As the horses were familiar with the route and needed no guidance, George laid down in the buckboard to catch a few winks while his horses headed for home. Along the way he was stopped by two men who had intentions of robbing him. George had a fair amount of cash on him from that day's receipts from deliveries, and losing it to a couple of low-life rogues would be catastrophic. The "would be" robbers quizzed George about who he was and what he was doing. Whatever it was that George said apparently convinced the duo of thieves there was nothing here to profit from and they allowed him to continue on his way.

Around 1910 George bought a farm on Omro Road just a few miles west of Oshkosh. He started by purchasing 15 acres, then purchased 80 acres more. George was ready to create his own farm market and that's when things started to change. Around 1911, George Miller decided to try his hand at farming horseradish after receiving advice from a neighboring farmer. This pungent root was not widely raised and Miller thought he could develop a business producing and selling horseradish. The 95 acre piece of agricultural land would become the Miller Horseradish Farm. He felt raising horseradish would enhance his produce market business. He also began a small dairy operation.

Miller's Farm Market stand on old Omro Road

Photo courtesy Robert Miller

A small, roadside building sat along the edge of old Omro Road. A gravel drive lined by a spilt rail fence invited cars to stop and purchase fresh fruits and vegetables. Refrigeration was still in its infancy and many of the local grocers did not have cold capabilities to offer fresh produce, meats and dairy. In fact, home refrigerators were not even common until the 1920s.

Like most small business, especially of this nature, it was truly a family affair. George's wife Edith worked alongside him, along with their son Lester. In later years, Lester would succeed his father as "horseradish king" and take over the business. Lester's wife Grace worked alongside him, and sons Richard and Robert helped when they were of age as well. Lester's mother, Edith, remained working in the family business until the age of 91 years old. George died in 1965 - Edith in 1972.

In October of 2016, I sat down with Robert Miller and his longtime companion, Pat. I also met with Richard Miller, who today lives in Texas, and his son, Mark. I wanted to hear first-hand how the Miller family operated the horseradish business. What better way to relive those days of the past than to speak directly with the two grandsons who as youths, worked on the farm.

Robert recalled having many jobs in the family business as a young boy. "There was a big hill back in the growing area and it was pretty sandy", Robert recalled. "It must have been good for growing horseradish roots because it did quite well growing there." Robert went on to tell me how he would help in the fall during the harvest time, digging the roots from the ground and transporting them to the "root cellar", a name he said they used to describe the storage building where the freshly harvested horseradish roots would be stored until they were processed. The storage area had a concrete floor covered with a mixture of sand. The roots were arranged inside and covered with the sand mixture to keep the roots cool and dry.

Growing horseradish is a bit more complicated than it seems. First, there is no seed for horseradish. During processing, small, fine roots are carefully harvested and stored under ideal conditions until spring when the roots are planted in trenches. Once in the ground, the plants must be cultivated, weeded and fertilized for harvest in the fall.

When it was time to process, the roots would be washed in a butter churn and ground by Lester, as it was the type of work that required someone older in years and more experienced than a young boy. Once the roots were washed, the roots, "eyes", and remaining dirt was removed by hand.

Robert also recalled another job that was not so pleasant. "The ground up horseradish was stored in large barrels waiting to be bottled. I would grab my buckets, close my eyes and run into the room, quickly scooping the buckets full and making a quick exit before the fumes would get to me." The buckets of horseradish were then taken into the bottling area where the jars would be filled and capped, then placed into cardboard boxes and ready for distribution. Each case would contain twenty-four jars.

There were several buildings and a silo made of wood on the Miller Farm as you would imagine. The building where the processing was done was large and served dual purposes. The lower level was the processing area and the upstairs was a dance hall. "My parents used to have square dances there," Robert recalled. Richard described the dance hall as being used by two local square dance clubs. "There were two clubs that would meet on alternating weeks. So, there was a dance every week. Sometimes the club would travel to other cities like Sheboygan or Green Bay and attend other club dance events. It was a big deal back then."

Richard then went on to explain some of the chores he was required to do on the family farm. "We usually processed horseradish twice a week. One of my jobs included screwing the caps on the jars and applying labels." As mentioned earlier, the Millers always had a small herd of dairy cattle. "My father told me that he promised his dad that as long as he was alive he would have cows on the farm. I don't know why he made that promise, but he did." The herd usually consisted of about 16 head of cows for milking. Richard recalled how much he disliked milking cows. "I hated that job," he said. "With cows it doesn't matter if you have 16 or a hundred. You still have to go through the work...and it was seven days a week, twice a day." He talked about sharing milking duties with his brother Robert and dad Lester.

Richard clearly remembered the old roadside farm stand building. "It was where we sold our farm-raised fruits and vegetables. I remember my grandmother Edith making homemade pickles in a barrel. She added vinegar, salt, dill and horseradish leaves to give the pickles a little zest. We sold them in the market stand. When a customer wanted to purchase pickles, we would reach down inside the barrel and pull out the pickles we needed and place them in a little waxed cardboard container with a wire handle...like the kind you used to get goldfish in!"

In the 1960s, the farm stand was discontinued and the building rented out to Koch Sales. Koch was a local merchant who went around the country searching to buy closeout items which he shipped back and sold in the little white building that once was the roadside market stand. There was everything from fishing gear to clothing, books, shoes, canned food...you name it. Koch would sometimes make large purchases and used the buildings on the Miller Farm to store his inventory.

The Miller Horseradish Farm was located at 3920 Omro Road, just west of Rasmussen's Apple Acres. In 1958 it was said that Miller was the only commercial horseradish producer in Winnebago County. I found that not to be particularly unusual as there was only a total of five producers in the entire State of Wisconsin.

At the height of the operation, Miller harvested between 15-20 tons of roots annually. During the peak of the processing season, the Millers would produce about 6,000 jars over a two week period. Lester delivered horseradish to local grocery stores for many years, just as his father did before him. In the 1960s and 70s I worked at Sawyer Street Super Valu and remember we carried two brands of horseradish...Miller and Silver Spring. The Miller brand was easily our best seller!

If you are not familiar with horseradish, it's quite an experience. Your senses come alive the moment you twist off the cap. The red label with white lettering that said "Miller Horseradish" assured you that you had just purchased the best horseradish around! Next, the "sniff test" would surely awaken your senses as the fumes from the horseradish can be as overpowering as the taste. In fact, during processing while grinding the roots, Miller would wear a mask similar to those used in the military to protect him from the effect of the fumes. Horseradish is a condiment with numerous applications. You can put it on hot dogs, sandwiches, seafood cocktail sauce…just about anything. My favorite use is with ham at Easter dinner. Similar to wasabi, just be careful how much you use. Horseradish is a member of the mustard family and unlike fine wine, its potency diminishes with time. For that reason, the Millers always preferred to process according to orders so what they were shipping was absolutely fresh.

What made Miller Horseradish so good you ask? Well, for starters it was made from pure horseradish root. The few ingredients that were added included vinegar, to help hold the nice white color and a bit of mustard oil. Both Robert and Richard commented that it was the mustard oil that really gave the horseradish the "kick". Additives like sugar and salt were <u>never</u> used. Secondly, it was grown fresh and produced right here in our own backyard. Thirdly, supporting local business and small business owners is always the right thing to do.

Millers made a few different products. Pure horseradish - a cocktail sauce that included catsup, vinegar, spices, and of course horseradish - a yellow mustard with Horseradish - and a zesty pickle relish.

But all good things must someday come to an end. In 1985, Lester Miller sold his horseradish business to Silver Spring of Eau Claire, Wisconsin. He continued to do some light farming after that, planting and selling "seed roots" to horseradish farmers.

In 1981, the *Appleton Post Crescent* interviewed Lester Miller and asked him after so many years in the horseradish business, did they ever grow tired of it? Lester's response was, "We have it on the table for the noon meal and dinner. We never get sick of it."

Lester Miller passed away on August 30, 1991.

Today, Richard lives in Texas, and is retired. Sadly, Robert L. Miller passed away on May 4, 2018. He was 75 years of age. The old homestead is still there, but the present owners have refurbished the main building into a residential home.

It is said one can still find horseradish root growing here and there around the old farm property and in the fence rows...the remaining remnants of what once was a thriving and unique business.

Sources: *Oshkosh Daily Northwestern*, Nov 11, 1958; Sept. 11, 1965; Oct. 24, 1970; Oshkosh Public Library Reference File-Miller Horseradish; *Appleton Post Crescent*, 9.27.81, pg4; personal interviews with Robert Miller and Richard Miller Oct/Nov 2016;

THE DAY THE SINGING COWBOY RODE INTO TOWN

I t's not often a famous entertainer makes a stop in Oshkosh, Wisconsin. But on occasion it does happen. When it does, it's a big deal.

On January 18, 1950, Gene Autry came to town and put on a live show at the Oshkosh Theater in downtown Main Street.

Known as "The Singing Cowboy", Gene Autry was one of Hollywood's biggest stars. His career spanned 70 years and he was famous in motion pictures, radio, television and as a recording artist. During his career, he wrote and sang hundreds of songs, starred in 93 movies and 91 television productions. In his later years, Autry owned a television and radio station on the west coast and even owned a major league baseball team, the Los Angeles Angels.[1] Some of his Christmas songs still get play and are popular today.

On that Wednesday, the city was "electric". The local Sears store on Merritt Street invited kids to come and see Autry's equally famous horse named "Champion" from 2:30-3:30pm. Free autographed photos of the famous cowboy were given to the first 1,000 kids in attendance.[2]

Two live performances were also scheduled that day at the Oshkosh Theater featuring a 4pm matinee and an evening performance at 8:30pm. The live shows were billed as "Gene Autry and his Melody Ranch Hands with Champion, the Wonder Horse". Also featured in the performance was Rufe Davis, Pat Buttram, the Cass County Boys, The Pinafores, Frankie Marvin and Little Champ. All seats were reserved with matinee seating priced at $1.80, $1.20 and 90¢, the evening show a bit more. The show included several songs made popular by Autry's movies and recordings, along with tricks performed by Champion and Little Champ. Rubber-faced comedian Rufe Davis "almost stopped the show" with his imitations.[2]

A touching scene took place between shows when Autry was made aware of a big fan of his that was too ill to attend. The *Oshkosh Daily Northwestern* reported the visit:

> *Perhaps the most excited little girl in Winnebago county Wednesday night was Edna Schinke, 6, a patient at Sunnyview sanitorium. Edna, unable to walk or even to sit up, was visited by her favorite movie star, Gene Autry, singing cowboy, who appeared with his western troupe yesterday afternoon and evening at the Oshkosh Theater.*
>
> *The youngster had been expecting a visit from the personable actor during the afternoon. Autry, however, was unaware the appointment had been made. Edna was deeply disappointed although she made every effort not to show it.*
>
> *Informed late in the afternoon of the slipup, the cowboy star said he wouldn't leave Oshkosh without seeing the youthful patient.*
>
> *Immediately after his matinee performance, Autry was whisked by auto to Sunnyview where the belated meeting took place.*
>
> *The movie star talked with the overjoyed little girl and presented her with a silver dollar which he told her "is the kind we use out west."*
>
> *Edna sang a little song for her ideal, after which Autry reciprocated with a selection from his show. His audience included a number of adult patients of the sanitorium and members of the staff. Autry had to cut his appearance short to return to the city for his evening performance at the theater, but he left behind him a very happy little girl.[4]*

Later that evening, Gene Autry had dinner with some friends at the Hotel Raulf. Joining him were Mrs. G.C. Mamer of 408 Grant Street, Oshkosh, and her sister from Savannah Georgia, Mrs. A.E. Satherley. Mrs. Satherley's husband was the Vice President of the Columbia

Recording Company and a personal friend and business associate of Mr. Autry.

Sources: (1) www.autry.com; (2) *Oshkosh Daily Northwestern*, January 17, 1950, Sears Ad; (3) *Oshkosh Daily Northwestern*, January 17, 1950, Oshkosh Theater Ad; (4) *Oshkosh Daily Northwestern*, January 19, 1950, pg2;

REPP'S BAR

Drive around the City of Oshkosh and you will notice there seems to be a bar on almost every corner. Neighborhood bars have been part of the charm and endearing charisma of our community since it was first settled by our European ancestors in the 19th century. We are the descendants of generations of hard working laborers who loved their beer – and maybe a shot of brandy or whiskey too.

Neighborhood bars were gathering places where mostly men would stop each day after work to wash down the dust and share stories of their day at the mill or factory. These bars were mostly privately owned, the exception being those owned by the powerhouse breweries of Milwaukee…Miller, Schlitz, Pabst, etc. that were looking to create monopolies with their brand. Some of the local breweries like Peoples, Oshkosh Brewing, Rahrs and others would contract with local owners to feature only their beer on tap.

Not every working man had the luxury of owning an automobile and many would walk to and from work. The neighborhood bars were a convenient stopping off point to "have a few" before continuing on home. In the days before television and the internet, the local tavern is where they would go to socialize, get caught up on the news and world of sports, and maybe play a few hands of cribbage or "sheepshead". Everybody knew almost everybody and the bartender always had a handful of jokes or stories at the ready to entertain his customers.

Oshkosh's past was built on a Mecca of manufacturing companies and those that worked in the mills and factories were hard working, blue collar laborers. The work was hard and often done under extreme conditions. When there was a shift change at the Axle, Leach Company, Oshkosh Truck, Diamond Match, or the Paine and

Morgan Lumber Companies, nearby bars would be ready for the rush of patrons leaving work.

This story is about one of those neighborhood taverns that was in business with the same family ownership for 75 years.

It was early in the summer of 2017 that I arranged to meet Alan Repp and learn the story behind a business that spanned almost 75 years. Al invited me into the tavern and led me over to the end of the bar where he had scrapbooks and newspaper clippings arranged awaiting my arrival. Without missing a beat, Al started right in at the beginning...

Alvin Repp purchased the tavern located at 168 West Algoma (today the corner of Oshkosh Avenue and Rainbow Drive) from Ed Bass in August of 1943. Ed Bass had owned and operated the Bass Tavern since 1939.

Young Alan Repp stands in front of the Bass Tavern in 1943

Photo courtesy Alan Repp

(The Grand Opening of the New Bass Tavern appeared in the Oshkosh Daily Northwestern on March 18, 1939) Shortly after taking ownership, Alvin moved into the apartment perched above the bar with his wife Dorothy and son Alan and changed the name of the tavern to *Repp Tavern.*

The area surrounding the bar was much different in the 1940s than today. Alan Repp remembers when much of what is Rainbow Park

Repps Tavern mid 1940s

Photo courtesy Alan Repp

Alan Repp circa 1945

today was occupied by the Paine Lumber Company. "It was a marshy area and Paine used the property to sort lumber. It was also the area that was used when carnivals came to town," he recalled. He went on to remind me that the north end of present-day Rainbow Park was once the West Side Bathing Beach and Tennis Courts. "The entire area was full of tall shade trees, that is until the Dutch Elm disease moved in and killed all the stately elms."

Across the street and to the south of the tavern was Pluswood, a manufacturing plant that produced wood products like plywood and laminates. All that remains on that site today is a tall, brick smoke stack which serves as a reminder to those who remember the days when Oshkosh was truly "Sawdust City". Alan recalls the Pluswood factory whistle blaring constantly signaling the end of World War II.

Oshkosh Avenue, previously known as West Algoma, was the business district for the rapidly growing west side of Oshkosh as residential areas were quickly expanding from Sawyer Street to the west. "There were six taverns and a liquor store in this first block," Alan stated. There was also Butzlaff Hardware, Mueller Potter Drugstore, Felda's Bar (later Mary's Toy and Togs), and a beer distributor for Blatz Brewing Company that later became a beer depot named West End Beverage. "I had a key for the beer depot so when we needed a keg, I would walk over there and get what I needed. It was the honor system," Repp told me. "We had limited refrigeration so keeping a supply of keg beer on hand was not feasible. It was a handy arrangement."

Another of Repp's neighbors included the Shubert Meat Market next door. Shubert's Meats was owned by Edward Shubert (1946-68). Prior to that the market was owned by Floyd Shurbert/Shurbert's Meats (1930-46), and earlier Ernest Westphal doing business as E. Westphal Market (1910-1930). Allen remembers sitting at his kitchen table eating lunch and looking out the window only to hear a gunshot from men stunning a cow or shocking a pig or wringing a chicken's neck. They were a custom meat processor as well as a fresh meat butcher shop, and fresh really meant fresh!

1953 was a special year for Oshkosh and its citizens as the community came together to celebrate its bicentennial anniversary. "The men all grew beards as part of the celebration and my dad had a great old bushy beard. I keep that photo of him hanging on the wall in the bar yet

Behind the bar with Alan and Alvin Repp and bartender Dick Voelzke

Photo courtesy Alan Repp

today." It was said that men who refused to sport facial hair during the celebration were sentenced to face a "kangaroo court".

The neighborhood tavern was run much like the Mom and Pop grocery store of the 40s and 50s...that is, on credit. There was trust and honor between the proprietor and clientele back then. The customers were "the regulars" and familiarity paid off for both sides. Credit was given in those days as it was just the way they did business. Men would come in during the week and run up a tab. On Thursday, the same men would return with their paycheck in hand, cash it and pay off their debt.

As Alan thought back to the days now past, he recalled those who made Repp's Bar what it is. "We had Germans, Poles, Rooshan's (Russians)...all came in here to play a few hands of cards, enjoy a few drinks, talk about the Packers, Braves and Cubs...and commiserate with their friends. They are all dead now." Some of the west siders still stop in but the after-work crowd is much thinner today than in years past as the manufacturing business has changed. Many of his customers today include folks who just finished a round of golf at the nearby Lakeshore Municipal Golf Course, stopping in for a beer or two and a sandwich. Repp still greets new arrivals with a basket of salted peanuts, inviting all to just throw the shells on the floor. This was a bit surprising to me as this is one of the neatest and cleanest bars in town! The long mahogany bar is covered with a grey Formica top, reminiscent to a time when Formica was chic, and enough sturdy, wooden legged stools to accommodate seventeen customers comfortably.

When cable TV was introduced in the late 60s and early 70s, customers who did not have cable at home would stop in to catch a ball game at Repp's. Alan put in cable so he could get the Cubs games. The Braves deserted Milwaukee in 1966 so a lot of local fans turned their allegiance to the Cubs.

In 1952, Alvin built a restaurant next to the bar and named it *Repp's Fine Foods Café*. Alvin began running the café in addition to the bar, then turned the café management over to his brother Henry Repp. Located adjacent to the tavern, the building would host several businesses over the years including *Father John's Chicken Coop* and *Gregory's Irish Shanty*. The building still stands today and sells bait and tackle to fisherman launching their boats in nearby Rainbow Park.

Alan's father Alvin was diagnosed with colon cancer and died on October 19, 1968 at the young age of 58. Alan took over the bar where he had started working in 1953 when he was in high school. After high school, Alan went onto college and enrolled in studies of music and journalism from Wartburg College. Today he still has a fondness for Big Band Music and Dixieland Jazz.

As Alan and I sat, reminiscing about the past, I discovered something strange and maybe even a little odd about the man sitting next to me. It turns out he is a Cleveland Browns fan! "How do you get by owning a bar in the heart of Packer country being a Browns fan?" I asked. "I've been a Cleveland fan all my life. My dad and I went to a Chicago White Sox/Cleveland Indian game in 1966," he said proudly. He still has the two pennants he acquired that day along with the ticket stubs that showed they paid only $2.50 each to attend that day's event at Chicago's Comiskey Park. The week of this interview, in honor of the Cleveland Indians reaching the 2016 World Series, Alan hung those same Indian pennants from his "back bar" along with the original ticket stubs from the 1966 game still stapled to each one. He also showed me a letter he received from Browns President Art Modell in 1966, thanking him for being a dedicated Browns fan living in Packer territory. Raising that subject stimulated another whole line of memories for Alan.

He recalled that back in the 60s, the famous Green Bay Packers linebacker Ray Nitschke would come into his bar on occasion. "He was a goodwill representative working for a liquor distributor during the offseason. The players back then didn't make the money that athletes do now." He also remembers Oshkosh native and Major League Baseball umpire Dutch Rennert working as a PR man for the Pabst Brewing Company. Local MLB Pitcher Bill Gogolewski lives just a "stone's throw" away from the tavern and at one time also tended bar for Repp on a part time basis.

One of the things that became crystal clear to me while we chatted was Alan's commitment to the Tavern League of Wisconsin, founded in 1945 in Racine. He is very proud of his trade association and will quickly tell you about all the good work that is done by the organization. The Wisconsin Tavern League is basically an organization that supports the tavern industry in Wisconsin. There are only three city chapters in the entire state (the rest are all county chapters) and Oshkosh is one of them. Alan is proud to have served as President of the Oshkosh Chapter for eight years. The League is funded strictly by donations from their membership. "Of all the bars in Oshkosh, only about half participate as members," Alan said. He gave me an example of some of the great work funded by the Tavern League which started year around here in December 15. 1985. The Safe Ride program provides *free* transportation home via taxi for anyone needing the service. During 2015-2016, across Wisconsin, the Safe Ride program provided 4,104 rides to patrons at a cost of $28,198. Since the inception of this state-wide program in 2003, there has been a 50% decline in alcohol related traffic fatalities. The League is also a lobbying group that works on behalf of the tavern industry on things like taxes and DWI laws.

Another unique thing about Repp's is the hours. When most bars are just warming up for the evening business, Alan is locking up and heading home. "My hours are 11am-6 pm Monday through Saturday. I close on Sunday and holidays. When people ask me how long I'm open I say 'as long as the till rings'." He pointed out that many other bars in town cater to a college or younger crowd and their hours vary significantly from his. He knows his customers. When he's not open, he's still there working, cleaning, ordering and stocking supplies, and banking. "I work seven days a week!" he says proudly.

He shared with me his age. Looking not a day over age 60, I was surprised to learn Alan was 78 years old in 2017 with no plans for retirement. He says he has a little arthritis but other than that he's in pretty good health. The bar is his business – his life. He and his lovely wife Barb married in 1966 and are still going strong today.

When you walk into Repp's Bar you immediately get that "*warm welcome*" kind of feeling. Alan Repp is a medium size man, bald with a friendly face like someone you've known your entire life. Women and children are welcome here in this family friendly atmosphere. "I have no pool table and no dice cup" he explained. The sound of that dice cup slamming on the bar was irritating to the *Slinger of Suds*, so he got rid of it in 1960. When he had a jukebox, it was one he owned, not leased from a vending company. "I owned my own jukebox so I filled it with *my own* songs…music I liked." One more oddity at Repp's is he has never sold beer by the pitcher, explaining "I never saw the need to."

Alan Repp, 1988

Photo courtesy Alan Repp

The sign on the wall says "Welcome To Repp's – The 3 B's – Beer, Booze and BS". You can bet there is plenty of all three to go around!

On December 30, 2017, Alan Repp turned the key for the very last time. Repp's closed and the building was sold to the City of Oshkosh, which plans to raze the historic bar to accommodate a new road system on Oshkosh Ave. I called Alan in early March and said we needed to finish this story. When I left him last summer, he had not yet made the decision to sell the bar.

My first question was…why?

"Randy, I'm 79 years old and I always said I would work until I was eighty. I'm almost there and the opportunity to do this was now," he replied with a tone of sadness in his voice. He went on to explain, "I haven't slept well since I closed the bar. That bar was my life. I hadn't taken a vacation since 1959. I was here…every day."

Alan continued to explain that there was no one in his family interested in the bar business in which to hand over the reins. And the city's controversial decision to sell Lakeshore Golf Course to a local manufacturer means the road system must undergo some significant changes. The writing was on the wall that one way or another, the bar would probably have to go. Repp also owned the bait shop next door to the bar and included it in the sale as well.

I asked the locally famous "suds slinger" what he will do with all his newfound free time. "Well, one thing I always wanted to do was to go to Branson. I always loved music and I've heard it's a great place for live entertainment." He also hinted that there may be another opportunity "behind the bar" waiting for him, but he wanted to take some time to think things through.

So, now its time to turn the page and bid farewell to another piece of Oshkosh's historic past...a neighborhood saloon that catered to the working man for three-quarters of a century.

To Alvin and Alan Repp...thanks for the memories!

Sources: Personal interviews with Alan Repp, 2016, 2018;

Pole Sitter Reaches New Heights

A t 12:05 pm, on May 2, 1931, pole sitter Betty Fox climbed a flag pole perched atop the Raulf Hotel. Her goal was to sit there regardless of weather conditions for 100 hours to break her former record of 96 hours. Fox received well wishes from hotel owners Conrad and Charles Raulf as she began her ascension to a 12 by 14-inch platform mounted at the top. Her attire was simply tennis shoes, white overalls, a jumper jacket and helmet. A telephone was installed at the top of the pole that allowed Betty Fox to take phone calls from well-wishers during her feat. She descended on the afternoon of May 6, breaking her former record. At the time it was also considered the world record for female pole sitters.

Sources: *Oshkosh Daily Northwestern*, May 2, 1931, p. 11; *Oshkosh Daily Northwestern*, May 7, 1931, p. 17

THE DELTOX AND WAITE GRASS RUG COMPANIES

During the early years of the twentieth century, Oshkosh had earned the reputation of the "Grass Rug Capital of the World". This badge of honor was anchored by two large companies that produced grass rugs.

Rugs produced by these two companies were made with a special type of grass harvested from local marshes in the Fremont, Zittau and Berlin areas. Vast marshlands here made the harvesting of "raw materials" easy due to its close proximity to Oshkosh and ample supplies. The grass was an abundant and renewable resource. Known to those in the business as "wire grass", its value to the rug business centered around being very durable and cost efficient to produce. In the early 1900s, grass rugs and woven fiber carpets were commonly found in most homes.

The Oshkosh Grass Matting Company began business in 1902 under the leadership of Emil H. Steiger, a sawmill operator from nearby Fremont. His business partners included Leander Choate – a banker and lumberman, and businessmen R. C. Brown and Frederick E. Waite. A few years later, it would become known as the Deltox Rug Company. It began in business with eight employees in a stone building on Ceape Street, then moved to the Wisconsin Avenue location in 1904.[4] The land on Wisconsin Street was acquired from William and Stephen Radford in 1903.

Emil Steiger was involved in several other Oshkosh businesses including the Oshkosh Pure Ice Company of which he was President. In 1890, Steiger was elected to the Assembly of the State Legislature.

His experience as a wholesale dealer in wood, potatoes, real estate and hay for the Wisconsin Grass Twine Company qualified him to be considered an expert in the purchase of suitable materials for making grass twine.[6-7] Other business interests included President of the Davis Hansen Pump Company, the Phillips Sprinkler Company, Treasurer of the Oshkosh Steamboat Company, manager of the Wegener Fuel Company, Treasurer of the Little Wolf Power Company, and others along with Mr. and Mrs. Leander Choate.

In 1914, the Oshkosh Grass Matting Company became the Deltox Grass Rug Company, then in 1924 became The Deltox Rug Company. Deltox owned 15,000 acres of marshland and leased another 10,000 in Wisconsin, Minnesota and Canada. It's first sale was to Marshall Field & Company in 1903. It is said that at one time, the Oshkosh Grass Matting Company produced over half of the grass rugs produced in the USA.[1]

In 1912, former US President Theodore Roosevelt used the "new" Oshkosh Grass Matting Company warehouse to give a speech. It was the only venue in Oshkosh during that time that could hold reportedly 10,000 people. The report says that 4,000 people were turned away.[1]

Emil H. Steiger ran the Deltox Company for almost three decades before dying of a heart attack while having dinner at his home on Elmwood Avenue on November 21, 1929. He was 58 years of age. His sons assumed leadership of the company with Carl E. Steiger as President and Emil L. Steiger as Secretary.

In 1907, Frederick E. Waite cut his ties with the Oshkosh Grass Matting Company to start his own business with his son, Ossian. The Waite Grass Carpet Company opened its first production facility on Pearl Avenue between Jackson and Market Streets. In 1910 they moved to their permanent location on Mt. Vernon Street, just a short distance from Harrison Street.

Frederick Waite was born in 1849 in Lakeport (Kenosha), Wisconsin.[8] His father Thomas, was head of *Waite & Company* of Chicago and published *The Daily Tribune* which later became the *Chicago Tribune*. Thomas Waite died in 1852 and his wife, Rhoda, married Ossian Cook in 1855 and moved to Oshkosh.

In 1874, Ossian Cook and business partner R.C. Brown and Ossian's stepson Frederick formed a company that later would become

Cook & Brown Lime Co. Waite sold his interest in that company in 1905.

Frederick and his only child, Ossian Thomas Waite, ran the company as business partners until Ossian's untimely death. Ossian T. Waite died in August, 1925 and his two sons, Stanley E. and Phillip C. Waite joined their grandfather Frederick in business. Ossian's death was sudden and unexpected. His father, Frederick, was traveling by automobile from Rochester, Minnesota to Oshkosh at the time. A story published in the *Oshkosh Daily Northwestern* indicated that Mr. Waite was unaware of his son's death and as he was traveling there was no way to reach him. The *Associated Press* became involved and radio stations in Milwaukee broadcast pleas for Mr. Waite to "hasten him home to the bereaved family of his son." [5]

Five years later, Frederick died at his home at 662 Algoma Boulevard on September 22, 1930. His cause of death was due to advanced age – Mr. Waite was 80 years old. His obituary informs us that Mr. Waite had few hobbies but was always interested in automobiles, "preferring always to drive his own machine". It is believed he also owned one of the first automobiles in Oshkosh.

When Frederick died, his grandson Phillip Waite assumed the position of President and Secretary.

Deltox grass matting shanties near Zittau
Photo courtesy Winchester Area Historical Society

But Deltox and Waite were not the first grass rug companies in Oshkosh. In 1901 the Crex Company was the first in Oshkosh to produce grass rugs but shortly after opening, the business was moved to St. Paul, MN.[1]

In the mid 1920s, the grass rug business started to feel competitive pressure from products manufactured in Japan. The Japanese used rice straw to make rugs that were less durable, but also cheaper. During this time, several grass rug companies across the US closed their doors, unable to compete in this changing market.

But the Deltox and Waite Rug Companies took a different approach.

Both companies dropped grass rugs from their line in 1924, moving toward kraft fiber rugs that were not only more durable, but could also be dyed with color. Deltox continued to make special order grass rugs until 1935. Also, key to the survival of Deltox was their decision to advertise in National publications such as *Life, The Saturday Evening Post* and *Better Homes and Gardens* magazines. This strategy broadened their reach into national markets which produced critical mass, enhancing production efficiencies.[1] That same year, the Waite Grass Carpet Company changed their name to the Waite Carpet Company.[2]

Deltox marsh press powered by a team of horses
Photo courtesy Winchester Area Historical Society

Grass harvesting was considered a critical activity and done mostly during the summer months. During this time, plant production at the Deltox was reduced to 25% to allow the male employees to participate in the harvest. Participation was not mandatory but was offered only to men, as the harvest involved the workers living in camps in the marshes. Between plant workers and hired locals, the harvest usually required several hundred strong bodies.

Each day, the horses were fit with "clogs". The clogs measured about 8 inches square and were bolted onto the horses shoes. Without these clogs, the horses would be unable to walk through the soft, mushy marsh bogs. Reaping machines similar to grain binders were used to harvest the grass. The machines would cut the grass and lay it aside in rows where men would hand-tie bundles and throw them into piles. The bundles were then placed into huge stacks about 15-20 feet high where they would wait until the winter months. Once the marsh was frozen, it was able to support the weight of the heavy machinery used to transport the stacks to the river's edge. In spring, two company-owned steamboats, The Evelyn and The Leander Choate, would collect the harvest and transport it to the piling-supported buildings at the Deltox along the Fox River. After the grass was unloaded, it was combed and fed into spinning machines that made it into twine. The spools of twine were then graded by color to produce a uniform finish when made into rugs.[1]

During the "wire grass" years, Deltox employed 250 workers. That increased to 400 employees when the company moved to kraft fiber and National advertising. At the time the company was sold to the Armstrong Cork Company in 1954, the workforce had increased to 550. The company was sold once again in 1961 to T.C. Widder, Ralph Petersen and John Miller. Deltox ceased production in 1968 and the buildings were used mainly as warehouses. The Deltox buildings were finally sold to the City of Oshkosh in 1983 and razed in 1984.[3]

The Waite Carpet Company ceased doing business in 1966 and sold the building to the Victrylite Candle Company who used the facilty for warehousing and shipping.

Today, the Waite building on Harrison is being renovated to provide low income housing.

Sources: (1) Historic American Engineering Record, National Park Service, Oshkosh Grass Matting Company, HAER No.WI 11; (2) Oshkosh Public Museum, Past Perfect, Deltox Rug Company, Catalogue Number 2009.44.42; (3) Oshkosh Public Museum, Past Perfect, Waite Grass Carpet Company, Catalogue P2010.48.2; (4) *Oshkosh Daily Northwestern*, 2.20.83; (5) *Oshkosh Daily Northwestern*, 8.15.1925, p.3; (6) *Wisconsin Blue Book, 190*, p.767; (7) *Oshkosh Daily Northwestern*, 11.22.1929, pp. 1,12; (8) *Oshkosh Daily Northwestern*, September 23, 1930, p. 1;

J. Frank Waldo

Through the years, Oshkosh has been the home of many local artists. Robert Lautenschlager, Ray Pable, Nile Behncke, Dan Radig…just to name a few.

John Frank Waldo was not an Oshkosh native, but came here in midlife and left his mark with some fabulous paintings, some depicting locally historical scenes. Born in Chelsea, Vermont in 1835, Waldo's interest in photography and art would take him on a journey across the United States that would include Wisconsin. In 1859 he married Esther Maria Bartholomew and together they made their journey to the Midwest. They had six children, Algernon born in Sumner, Kansas, Maria born in Racine, Wisconsin, William born in Kenosha, Wisconsin and Ralph, Edward and Frank born in Oshkosh between 1866 and 1883.

Waldo lived in Sumner, Kansas for two years (1859-60) before moving to Central City Colorado to work as a photographer. By 1863 the family moved to Racine, Wisconsin where they only lived one year before moving to Oshkosh in 1864. Waldo went to work here with the Rudd & Holden Carriage Company as a painter of carriages and signs.

Waldo enjoyed this work as a painter and decided to expand his skills as an artist. In 1866 he began taking art lessons from a well-known local artist named Mrs. Thomas P. Russell. As he worked to hone his newly acquired skills, Waldo began working as an artist and fresco painter in the Oshkosh area. Some of his creations can still be seen today at the Hearthstone Historic House Museum in Appleton, Wisconsin where he was contracted as a fresco painter to work in the William Waters designed home of Henry J. Rogers, a local business leader in the early days of the paper industry. His beautiful frescoes still cover the walls and ceilings of this historic landmark.

An article in the *Oshkosh Daily Northwestern* gave a fine illustration of Waldo's work:

Waldo's Work

J.F. Waldo, the artist, returned on Saturday evening from Appleton, where he has completed the frescoing in the Commercial Bank building. 'The Crescent' speaks in the highest terms of Mr. Waldo's work. The ceiling is frescoed in a large circle with conventional flower wreaths of oak leaves and acorns, bars, etc. the effect being in fine harmony with the sides, the base being a gray Bismarck border, floral relief. The right side is ornamented with a fine view of the factories and the water power, including the Rogers paper mill, Kimberly & Clark flouring mill, paper mill and several others, with an excellent view of the government works and the valley of the Fox from an original sketch by Mr. Waldo. Mr. Waldo is enthusiastic in his praise of Appleton, which he pronounces one of the handsomest and most enterprising cities in the west.[2]

Waldo's frescoes found their way into more than just banks and businesses. Some of Oshkosh's prominent citizens commissioned J. Frank Waldo to paint frescoes in their private residences – O.D. Peck, Edgar P. Sawyer, Mayor Pratt, George M. Paine, W.T. Ellsworth to name a few.[4]

Another beautiful example of his work caught my eye at the Oshkosh Public Museum. His painting, "View of Island Park", depicting the British occupation of Garlic Island, was hanging on display. Because of my interest and affection for Garlic Island, I instantly fell in love with it. I was delighted to find out the Museum had prints of this original painting available for sale and I purchased one. Today the print hangs proudly over my fireplace and seldom does a guest get by without a quick mention on this important piece of local history.

His work was mainly oil and watercolor based and he loved to paint landscape scenes. Some of his local subjects included Lake Winnebago scenes and a wonderful painting titled "Matchstick Factory". Waldo is also credited as the artist who hand-painted the drop curtain, walls and ceiling inside Oshkosh's Grand Opera House. He also was consigned to decorate the walls of the new Appleton opera house which opened in 1882.

Waldo traveled across the US making sketches, most notably in California and the Lake Superior Region. He would later use the sketches to paint his masterpieces.

On February 1, 1883, Waldo's Washington Street studio was destroyed by fire. The fire broke out around 2 am in the building where Waldo kept his studio. The fire was blamed on a furnace in a Turkish Bath which shared accommodations in the same building. The Turkish Bath business recently was having problems with pipes freezing and an employee whose job it was to prevent that is blamed for the tragedy. Reports say the employee stated he would "keep a rousing fire and stay up all night to keep the pipes warm". Local newspaper, *The Oshkosh Times*, was also destroyed by the blaze.[7]

The loss included many paintings and sketches Waldo had accumulated over many years. Also lost in the blaze were all his patterns for ceiling and wall decorations, and a number of valuable paintings he had been working on, along with many miscellaneous pictures. He was not insured.[7] It was nearly impossible to put a dollar value on the loss as many would say certain works of art are irreplaceable.[1] Among the items salvaged from the fire was a medal which Waldo designed for the Great Northwestern Sanitary fair held in Chicago in 1865. Waldo's design for the medal was selected by committee from among the twenty entries submitted that year. The medal was cast in bronze by the US Mint at Philadelphia. [3]

Two years later, he moved to Chicago, where he worked as an art school teacher for artist Frank C. Bromley.[5] Before departing from Oshkosh, Waldo offered to the public a large exhibition of his artwork in the Washington Street art studio of Edmund and Mary Osthaus, and over several weeks sold many paintings from his collection. The remainder of his large collection was then shipped to Chicago.[6]

On April 27, 1883, the *Oshkosh Daily Northwestern* reported that Waldo had just returned home from Shawano where he was frescoing a Presbyterian church. Upon his arrival home it was learned that his wife was suffering "from an acute form of delirium, arising from puerperal disturbance, and fears are entertained that she may become deranged." Court records indicated he divorced her in 1890 and re-married that same year. His first wife, Esther, remained here in Oshkosh until at least 1905.

Waldo moved back east in 1897, and in 1902 his works received distinguished recognition in several New York galleries.

The final five years of his life were spent living in Los Angeles where he died on May 29, 1920 at the age of 85 years old.

Sources: Oshkosh.pastperfectonline.com,catalogue number P2002.3.202; thegrand oshkosh.org/history/early-years.html; http://www.focol.org/hearthstone/; (1) *Oshkosh Daily Northwestern*, February 7, 1883, p. 4; (2) *Oshkosh Daily Northwestern*, September 11, 1882; (3) *Oshkosh Daily Northwestern*, February 12, 1883, p. 4; (4) *Oshkosh Daily Northwestern*, July 20, 1882, p. 2; (5) *Oshkosh Daily Northwestern*, October 28, 1885, p. 8; (6) *Oshkosh Daily Northwestern*, February 5, 1885, p. 3; (7) *Oshkosh Daily Northwestern*, February 1, 1883, p. 8;

ALICE WASHBURN

Oshkosh's First Motion Picture Star

By Dan Radig

I invited Dan Radig to join me in this venture as there is no one I know today that has a deeper knowledge or greater passion for Oshkosh's local history. Aside from being born and raised as an Oshkoshian, Dan is a friend, a well-versed historian, an author, and a wonderful and locally famous artist. Dan also collects historic photos and is a regular contributor to several of the local social media sites on Facebook.

When I asked Dan if he would like to contribute to this project, he eagerly agreed. I told him he could choose the story he wanted to tell and without hesitation he said, "Alice Washburn…Oshkosh's first motion picture star".

Here is Dan's story.

The best way to introduce this story is to include an excerpt from the *Edison Kinetogram*, dated January 1, 1914, Vol. 9, No. 11…

Alice Washburn made her first bright remark in Oshkosh, Wisconsin — yep, Oshkosh — at the age of several minutes and began amusing audiences of varying sizes ever since. She is the youngest daughter of the late Judge G. W. Washburn of – well let us not be cruel - and while her father was named after the hero in FORTY THIEVES, Alice said all she ever knew he stole was a few naps daily on the family sofa and did that duty for over sixty years.

Miss Washburn did not officially start the laughter microbe going, however, until she abandoned Hellard's Fifth Reader for the Sixth — giving DARIUS GREEN AND HIS FLYING MACHINE. She won her first professional spurs in Boston - quite a jump from Oshkosh to the hub of the universe - where her rendition of humorous characters and weird interpretations attracted much attention.

She studied under several of the best teachers in the country, among them the celebrated Leland Powers who said of her: 'As a humorist, Miss Alice Washburn occupies a field entirely her own, and in which her success is unquestioned. The public is quick to appreciate that which is unique and unhackneyed, especially if artistic, and Washburn, rarely gifted by nature for her special line of work, cultivated by careful study and training, presents herself backed by the capable opinion of critics of the highest standing.'

Miss Washburn made her professional bow as La Frochard in the TWO ORPHANS. Next came the roles of Mrs. Tattleby in OUR NEW MINISTER, Priscilla Filkins in CAROLINA, and Mrs. Madge Holcomb in MLLE RICCI.

She then became a member of Proctor's Fifth Avenue Company and later joined the Friend Players of Milwaukee, playing important roles in many of the best-known comedies and dramas. Her whimsical mind next found vent in the moving pictures where she appeared in Powers and Kalem Photoplays and then joined the Edison Players. Her first performance for Edison was in HOW THE TELEPHONE CAME TO TOWN, which she made a tremendous hit. Some of her best remembered parts are STAGE STRUCK LIZZIE, HOGAN'S ALLEY, NO PLACE FOR A MINISTER'S SON, BRIDGET'S SUDDEN WEALTH, HOW A HORSESHOE UPSET A FAMILY, PROPOSAL UNDER DIFFICULTIES, A PAIR OF FOILS, AT MIDNIGHT, THE COMEDIAN'S DOWNFALL, WHY GIRLS LEAVE HOME, and PORGY'S BOUQUET.

Miss Washburn is blessed with an irrepressible sense of humor, keen and subtle. She has an unerring eye for detail in designing her marvelous costumes which constitute a comedy in themselves. The fact that Miss Washburn is known to the public as a comedienne is due solely to her preference for humorous roles, as she is as versatile as she is clever. Upon several occasions, she has given convincing interpretations of difficult dramatic parts, putting into them all the realism and spirit which has always characterized her performances.

Though she preferred to wear the cap and bells and had won her place as the foremost motion picture comedienne, Miss Washburn might cast aside her present laurels and win them anew as a dramatic actress were she so inclined. For hers is the true genius which finds expression in whatever phase of the art Miss Washburn undertakes.

Oshkosh's first motion picture star, Alice Washburn, is said to have been an outgoing and precocious young girl, the daughter of a pioneer family.

Miss Washburn and her brother were born as twins in Oshkosh on September 12, 1861, to Ganem & Sarah Strickland Washburn. Mr. Washburn was born in Livermore, Maine, October 29, 1823, the son of Rewel Washburn, a Maine lawyer. He attended Bowdoin college at Brunswick, Maine, and graduated from the law course, after which he came west and settled in Oshkosh around June, 1847. He was considered one of the earliest settlers in this vicinity.[1] Her mother was born in Maine on October 8, 1826 and came to Oshkosh in 1850. On November 19 of that year she married G. W. Washburn, placing them among the earliest pioneer families to settle in Oshkosh. The Washburns were prominent in the early growth of the city. Judge Washburn was the first circuit court judge in Winnebago County. In addition to his judicial duties, he was also connected with other local business ventures.

Alice spent her youth at 92 Jefferson St. (now 524 Jefferson) along with her brother John and sisters Clara and Mary. Her twin brother, Benjamin, passed away less than a year after being born. She most likely was educated at the "old" Fourth Ward School at the corner of Jefferson and Merritt, a block from her family home. Little is known of her younger years growing up in Oshkosh. She did graduate from Oshkosh High School in 1880 with the intentions of becoming a teacher - something she did do off and on for several years.

The first public notice of her as an actress appeared in the local paper playing the character "Rose, the waiting maid" at the North Side Turner

Washburn Residence at 92 Jefferson Street (now 524 Jefferson Street) 2015.

Photo courtesy Dan Radig

Hall in the play *RENDEZVOUS*, on October 24, 1879. [24] Because of their family prominence, stories appeared in the local newspaper about Alice and her friends who also came from other well-known families in Oshkosh. These young adolescents would gather at the homes of their parent's and recite dramatic readings, and perform plays and music shows for family and friends, sometimes lasting late into the evening.

After high school Alice attended the Oshkosh Normal School where she graduated in 1882. She was assigned as a teacher's aide at the Frentz School in Oshkosh but in July of that same year decided to turn down the offer and accepted a position to teach at the Dale School in 1883.[3] Always looking for change, she only taught at that school for a couple of years. Alice then accepted a job in Menominee, Wisconsin in 1887.[4] There she taught grade school for a couple of years and then off again, this time out east, to attend the Boston School of Expression at Massachusetts, where she was said to have been an exceptional student. Miss Washburn received several favorable reviews in the Boston papers for her writing and dramatic readings and graduated from that institution in 1891. On her return visits home, she found herself high in demand for her oratory skills which she obliged by giving readings at women's groups, churches, etc. She also coached the local high school students in their drama & musical productions.

Oshkosh Daily Northwestern, September 12, 1890

Miss Alice Washburn made her first public appearance in this city last evening, when she recited 'Susan's Escort' a selection written by Edward Everett Hale. Miss Washburn was encored. Later in the evening she recited an Irish piece, which evoked considerable laughter, and won her another recall. Her work last evening is indicative of the fact that her studies in Boston have born much fruit. Her enunciation was distinct, and her powers of imitation apparently well developed, so that she cannot but please an audience whenever she appears.[5]

The following spring the *Oshkosh Daily Northwestern* reprinted an article from the *Boston Times*:

Miss Washburn has made a striking scene of her dramatization of the WITCH'S CAVERN, and her personification of the Witch was notable for its weird successfulness. Miss Washburn shows always an intensity of thought and feeling that points the genuineness of her individual talent. Her powers are markedly strong, and she is to be congratulated on the continental and perceptible progress made to their full expression.

Alice returned to Oshkosh in 1892 and began performing in many local musical and dramatic productions.[6]

After a short visit back home, Alice returned east and worked with several acting groups including performances at the Colonial Theater in Boston. This time she had numerous mentions in Boston's papers about her acting performance on stage, but then once again she went back to the classroom teaching elocution at the university level.

She was asked to teach elocution at Columbia College of Music and Oratory, Columbia, Missouri, in 1893, a job that interested her. However, she only taught there for one year and apparently had a change of heart and returned to Oshkosh. Upon her return she took the former position as a grade school teacher at Dale School from 1894-1896. Miss Washburn was later appointed to the position of drama and elocution teacher at Oshkosh High School, a job she held for the next two years. According to the *Oshkosh Daily Northwestern*, Alice opened a school of elocution at the family home on Jefferson St. in October of 1898. Lasting only two years, she then closed her tutorial school and moved to Milwaukee in hopes of more success.[7] However, that too closed down in 1903 and with that, she decided to start a professional acting career.

ADOPTS PROFESSIONAL CAREER

Oshkosh Daily Northwestern, August 15, 1903
   Miss Alice Washburn of Milwaukee, formerly of Oshkosh, has accepted an offer to play La Frochard in THE TWO ORPHANS this season under the direction of Gilbert Faust, formerly assistant stage manager of the Thannhauser Stock Company, Milwaukee. The company opens there in the Pabst theater state fair week, after which they play through Illinois, Indiana, Missouri and Iowa. There is probably no character any better suited to Miss Washburn's peculiar abilities than this woman of the slums. Miss Washburn has always enjoyed portraying grim humor and eccentric, grotesque characters. Her originality, magnetism and a certain ideality lifting them above vulgarity and coarseness, though always consistent. Miss Washburn has enjoyed a varied career. She has been popular in society, she has been bookkeeper, school teacher, a successful public reader, a favorite amateur and once while studying in York, she played professionally for a week in MAKE WAY FOR THE LADIES, Jersey City. She is a still member of the Study class, the oldest woman's club of Oshkosh, and was the original director of the Searchlight club, where extemporaneous speaking only is in order. In literary works she has written a short story. THE MYSTERY OF THE SACRED HEART, published in The Literary Independent; was one of the authors of the Mystery Revealed, produced by the minstrels last winter. She wrote a still more successful and witty farce for girls. COLUMBIA'S DIPLOMACY, or A CONVENTION OF THE SPOOKS, produced in Plymouth Church, Milwaukee. The Evening Wisconsin declares the plot unique and the play of

unusual literary merit. Miss Washburn is a member of National Association or Elocutionists and by some was considered the best critic on the floor of the convention this year in Denver. She has trained many of the oratorical contestants; one pupil, Miss Beulah Hibbard, tying this year with Miss Furber of Appleton at the state declamatory contest in Madison. Walter Pyre, coach of the University Dramatic societies and one of the judges at this contest, declared Miss Hibbard's work the most finished of the kind ever given in Madison. The Oshkosh amateurs have Miss Washburn's helping hand in their plays. They consider her stage direction for smoothness, dash and spirit unusually good. Miss Washburn leaves Wednesday for Milwaukee to begin rehearsals. Her friends are confident of her success and some of them intend to form a theater party and go to one of the matinees. [8]

After working on the Milwaukee stage, Miss Washburn returned to Oshkosh in 1904 to reprise her role, playing the character *Dorcus Tattelby*, the town gossip in the play *OUR NEW MINISTER* at the Grand Opera House, a character she played off and on for the next few years.

In 1907, while she was on tour with the cast of *OUR NEW MINISTER* in Waterloo. Iowa, she received a telegram telling of her father's death:

ACTRESS GETS SAD NEWS
Miss Alice Washburn
Has to Play Her Part
With Death Telegram in Pocket
Oshkosh Daily Northwestern,
October 10, 1907

Information received from Waterloo, Ia. is to the effect that Miss Alice Washburn played the part of Dorcas Tattleby in OUR NEW MINISTER theatrical company last Tuesday night while she carried in her pocket a telegram announcing the death of her aged father, Judge G. W. Washburn, of this city. A Waterloo dispatch states: 'The

GRAND OPERA HOUSE

TUESDAY NIGHT, SEPT. 6,
Return of Last Year's Triumph

OUR NEW MINISTER

By the Authors of
THE OLD HOMESTEAD.

Direct from its four months' New York run, and with the same great all-star cast.

"IT'S UP TO YOU, OBADIAH!"

Prices—Gallery 25c, Balcony 50-75c, Lower Floor 75c and $1.00. Seat sale at Hannan's drug store Tuesday morning.

Ad in the Oshkosh Daily Northwestern, September 3, 1904

death message came a day before Miss Washburn's arrival here but was held in this city and the announcement broken to her shortly before she went on the stage. She portrayed the character with the vivacity characterizing her work in the past but collapsed at the end of the performance. Owing to the delay in the delivery of the telegram, she was unable to attend the funeral.'

That Miss Washburn had a most difficult task in going on with her part under such trying circumstance is easily realized. She has been on the stage for several seasons, having been with OUR NEW MINISTER company for three years. She has also been with other companies. Previous to going upon the stage, Miss Washburn was an instructor in this city and in Milwaukee. She was formerly a member of the Oshkosh High school. While the theatrical season was closed this summer, Washburn visited at her home here. [23]

PLEASED WITH STAGE, ALICE WASHBURN, OF OUR NEW MINISTER COMPANY, TELLS OF SEASONS WORK

She Enjoys Being a Professional Actress After Much Success as an Amateur-Will Continue with the Company Next Season-Characters Taken From Real Life-Chat With Miss Washburn
Oshkosh Daily Northwestern, July 10, 1905

Miss Alice Washburn has returned to this city to spend her vacation after a thirty-week tour with OUR NEW MINISTER company. Miss Washburn will remain here until sometime in August, when the company will open its season for next year at Watertown, Wis., August 28. The company appeared in Oshkosh last season with Miss Washburn in the role of Mrs. Tattleby, a comedy part in which she made an excellent impression. Miss Washburn has for several years been recognized as an excellent delineator of character parts and in OUR NEW MINISTER she found a vehicle which gives her ample opportunity to make a hit. She took advantage of the opportunity and it was not through any partiality, because of her being an Oshkosh resident, that she was given a very rousing reception upon her appearance here. The company will play in this city early this fall, and with but two exceptions the company will be the same as last year.

Mr. Brown who played Skeezicks and Louis Fierce who played Obidiah Blurton have left the company, but all the others have been re-engaged for next season.

Theatrical Life Delightful

Miss Washburn says that she has found the theatrical life most delightful, the members of the company all ladies and gentlemen and congenial and there has been nothing but pleasure in recalling the season. The company had a phenomenally successful season, in a period which proved one of the most disastrous in years for many companies. This company opened last season in Milwaukee and played in various cities in Wisconsin. Other states visited were, Minnesota, Indiana, Ohio, Illinois, West Virginia, Pennsylvania, New Jersey, Delaware, Massachusetts, New York, New Hampshire, Vermont and Missouri.

In every state where the company appeared the play seemed to draw well, but in some of the New England states where the prototypes of many of the characters may be found, Miss Washburn states, there was a peculiar air among the members of the audience showing that they recognized themselves. Miss Washburn met the village constable, whom Mr. Conyers of the company represents as Darius Startle and the resemblance is marked. Mr. Conyers exaggerates the original in some respects but the make-up, the laughable little teeter and swinging of the head, and the same important air could not be mistaken. Mr. Conyers had known the man for some time and had made a study of his every action and mannerism for some months. The man came upon the stage after the performance and Miss Washburn had an opportunity to converse with him. If he recognized himself in the character of Darius Startle he did not let the fact be known but expressed pleasure at the performance. In many places in the east types of the various characters were to be found, which showed that the original was not strongly exaggerated in the performance.

Business Was Good

The business done by the company and the excellent newspaper criticisms given prove the play to have been one or the most successful of the season. The company played one-night stands chiefly, but played a week's engagements in Milwaukee, St. Paul, Minneapolis, Detroit, Cleveland, Brooklyn, Jersey City, Cincinnati, Kansas City and two weeks in Chicago. In several other places they played two or three nights consecutively. Miss Washburn said she is thoroughly in love with her work and while she will relish her vacation she will take up her work again with pleasure and will enjoy being with the members of the companionable company again. [9]

Alice toured with the OUR MINISTER CO. through 1908 and then went to New York for a short time, where she signed on to a fifteen-week stint with The Alexander Pantages Circuit working in Vaudeville throughout Canada and the Pacific Coast of the United States.[10]

The summer of 1910 saw her working for the Gardner-Vincent Co. in New Castle, Pennsylvania. Her performances were held in the New Castle Opera House. In between all her traveling, when she would return home she would unselfishly volunteer at the Oshkosh Normal School to direct and give assistance in their drama and musical programs.

1911 found Alice in New York City, starting a new form of dramatic expression - film. It is unknown how she actually became discovered, but her many theatrical friends on the East Coast could have been the conduit for such an introduction. Filming was done in Edison's "Black Maria" studio in Orange, New Jersey. The films were originally one reel and about ten minutes in length. Several movies would be filmed each day of production. According to the International Movie Data Base and the *Kinetogram Magazine*, Alice is credited with nine films in 1911, but she more than likely made many more since early films were very much disposable and detailed records were not well kept. When winter set in, the entire production was moved to Florida. Within a few years, that move would be the beginning of the end of Miss Washburn's film career.

Edison's Black Maria Studio

Photo courtesy of Dan Radig,

When Edison started publication of the *Kinetogram Magazine* in 1908, it started to put forward information on the movies content and names of the actors and their characters.

From 1911-1916 Alice is credited with at least 104 short films for Edison. Prior to Edison, Alice said she worked for the Kalem Company, a New York based film company, and the Powers Company.[13] No record of her films or work could be found with these two companies.

Miss Washburn was not only an actress; she was also a seamstress and costume maker. Her characters always had lavish and over-the-top costumes and especially her hats that she would make herself. She could also be seen wearing some of those hats while strolling through the streets of New York.

The one exception was a hat sent to her by an elderly fan.

This article from the *Anaconda Standard*, Anaconda, Montana, February 22, 1914, shows how even early film actors did have an impact on their fans:

Alice Washburn has added much to the enjoyment of Edison comedies by her fantastic headgear. She believes and has proven her theory beyond question-that the hat of the comedienne can be made to express a character to a remarkable degree. Her reputation for these grotesque hats has caused several ardent fans to send her marvelous contrivances which they dignify by the name of the hat. She recently received one from a Jacksonville native, aged 81, accompanied by a note saying that she wanted Miss Washburn to have this 'bunnit'. 'These lilacs were sewn square on the front of it. I got it 35 years ago for $1.25, but you've made me laugh many days when I've been lonely and if it will do you any good you are welcome to it'. It was just what Miss Washburn wanted for ON THE LAZY LINE and it finished off her costume as Samantha in capital style. In this ridiculous film Miss Washburn adds her quota to the fun by calmly walking alongside of a near-train, gossiping with Arthur Housman, the engineer, while it is going full speed. [11]

The year 1913 was an exceptional year for Alice making as many as thirty short films. But as 1914 rolled in she was beginning to feel the strain of the non-stop film and stage work to the point that on March 27, she had a nervous breakdown while filming in Florida. Alice was admitted at New York's Belleview Hospital for recuperation. After her release, she went to stay at her brother's farm in the town of Algoma near Oshkosh's west side. Today, the frontage road we know as Washburn Street is named for this family whose property was located near the intersection of Highways 21 & Interstate 41.

MISS WASHBURN IS ILL

The Popular and Successful Oshkosh Actress Suffers Nervous Collapse Because of Overwork-Has Been With Edison Company.
Oshkosh Daily Northwestern, April 1, 1914
Miss Alice Washburn, sister of John R. Washburn of Oshkosh and formerly a teacher in the local high school, is in a New York sanitarium suffering from a nervous breakdown. The collapse came last Friday at Jacksonville, Fla., where Miss Washburn was working with the Edison Film company, of which she is a member.

Her brother has heard but the bare announcement of the breakdown, by telegram. He expected a letter with every mail, so as to learn more details. He fears the breakdown was due to overwork. Miss Washburn has been having marked success as an actress for moving pictures.[14]

MISS WASHBURN BETTER

Condition of Motion-Picture Actress is Greatly Improved and She May Return Here to Recuperate
Oshkosh Daily Northwestern, April 8, 1914
John R. Washburn has received encouraging information concerning the condition of his sister, Miss Alice Washburn, who was taken to Bellevue hospital, New York, following a nervous breakdown. The health of the motion picture actress is improving rapidly. She is resting comfortably in the sanitarium to which she has been taken from Bellevue. She may come to Oshkosh to recuperate, when her condition is such that she be will able to travel.[15]

Later that same year, Miss Washburn's health looked to improve.

Oshkosh Daily Northwestern, November 18, 1914
Miss Alice Washburn, who has become famous through her eccentric, character work in moving-picture comedies, will remain in this city this winter. Miss Washburn has been visiting here for some time, but recently went to New York and dismantled her flat there, planning to remain in Oshkosh until spring. She completely recovered her health several months ago, after a nervous breakdown, but has remained with relatives indulging in what she is pleased to term 'the simple life of raising chickens.'[17]

Alice took a year off to recuperate. One of her rare public appearances during this time was a short talk given at the Orpheum Theatre in Oshkosh following the showing of two of her films.

Two days later, the local newspaper offered the featuring story on Miss Washburn's appearance.

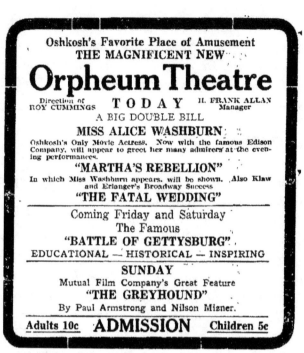

Oshkosh Daily Northwestern Ad on August 6, 1914 announcing Alice
Washburn's personal appearance at the Orpheum Theater

Oshkosh Daily Northwestern, August 8, 1914

*A very large number of the friends of Miss Alice Washburn,
who is visiting at the home of her sister, Mrs. L. D. Harmon, 280
Winnebago Street, took advantage of the announcement that she
would give a talk on moving pictures at the Orpheum Theater
Thursday evening. Miss Washburn gave a five-minute talk at
each of the two performances and was greeted by a capacity house.
Her appearance was the signal for an ovation and Oshkosh's only
moving picture artiste was presented with a very large bouquet of
flowers as a token of the appreciation of her friends.*

*Miss Washburn told how moving pictures motion are made,
explaining that the scenes are in various cities. The animal
pictures are made largely by the Selig company, she said, which
company has the largest zoo on the Pacific coast. The Pathe
Company, last year, she said, leased a large menagerie at St.
Augustine where it had gone for winter quarters. She stated that
the pictures are all rehearsed in advance and timed like a horse*

race, one minute of action requiring fifty feet of film. Therefore, careful estimates must be made and as films are made in lengths of from 1,000 to 3,000 feet, if the action runs over, sections must be cut out. Miss Washburn has been employed by three companies, the Powers, the Kalem, and for the last three years by the Edison company. Following her talk, a picture series, MARTHA'S REBELLION, was shown in which Miss Washburn appeared in the title role. She explained that the pictures were taken at Jacksonville, Fla, and that the Orpheum Theater shown in the reel is at that city. She told two or three amusing incidents in connection with the taking of the pictures, which made it more interesting. Preceding her engagement with the movies, Miss Washburn appeared in a number of metropolitan theatrical companies, one of which, OUR NEW MINISTER, appeared in Oshkosh several years ago, with her in the role of Mrs. Tattelby. She has been recently ill but has nearly recovered and after a few weeks will resume her profession, but she has no definite plans to announce yet.[18]

The following excerpts are reviews from across the nation.

The Anaconda Standard, Anaconda, Montana, May 10, 1914

Cheer Up! There is still another white hope to be reckoned with-and all bona fide sports are hereby officially advised to place their money on this sure thing. Alice Washburn is the latest addition to the long list of notables who have assumed this title, her claims being based upon her display of fistic ability in the MARTHA'S REBELLION. After training diligently under the direction of Harry Gripp, she reduces her bulling husband (William Wadsworth) to a veritable pulp when he attempts to abuse her.[16]

Bradford Era, Bradford, PA, March 25, 1914

Alice Washburn, considered by many the funniest woman on the screen, has a great role in A STORY OF CRIME. a burlesque that stirs laughter from the very first to the end. As a cook in a family of newlyweds, she overhears a remark that she exaggerates to another cook.[19]

Sheboygan Press, Sheboygan, WI, September 20, 1915

Laugh! THE TWO FLATS Shout!

Alice Washburn the immutable comedienne. appears in this side-splitting comedy. New! We venture to say that it is a long time since you have seen Miss Washburn and it will be a still longer time before you will see her again. So, come out and greet her.[20]

Colonial Theater as it appeared in 1912

Colonial Theater Ad August 10, 1915, Oshkosh Daily Northwestern

Photos courtesy of Dan Radig"

TO RE-ENTER MOVIES – After a period of rest, Miss Alice Washburn, Oshkosh Reader and Actress, Who Won Fame in Speaking Comedies and Motion Pictures, Will Resume Work Before Camera-Services in Demand

Oshkosh Daily Northwestern, March 17, 1916

Miss Alice Washburn will leave tomorrow morning for Brooklyn, N.Y. to enter upon the fulfillment of the contract with the Vitagraph moving picture company. She is to work with

Frank Daniels in the Blue Ribbon feature comedies, which have their first appearance in the Broadway theaters. Miss Washburn concluded negotiations yesterday with the company and is today busily engaged in preparations for the trip and engagement. The contract Miss Washburn negotiated by C. J. Williams director of the Vitagraph Blue Ribbon features, who was director of the Edison Film Company with which Miss Washburn worked for several seasons until compelled to take a rest. Since that time, she has been recuperating at her home in this city and occasionally entertaining audiences with some of her character recitations. In conversation with Mrs. R. W. Wilde, formerly of Oshkosh, Mr. Williams said of Washburn that she was the highest salaried character woman in the film business and made the statement to Sidney Vaughn, his assistant, known as 'The Candy Kid', that she was the 'only woman in the Edison company who could do his comedy parts with success and put it big.' Mr. Vaughn's name, 'The Candy Kid' came from the part he played as the candy peddler in MARTHA'S REBELLION, Miss Washburn's last Edison Work.

Previous to doing moving picture work, Washburn played in the regular drama and as Mrs. Tattleby in OUR NEW MINISTER she made a great hit and later in the same part in the movies. Director Joe Conyers pronounced it 'the best Tattleby ever seen in the part.' Miss Washburn has been seen by Oshkosh audiences in both forms of production of that part. Not only because she is well known, but also because she is an artist of superior type. Miss Washburn has always been a great favorite with her home people as well as with the American public generally and future successes will be awaited by a large number of Oshkosh people.[21]

MISS WASHBURN IN PICTURES

Oshkosh Actress is Now Performing at Vitagraph Studios at New York City - Her Plays
Oshkosh Daily Northwestern, April 1, 1916
Information coming from New York indicates that Miss Alice Washburn, the Oshkosh character actress recently signed by

the Vitagraph Motion Picture Company, is having much to do and is performing capable services for her new employers. Miss Washburn's principal motion picture work has previously been done by the Edison company. Her first Vitagraph assignment is the closing scene in WHO'S LOONEY? Her next is the janitor's wife in MR. JACK TURNS JANITOR. Both of these feature Frank Daniels, one of the finest comedians in the business. Mare McDermott, the versatile Edisonian, was to join the Vitagraph forces today. Viola Dana has just Metro.

Miss Washburn writes. "Everything so far seems made to order and my director says... 'Now I have a real company.' You may remember that the vice president and secretary is J. Stuart Blackton, who produced THE BATTLE CRY OF PEACE. Vitagraph has fifteen directors, two only doing comedies." Oshkosh people have always taken a lively interest in Washburn's work and the productions in which she appears will be watched for here. [24]

Alice's last performance on film was her biggest, her characterization of Witch Hex in the first ever film production of the Grimm Brothers story of SNOW WHITE. The film was shot in 1916 by the Famous Players Film Co. (Paramount Pictures Corp., distributor). *Director:* J. Searle Dawley; *Cast:* Marguerite Clark (Snow White), Dorothy G. Cumming (Queen Brangomar, her stepmother), Creighton Hale (Prince Florimond), Alice Washburn (Witch Hex). *SNOW WHITE* was known primarily from Walt Disney's recollection of seeing it at a Kansas City matinee for newsboys. *SNOW WHITE* stuck in his mind, he said, partly because of an unusual exhibition format in which the film was rear-projected onto four screens arranged in a square around which the audience sat. From his seat the fifteen-year-old Disney could see the film twice. His memory was inspiration for *SNOW WHITE AND THE SEVEN DWARFS* (1937), his first animated feature. [22]

It is interesting to note that when *SNOW WHITE* played in Oshkosh at the Orpheum Theater, Miss Washburn's name is missing from the advertising in the paper and in the film company's national advertising. A few ads from other papers did give her credit though, like *The New Castle News*, from New Castle, Pennsylvania, her old stomping grounds in the summer of 1910.

New Castle News, Feb. 22, 1917

One could reason her name was left out of promotional advertising most likely was that Miss Washburn had a second mental breakdown in 1917 - one she would never completely recover from.

The actress would be institutionalized and never perform in public again.

This from the *Oshkosh Daily Northwestern* dated October 29, 1917:

John R. Washburn of this city has been appointed by the county court as guardian of the person and estate of his sister, Miss Alice Washburn, former well-known elocutionist and actress, who is now a patient at a sanitarium at Dearborn. Mich., and incompetent to have the care and management of her own property. In the petition for the guardianship it was stated that Miss Washburn is possessed of personal property of the probable value of $15,000 and real estate from which there is a revenue of about $100 a year. Mr. Washburn is required to furnish a bond of $1,000 before his appointment guardian is made effective.

Alice was later moved to Oshkosh where she was admitted to the Northern Wisconsin Hospital for the Insane. She is listed as a patient there in 1920 in the United States Census. Eventually she was released and spent the last few years with her brother on his farm. From there, she appears to have been forgotten by her hometown, no more mention of her was found from 1917 until her death in 1929. She did receive mention upon her death in papers throughout the country.

Alice Washburn died on November 18, 1929. News of Alice Washburn's death made headlines.

Pioneer Movie Comedienne with Bunny Dies in Oshkosh (UP) Funeral services were planned here today for Alice Washburn pioneer comedienne in moving pictures. Miss Washburn who began her career on the legitimate stage, died here Thanksgiving Day after a long sickness. She was 68. It was 15 years ago that Miss Washburn played her last cinema role in the production Snow White. She was a contemporary of John Bunny, early screen comedian.

OSHKOSH, Wis. - (AP) - Onetime noted comedienne in the movies early days, Alice Washburn today was cast in a tragedy role. For the 68-year-old woman who died almost forgotten by her townspeople and thousands who once acclaimed her, a simple private funeral service was arranged and intimate friends and relatives invited. In 1915 *(correction, should be 1914)*, broken by the work, she retired to Oshkosh. Five years ago *(correction, should be twelve years prior to her death)* she was committed to the county asylum there. As her mind gave way she lived again her movie life and often, attendants said. She acted out the roles which brought her to prominence.[25]

Alice Washburn -1916

Photo courtesy of Dan Radig

OSHKOSH WOMAN ONCE FAMOUS COMEDIENNE, DIES

Miss Alice Washburn Passes Away,
Was Actress of Prominence in Spoken and Silent Drama

Miss Alice Washburn, formerly an actress of national prominence, who resided near city highway 21, passed away Thursday morning at St. Mary's hospital, shortly after 4 o'clock. Miss Washburn was the daughter of the late Judge and Mrs. G. W. Washburn. She was born in this city, and Oshkosh had been her home all her life.

PROMINENT ACTRESS

She was for a number of years prominent before the American public as an actress, first in the spoken drama and later in the movies, and she was recognized as one of the leading comediennes in the country. From early girlhood she exhibited unusual talent and after an extended course in dramatic art she taught elocution in the high school and appeared first in readings and sketches in the local entertainments and later as a professional life a number of years ago.

FUNERAL WILL BE PRIVATE

Her survivors are a brother, John R. Washburn, and a sister, Mrs. L. D. Harmon, both of Oshkosh. The funeral will be held Saturday afternoon in private at 4 o'clock from the Spikes & McDonald funeral home, Court and Otter streets, with burial at Riverside cemetery. Rev. J. N. Barnett of Trinity Episcopal church will officiate. [29]

WASHBURN - *Final rites for Miss Alice Washburn were held Saturday afternoon at 4 o'clock in private at Spikes & McDonald funeral home. Rev. J. N. Barnett of Trinity Episcopal church officiated. The remains were placed in receiving vault at Riverside cemetery and will be interred later. Several organ selections were played at the funeral home* [26]

FORMER FILM STAR LEAVES BIG ESTATE

Ask Appointment of Administrator for Property of Late Alice Washburn
A petition for letters of administration in the estate of Miss Alice Washburn has been filed in county court. The value of the personal property is estimated at $50,000.

The petition is signed by a brother of the deceased. John R. Washburn.

Judge McDonald set the hearing for Dec. 31.[28]

With her brother John's petitioning of his sister's estate came the last mentioning of Alice Washburn. It was a lifetime distance from her first ever mention in the *Oshkosh Daily Northwestern* of her written essay "Growth" as a sophomore at Oshkosh High School at the age of eighteen.[27]

Many of her films are now in the New York Museum of Art. Some can still be found on YouTube for viewing, and SNOW WHITE can still be purchased on the internet.

Alice is buried alongside her twin brother Benjamin, who died one year after his birth in 1862. He and Alice are resting in Oshkosh's Riverside Cemetery.

Sources: (1) *Oshkosh Daily Northwestern*, October 7, 1907; (2) *Oshkosh Daily Northwestern*, February 9,1912; (3) *Oshkosh Daily Northwestern*, March 23, 1883; (4) *Oshkosh Daily Northwestern*, November 26, 1887; (5) *Oshkosh Daily Northwestern*, September 12, 1890; (6) *Oshkosh Northwestern* reprinted from the Boston Times. May 30, 1891; (7) *Oshkosh Daily Northwestern*, July 21, 1900; (8) *Oshkosh Daily Northwestern*, August 15, 1903; (9) *Oshkosh Daily Northwestern*, July 10. 1905; (10) *Oshkosh Daily Northwestern*, December 15, 1910; (11) *Anaconda Standard*, Anaconda, Montana, February 22, 1914; (12) *The Kinetogram*, Vol. 10 No. 10 July 1914; (13) *Oshkosh Daily Northwestern*, August 8, 1914; (14) *Oshkosh Daily Northwestern*, April 1 ,1914; (15) *Oshkosh Daily Northwestern*, April 8, 1914; (16) *Anaconda Standard*, Anaconda, Montana, May 10, 1914; (17) *Oshkosh Daily Northwestern*, November 18, 1914; (18) *Oshkosh Daily Northwestern*, August 8, 1914; (19) *Bradford Era*, Bradford, Pennsylvania, March 25, 1914; (20) *Sheboygan Press*, Sheboygan, Wisconsin, September 20, 1915; (21) *Oshkosh*

Daily Northwestern, March 17, 1916; (22) Internet, *National Film Preservation Foundation* website; (23) *Oshkosh Daily Northwestern*, October 10, 1907; (24) *Oshkosh Daily Northwestern*, April 1, 1916; (25) *The Capital Times*, Madison, Wisconsin, November 30, 1929; (26) *Oshkosh Daily Northwestern*, December 2, 1929; (27) *Oshkosh Daily Northwestern*, March 29, 1878; (28) *Oshkosh Daily Northwestern*, December 12, 1929; (29) *Oshkosh Daily Northwestern*, November 29, 1929

WHO TURNED OUT THE LIGHTS?

Is it the end of the world?

Darkness, our most primeval fear: we fear darkness before we know death exists. The second verse in the Bible establishes darkness as an ancient infinity, a view science still holds. Then in Exodus 11:22, "Moses stretched forth his hand toward heaven; and there was a thick darkness in all the land of Egypt for three days." Thus, the last plague of Egypt. At the crucifixion of Christ, "It was about the sixth hour, and there was a darkness over all the earth until the ninth hour," said Luke 23:44.

Friday, March 19, 1886, was a bright, windless day in the city of Oshkosh. That was until midafternoon when the city experienced sudden darkness from a blackout of unknown origin that was not an eclipse. It occurred about 3:00 pm and lasted about 10 minutes, plunging the city into pitch darkness. It moved from West to East and looked like a dense black cloud of mist. There was no wind, but lightning in Berlin and rain in Winneconne. Experts felt the phenomena was cyclonic in action but that air currents were too high to cause damage. Nobody has definitively explained the unusual event, which is sometimes referred to as Black Friday.

Sources: *Jamestown Post-Journal*, Norman Carlson Article, 1986; (see http://the-red-thread.net/dark-day.html)

THE FOOTE BROTHERS

By Dan Butkiewicz and Randy Domer

This is a story that is a bit strange, but true. Perhaps not odd enough to be categorized under the *Ripley's...Believe It or Not* column or the front page of the *National Enquirer*, but intriguing enough that the story deserved its rightful place in this book.

The tale of the locally famous Foote brothers and their infamous mansion have been part of local lore since the early 1900s. For years, many different stories of the odd arrangement between two brothers that were bonded to each other their entire lives have been told. People claim the property may have once been the hideout of Al Capone. Some say the mansion once harbored runaway slaves and was part of the Underground Railroad network due to the presence of strange, tunnels found in the basement...now sealed tight. Others even claim the place was haunted!

As I began to research this story, I became acquainted with a man who has studied the history of this family for more than 25 years. Dan Butkiewicz lives today in nearby Hortonville but was raised in Eureka where much of this story takes place. I contacted Dan and we began to share information including notes he derived after many hours at the Oshkosh Public Library and the Winnebago County Courthouse. After lengthy discussions, we decided the best way to pull this all together was for he and I to write this chapter in tandem.

Here is our story.

Augustus Ira Foote and Argalus Isaac Foote were twin brothers.

They were born on March 23, 1817 in Lanesborough, Massachusetts, the sons of Joseph and Rebecca Foote. Identical twins at birth, it was said that it was difficult to distinguish one over the other...even into adulthood. Unusual or not for twins, their bond and love for each other made them virtually inseparable for much of their lives. The Foote twins had eight other siblings that included seven sisters and a brother. Their father, Joseph, died in 1825 when the boys were only eight years old. It was always their firm commitment and belief since their early age that they would work to support themselves and their widowed mother Rebecca. They lived true to that commitment and always shared what earnings they had in common and always displayed a strong loyalty to each other and their mother. Only the twin brothers and their eldest sister Sarah (Sally) and mother Rebecca would someday make the long journey to Wisconsin.[5,7]

The connection between Augustus and Argalus continued throughout their life, including marriage. Augustus married Anna and Argalus married Adelia making the four of them recognizable with the initials "AF".

In 1849, Augustus moved to Wisconsin and initially lived with the Luther Parsons Family who owned a grist mill near Waukau. In 1851, Argalus arrived along with their mother Rebecca and sister Sarah. Together, they purchased a plot of land in the Township of Rushford near Eureka, Wisconsin. Over the next few years, the family purchased additional parcels until 1856 when it totaled 320 acres. A plat map dated 1862 shows they expanded their land ownings to 560 acres, but the additional acreage would be sold off in later years leaving the estate situated on the same 320 acres as it is today.

Located only about 10 miles west of Oshkosh, Eureka was a new settlement platted in 1850 by a group of three men including Mr. Walter Dickerson. Dickerson is credited with giving the new village its name. **Eureka**, derived from the Greek word which means "*I have found it*", was perfect for this setting as Dickerson was looking for a place to live with a great view of the river, ground that was high and dry, and plenty of natural springs.[3]

It was no doubt this same natural beauty that attracted the Foote family here. On this land in 1852, the Foote brothers built a marvelous 30 room mansion with the idea in mind the two brothers and their families would share the living space. The remaining acreage would be farmed by the brothers.

The mansion was built with mirrored floor plans on each side of the home. Even here, they wanted their home to be as identical as they were. The home featured two identical sets of 15 rooms, separated by a grand hallway in the center. Reports say the home was decorated to the highest quality of furnishings. The home was the "jewel" of the area as no other building of this prominence could be found in this new frontier.

Their life's dream started to progress. Argalus and Adelia raised three sons – Andrew, William, and Frank. Augustus and his wife Anna were pregnant with their first child.

It is here where the dream started to crumble.

Less than a week before Christmas in 1855, Augustus' young wife Anna died giving birth to their daughter Mary. A few months later, baby Mary died too. It was said that Augustus was inconsolable and understandably racked with grief. He spoke of leaving the mansion, the thought of being surrounded with his dream would be a constant reminder of his tragic loss. Something he felt he could not bear. But after long and thoughtful consideration, Augustus finally decided to remain and carried on his life on the farm. He continued to share his half of the living quarters with his mother Rebecca and his sister Sarah until their death in 1865 and 1868 respectively.

In 1867, Augustus invested in a sawmill located in Eureka. He maintained ownership of the sawmill until 1870 when records show he decided to sell it. By 1870, the US Census indicated Augustus no longer lived in the mansion and had sold his interests in the Eureka sawmill business. He had purchased another property in Eureka and lived in a house there after moving out of the Foote Mansion.

In 1872, the brothers acquired more land – about 200 acres in the Black River Falls area and operated a cranberry marsh there. In 1874, the Foote Brothers purchased land near Lake Superior where they would conduct business in the lumbering industry. The land was purchased from George Wakefield. As the result of three different transactions that year, the brothers accumulated approximately 2500 acres. It was estimated the wood value there was equivalent to some 200 million board feet. Over the years they expanded their lumber interests by purchasing land in Minnesota and also near the Wolf and Embarrass Rivers.

FOOTE BROTHERS & CO.

Wakefield's Mill and Elevator,

MERCHANT & CUSTOM

MILLERS,

FLOUR

Grain & Feed.

Advertisement for Foote Bros. & Co. Flour Mill

Photo source: Holland's Oshkosh City Directory, 1879-1882

Then in 1875, the Foote brother's business ventures took them in yet another direction. The brothers and their families moved to Oshkosh where they purchased a home on the western foot of New York Avenue as it is known today. (In the late 1800s, the street that ran from Algoma west to the Fox River was known as Vermont, then later James Street) It would be here that Argalus' sons, Andrew, William and Frank Foote would become proprietors in a flour mill previously owned by George Wakefield. Wakefield Flour Mills, Foote Brothers & Co. was run by the three Foote brothers and business partner Warren Nutting of nearby Berlin, Wisconsin. The mill was a four-story brick building located north of the Fox River on the corner of River and Broad Streets in Oshkosh. Reports indicate the mill was capable of producing 150 barrels of flour per day using the patented "roller process". An elevator with a 10,000-bushel capacity enabled the Foote brothers to purchase all the grain offered in this area. Their product was branded as "Pride of the West -Queen of the Valley-King of the Forest". It was said their quality was unexcelled and therefore was able to bring the highest prices in each market for its superiority.[4] Andrew, William and Frank along with their father Argalus would invest $40,000 in the flour mill business, but would see little return for their investment.

During this time, the mansion went into foreclosure due to financial strains caused by the flour mill's lack of profitability. Financial woes began back in 1874, when the brothers agreed to sell the mansion to one H.G. Powers for the price of $14,000. The agreement included a clause from Powers, demanding the house be finally bricked up (the brick siding was never finished during original construction). The case was carried on through the courts for the next three years. In the end, the Foote's lost the court case and the house was sold to H.G. Powers in a sheriff's sale. An auction was held that included the sale of sheep, hogs, cattle and horses. Powers would live there until 1890. The house would be sold to numerous parties over the years. Owners included hog farmers, a place of many cattle auctions, and a creamery. The present owner bought it in 1934.

The Wakefield Flour Mill went into foreclosure in 1890. The once state of the art grist mill suffered a fire around 1900. The building still stands today near the south end of Broad Street, one block north of the Fox River.

The legends surrounding the Foote brother's mansion continue to be told today. Social media is full of photos and tales of what have all taken place there so many years ago.

Stories run rampant of covered trucks coming and going under the cloak of darkness in the night, while the possibilities of gangsters hiding away there made for some sleepless nights for several concerned locals. Rumors included speculation of a machine gun having been mounted in the cupola – an obvious advantage point for lookouts. Some say it was the notorious Al Capone and his gang hiding out here until things "cooled off" down in Chicago.

In 1935 a local women's group held a Halloween party there. It was said folks traveled great distances for the chance to see the already legendary house.

Evidence of wrong doing in the mid 20th century came in the form of coils and boilers from moonshiners found outback by a shed.

Signs of the fabled tunnel are still there, although the entrance has since been mortared over. Many have surmised it was used to hide runaway slaves, or maybe it was just simply a root cellar. This secret will be buried along with the memories of a better time in life as the deteriorating structure continues to crumble and fall. [2]

In 1876, Argalus' wife Adelia died.

Argalus' son Frank passed away in 1890 at the very young age of 36. His son Andrew moved to New London and operated a flour mill there. He died in 1904. William lived to the ripe old age of 82 years, dying in 1934.

Augustus and Argalus lived out their lives together in New London in the New London home of Argalus' son Andrew. Augustus passed away on February 17, 1901.[5] Argalus died on May 6, 1902.[6]

Both men are buried in Eureka Cemetery. Augustus lies next to his wife, Anna and daughter Mary. Argalus rests next to his wife, Adelia. As

Foote Mansion in 1993 showing signs of deterioration

Photo courtesy Dan Butkiewicz

they were in life, the twin brothers now lie together for eternity in Section 3, Row 7…a short mile from the crumbling ruins of the Foote Mansion.

Today, the mansion is well beyond repair. Remnants of the grand old house are barely visible as much of the building has now been claimed by untethered vegetation…it's appearance despicable.

Soon it will be gone entirely and all that will remain will be the lore of its legendary past.

Author's Note: Dan Butkiewicz's interest in this story began around 1991. That interest quickly turned into a passion which drove Dan to want to learn more. In the 90s the house was still relatively safe to enter, and Dan did just that. As he explored the house he took measurements and photographs, documenting what he saw. He took these notes and created a blueprint of the floor plan on both stories including the basement and cupola. He also created scaled drawings of the elevation. Much of the details we include here are based on Dan's first-hand experience and observations made inside the mansion. Today Dan shares his knowledge of the Foote mansion through presentations he does with local historical societies and social media. He has also written a fiction novel based on factual information on the lives of the Foote brothers.

A word of warning. We strongly advise against any notions to visit the house today. Not only does it reside on private property, but the condition of the house is extremely precarious.

Sources: (1) Oshkosh Public Museum, oshkosh.past perfect-online.com, keyword Foote; (2) Personal Interviews with Dan Butkiewicz of Oshkosh, WI; (3) Oshkosh

Public Library, Historical File – Foote Mansion; (4) *Holland's Oshkosh City Directory*, 1879-1882, p. 83; (5) *New London Republican,* February 21, 1901, Augustus Foote Obituary; (6) Argalus Foote Obituary, *Oshkosh Daily Northwestern* May 7, 1902; (7) *Foote Family: Comprising the Genealogy and History of Nathaniel Foote of Wethersfield, Connecticut,*.p1284; Powers vs Foote and Foote etal, 1880 case# 5244, Call# Winnebago Series 108, item# 12899

Oshkosh Boys Spot Flying Saucer

O n August 21, 1956, the *Oshkosh Daily Northwestern* reported the sighting of UFO's over Oshkosh. The headline read: **Flying Saucers Are Back Again! Boys See Them**

The article went on to report that 13-year old Richard Kaufmann of 193 Cedar Street claims he saw "round, shiny objects high in the sky, traveling very fast", not once but twice that morning. At 11:15 that morning, Kaufmann and his friends say they heard the sound of a jet passing overhead but when they looked up, no aircraft could be seen. Only a small white dot, moving very fast, then paused briefly before disappearing toward the sun.

About a half-hour later, they heard and saw jets circling around and also a disc-shaped object that seemed to be sporting a small tail of sorts. This time there were six boys who witnessed the event.

Source: *Oshkosh Daily Northwestern*, August 21, 1956, p.4

A CHILD DISAPPEARS

The Story of Little Caspar Partridge

by Patti Yana

*T*he following story is written by a colleague of mine, Patti Yana. This story first appeared as a seven-part series in the newsletter of the Butte des Morts Historical Preservation Society in 2016-17. I decided, with Patti's approval, that this story be included here where it hopefully will reach a wider audience. Patti, is a retired school teacher, a member of the board of two local historical societies, volunteers at the Oshkosh Public Museum and the Grand Opera House and is a local historian who resides today in Butte des Morts with her husband, Joe. She and Joe took a personal interest in the story of the disappearance of a young child in the 19th century from the Allenville area, just a few short miles northwest of Oshkosh in the Town of Vinland. Here is her story...

A Child Disappears

Nothing strikes more fear into a parent than a missing child.

Young Alvin and Lucia Partridge were no different. During the era when pioneer Augustin Grignon was building his hotel in Butte des Morts, the young Partridge family from McHenry, Illinois arrived not far away in Vinland Township in 1846, just north of what we know today as Allenville, Wisconsin. They had two small children in tow; two year old Loretta and 6 month old Caspar. This young pioneer family was ready to settle in this wilderness area on the 40 acres of land that Alvin purchased for $50. Wisconsin was not yet a state. This farming family worked hard, prospered, and settled into the farming life with sugar bush just waiting for them to tap for syrup. Little did they know that one day their adventure into the sugar bush would soon turn into the most talked about story for decades.

Alvin Partridge was followed to Winnebago County by his father Wakeman, the patriarch of the Partridge family. Wakeman and his wife Mary Elizabeth moved to the area, as did sons Frederick, William, and George. Alvin soon expanded his 40 acres bordering the line between Vinland and Clayton in an area known as Ball Prairie. Farming life moved forward, despite the harsh Wisconsin winters.

These pioneers adjusted to living near the local Menominee tribe, sometimes attending church together. Father Florimond Bonduel conducted the services, assisted by Mrs. Rosalie Dousman. In 1848 Wisconsin became a state, with Nelson Dewey the first governor. Through a treaty, the Menominee surrendered 4,000,000 acres of land to the whites. Life was moving along.

But on April 19, 1850 the lives of the Partridge family would forever change.

Alvin and his young family were gathering sap at the sugar bush. Four year old Caspar was said to have lost one of his tiny shoes on this adventure. While wandering around poking a stick, he soon disappeared into the wilderness. When his parents came to realize he was missing, Lucia immediately feared he had been taken by Indians. According to author William Converse Haywood in *Red Child, White Child*, that fear had been ingrained in many of these frontier mothers, having been conditioned by stories of Indian ferocity against whites.

After a frantic, yet fruitless search, Alvin rode off to seek help assembling a search party of local farmers. Despite not having a 24/7 news cycle like we have today, word spread to Neenah and the search party eventually numbered one thousand or more. The continuing search turned futile and little Caspar was not found. Having found no sign of his son, Alvin too began to assume Caspar had been abducted by Indians. A $2,000 reward was offered on printed handbills, and a notice put in the *Oshkosh Democrat*, a local newspaper at the time.

Because of his growing concern that his son had been abducted by local Indians, Alvin and his brother Frederick hired Archibald Caldwell to question said natives at the Rat River sugar camp, some 8-10 miles from where Caspar disappeared. Caldwell was an Indian trader married to a Menominee, and conversant in their language.

A final search for little Caspar failed to turn up anything. The family arranged a memorial near the area where he disappeared. Alvin built a farmhouse to replace their shanty and the family moved on with their lives after the loss of their only son, still hoping he would turn up. But would he?

Whose child is this?

Life moved on for the Partridge family. Their farm prospered. Another daughter (Amelia) was born. North of Vinland, in what was called Waupaca Falls (near Weyauwega in Waupaca County), a band of Menominee Indians had set up camp. Alvin Partridge's sister, Maria Partridge Boughton, lived nearby. She was the aunt of the missing little Caspar. Several white community members noticed a young child among the Menominee who appeared lighter skinned than the rest, and spoke a bit of English, unlike his three siblings. Suspicion emerged that this was the missing white child from Vinland Township. Word soon spread to Caspar's aunt, Maria Boughton.

In the fall of 1851, almost 18 months after Caspar disappeared, the child, whose name was Oakaha, was spirited away to a house in Waupaca for Maria to examine him. Although Maria had never actually met Caspar, she was convinced it was her nephew, having noticed a scar on his foot that she had heard of. The child was questioned intensely. He would nod his head or respond in limited English. He was a child who appeared malnourished and was plied with food to get responses. Maria's husband, Myron Boughton, trekked to Vinland Township to fetch his brother-in-law to positively identify the young boy as Caspar. He announced his finding of the young boy in Alvin's church.

Caspar's father Alvin, Alvin's brother Frederick, and a party of others headed to Waupaca County. Because they arrived at dusk, they waited until morning to examine the child. Alvin did not recognize this emaciated child as his own. However, Frederick insisted that the little boy was indeed Caspar. His examination of Caspar's skull through his own study of phrenology was all he needed to convince everyone that this was his missing nephew.

The child's Indian mother, Nahkom, was talked into accompanying the whites back to Vinland Township where Caspar's mother, Lucia, could identify her son. Lucia and a large crowd had gathered for this examination. She washed him thoroughly, hoping to make him a bit lighter than he appeared. Although he had features similar to Caspar, even his own mother was not convinced it was her son. He spoke Menominee, which made questioning him difficult. Ultimately he was sent back with the Indians, who were now settled in Poygan.

Father Bonduel protested how the whites had "illegally" handled the situation and was outraged. His assistant, Mrs. Dousman, was equally indignant at the behavior towards Nahkom and her son. However, Caspar's uncle Frederick was adamant the child was in fact his nephew. He insisted they retrieve the child immediately. A writ of *habeas corpus* (to return the child to the Partridges) was sworn out by Judge Jedediah Brown in the name of William Partridge (another of Caspar's uncles). The Partridge family chose to put William's name on the document purposely. If they lost in court and were made to pay costs, William lived with his parents and owned no property. Alvin's farm would be saved in the event they lost this court case.

The sheriff appeared at the Indian camp with the writ and Nahkom was forced to relinquish the child. Little Oakaha was to stay with Deputy Sheriff Kendrick Kimball until the case came to court. Because this case attracted so much attention, it was agreed the trial needed to be held in a larger venue than the courthouse in Oshkosh. The Methodist Episcopal Church was chosen to hold the trial, which began February 12, 1852.

The Trial Begins

Townsfolk traveled by buggies, wagons, sleighs, and horseback from as far away as 20 miles to witness the trial. They packed the church gallery to capacity. It was indeed the most talked about trial in Winnebago County. Farmers, Indians, interpreters, traders, missionaries, and general spectators were there to witness the most excitement this area had ever experienced.

The trial was to be conducted by a 26 year old, rather inexperienced, court commissioner named Edwin L. Buttrick. He was appointed by Judge Jedediah Brown. The Partridge attorney was Leonard P. Crary, the Indians having hired Jackson Whitney as their attorney. James Densmore, the editor of the *Oshkosh Democrat,* was appointed court clerk. He recorded every word, filling 150 pages. Following the trial, he announced that the transcript was too voluminous to publish in the paper, but he would later publish it in a pamphlet for the public to read.

Dozens of witnesses were called, each proclaiming to know the said boy as either the son of Nahkom or the son of the Partridges. Community opinion favored the respectability of the whites, especially the Partridge family. The trial lasted one week with morning, afternoon and evening sessions. Even Augustin Grignon from Butte des Morts testified.

The child in question was placed with Sheriff Cooley during the first adjournment. Caspar's mother, Lucia Partridge, complained because the Indian mother Nahkom was granted free access, but she was not. When the child appeared in court he was often dirty, looking much darker. Thus the sheriff was accused (mostly by the court reporter/editor Densmore) of allowing the Indians to paint the child to appear more like an Indian. Dr. LaDow even testified that the child's hair appeared dyed darker. The court ordered the boy washed and combed. He appeared dramatically different after that washing. The plaintiff was ready to present their case. It was February 12, 1852.

The Trial Continues

The trial key testimonies for the plaintiff are as follows:

William Partridge (Caspar's uncle) was the petitioner. He simply testified to that. He later testified he had no doubt the child in question was his brother's son even though he only saw him a few times before he was lost. He said the child understood him when he spoke English.

Alvin Partridge (Caspar's father) testified as to Caspar's disappearance while gathering sap at sugar camp. He said that the marsh west of sugar camp had tracks leading to the marsh and ant mound. He followed these tracks to no avail trying to find little Caspar. Alvin then gathered a search party (up to 1,000) who searched for six days. On January 4, 1852 a messenger announced that Alvin's child was living among the Indians in Waupaca Falls. He ventured to their camp but did not recognize the child at first. He said the boy was crying and frightened and did not look natural then. However, he now definitely recognized the child in question as his son Caspar. He said the boy understood English, but now speaks Menominee.

Mrs. Lucia Partridge (Caspar's mother) testified to having 4 children. She stated that her only son disappeared on April 19, 1850 while making sugar 5 miles north of their farm. She spoke of the search party looking for 6 days and finding small tracks indicating one shoe and one stocking foot, but no child was found nearby. (Alvin had said Caspar lost a shoe that day.) She testified the child in question was found among the Indians, but was indeed hers. She claimed he recognized objects in their home. She also said the Indians colored his hair and skin to appear darker, but after washing, he looked more like a white child. He spoke some English. She spoke of a scar she recognized on the boy. She was upset that she did not have more access to the child before the trial as the Menominee family did.

Frederick Partridge (Caspar's uncle) said he examined the boy closely and was convinced that the boy was his brother's child because of features. He said he knew it was Caspar as well as he did his own children.

A few others testified for the claimant. Then the defense started. Many witnesses came forward, including Mrs. Dousman, Sheriff Cooley, William Powell, and Archibald Caldwell. Many witnesses were cross examined and then rebuttal testimony was heard.

The Trial Concludes

The trial in 1852 continued with the defense making their case for the little boy who lived among the Menominee. Their key testimonies are summarized as follows:

Augustin Grignon testified (in French through a translator) that he had known Nahkom since she was a child. He also knew the child in question since he was born. Many witnesses that testified connected sightings of the child to land payments that were made to the Indians. Augustin specifically remembered seeing Nahkom and her son in his store and/or house.

Augustin Grignon's nephew **Robert Grignon** testified through an interpreter that he also had known Nahkom for 20 years and had first seen the child at Poygan 6-7 years ago. He saw the boy several places including at his uncle Augustin's place. He knew of the boy speaking Menominee, but not English. He testified that the Rat River where the Partridge boy disappeared was not on Indian land.

Louis B. Porlier (Augustin Grignon's son-in-law) also testified as to having known Nahkom and her son before Caspar Partridge was reported missing. He remembered selling Nahkom cradle bands in 1844 (two years before the Partridge family moved to the area) for the child. He said if she had lost a child he would have sold her funeral clothes to dress the child.

Just as convinced, was **Nahkom's sister** who actually nursed Oakaha as an infant. (This duty was shared back then.) She said the boy was nearly 8, while Caspar would be turning just 6.

Nahkom testified that her husband (Pi-ah-wah-tah) was a full blooded Menominee, as was she. She was trying to discredit the rumor that the child was light skinned because he was a half-breed. However she admitted previously telling Mr. J. H. Smalley (former Indian trader) that the child's father was Archibald Caldwell (a white local trader). On the stand she said she was not acquainted with Caldwell. She also indicated she could identify the boy by a mark on his foot made from a cut with a knife.

J.H. Smalley (former Indian trader) testified that Nahkom had first told him her husband was the father of the young boy. But when he pointed out the child appeared to be a half-breed she quickly told him that Archibald Caldwell was the boy's father. (Note how she explained this above.) He said his experience with the boy was that he refused to speak English, stating his mom would "whip him" if she caught him speaking English.

Archibald Caldwell (white trader) testified he met Nahkom in January, 1844 and that her husband died shortly thereafter. He knew because he made the coffin. He first met the child some 10 months later. He said others joked that the child looked like him. He claimed he went among the Indians at Alvin Partridge's request in April 1850 to inquire about a missing boy. He testified Indians were friendly and the chiefs honest. He also said that he saw this same boy, belonging to Nahkom in 1848 and 1850.

The paternity trial ended and the decision went to the inexperienced court commissioner, Edwin L. Buttrick.

Author's Note: The previous trial testimony summaries were reviewed from abstracts written by Freeman Dana Dewey (first settler of Waupaca Falls who published a story called Indian Child), F. B. Plimpton (The Lost Child), William Converse Haygood (Red Child, White Child), and the Oshkosh Democrat, James Densmore, editor. Densmore agreed to publish these abstracts in a pamphlet after he realized they were too voluminous to print in the paper. Mr. Alvin Partridge tried to buy the transcripts and self-publish. After finding out what the cost would be, he relented. Public outcry demanded these abstracts be publically available so Densmore eventually published them in the Oshkosh Democrat newspaper.

Following the trial, Caspar's father, Alvin Partridge, put up a $2,000 bond to allow the child to stay with them until a decision was reached.

A Decision is Reached, but Saga Continues

After unsuccessfully trying to shift the decision to circuit court, Commissioner Buttrick ruled in favor of Nahkom (the Indian mother). He felt the whites had "impressions" that the boy was theirs, whereas the Menominee proved facts. Sheriff Cooley was ordered to retrieve the child from the Partridges and return him to the Menominee. He was met by a few dozen white friends of the family who would not allow him to take the boy. The family ultimately fled to Ohio with the little boy. Alvin sold his farm to his father Wakeman Partridge to avoid losing it.

Alvin Partridge then hired Florus B. Plimpton to write the story of his missing son and subsequent trial. The story was published that same summer following the trial in 1852. It was entitled *The Lost Child; or The Child Claimed by Two Mothers*, and copyrighted in Alvin's name. The author concluded that court commissioner Buttrick erroneously ruled in favor of Nahkom, even referring to her as the "pretend mother". Alvin Partridge, through Author Plimpton, was trying to regain public sentiment.

However, the discovery of a skull and bones of a small child altered the public's sentiment in a different direction. A hunter discovered these bones in May, 1853 in the vicinity of where Caspar Partridge disappeared around Ball Prairie. But by this time the Partridges were no longer in the area. Members of the Partridge family had already fled with the boy and records indicate in 1852 family patriarch Wakeman Partridge sold his Wisconsin farm back to Lucia Partridge who lived in Ohio.

The young boy was eventually located and Dr. Franz Huebschmann (Superintendent of Indian Affairs) brought him back to Milwaukee. In December, 1854, he sent a letter to Lucia Partridge (Caspar's mother) telling her she was mistaken about the identity of the boy. He was, in fact, not her son Caspar. Alvin Partridge swung into action and again delivered a *writ of habeas corpus* to Huebschmann. He demanded a second paternity trial before Judge Abram Daniel Smith. During this unsettled time, the boy was to live with Undersheriff Samuel S. Conover until the March 6, 1855 trial.

Formerly the Wakeman Partridge Homestead in the Town of Vinland,

Photo courtesy of Patti Yana

To help pay for the upcoming court proceedings, Lucia soon sold the family's Vinland farm to Charles Church. The trial was not to be. On March 5 the young boy was again abducted by members of the Partridge family and they vanished without a trace. They completely ignored the news of the young child's skeleton found on Ball Prairie. Hueschmann hired Pinkerton & Co. to search for the boy. However they were unsuccessful in locating the boy. He was living in Tennessee, where they never searched. Family patriarch Wakeman Partridge died at age 73, followed years later by Elizabeth who died at age 93.

Growing up in the Partridge Family

Oakaha (the young boy) eventually returned to live with Alvin and Lucia Partridge, who claimed to be his parents. He was renamed Joseph Wakeman Partridge, hoping folks would forget about the missing Caspar. In 1864 "Joseph" enlisted in the Union Army, where he was described as the white race, yet dark skinned with black hair and eyes. "Joseph" farmed over the years in Indiana and Michigan. Alvin died at age 72, leaving money to his "son" Joseph.

Joseph first married Mary Jane Taylor. They "divorced" (not officially) in 1877, but remarried in 1878. They had a daughter Cora, and later separated for good. Mary changed her name to Mabel and "remarried" (again may not have been official). She died in 1895 at the young age of 37. Joseph Partridge married Clara Hoxter in 1881. He was 35 and she was 19. Her family allegedly believed that Clara was marrying an Indian. The marriage may not have been legal because he likely never officially divorced his first wife. Joseph and Clara had 3 children who survived (Carl, Lulu and Fay). Joseph drifted and again changed his name, this time to Charles Parker. He eventually ended up back in Wisconsin. However there is no evidence he ever returned to the Menominee to find Nahkom. He died in 1916 and was buried in Camp Douglas Cemetery, his marker reading "Joseph Parker". His wife Clara died at age 93.

Conclusion

Perhaps Alvin and Lucia were deluded into believing that Oakaha was their only son Caspar, the truth being too much to bear. According to a nephew, they never acknowledged any doubt to the boy whom they raised as their son. Joseph's wife Clara was unsure if her husband was white, but apparently it didn't matter.

There is no definitive history about what happened to Nahkom. No one knows the whereabouts of the bones of little Caspar Partridge.

Author's Note: A special thanks to John Allen, Vicki Weise, and Dave & Jenny Tovar in helping to locate this homestead.

© Patti Yana, 2018

Sources: Much of the information was gathered and summarized from the *Oshkosh Democrat* newspaper (1850-1852), which published transcripts from the trial. Trial transcripts were edited by James Densmore, editor of that paper; *Lucia's Child/Nahkom's Child* written by Dr. Neil T. Eckstein and published in Chapter V of *Prairie*; *Pines and People* edited by Jim Metz; *Red Child, White Child* by William Converse ©1975; Newspapers researched: *Oshkosh Democrat*, James Densmore editor 1852, *Fond du Lac Journal, Oshkosh Courier, Herald Times Reporter, Democratic State Register, Madison Daily Democrat, Milwaukee Daily Sentinel, and Menasha Advocate*; *Was He Son of Indian Woman or White Mom?*, article by Silas Anderson published in *The Oshkosh Daily Northwestern*, June, 1931; *Oshkosh Biographies* at the Oshkosh Public Library included the Partridge case of 1852; Trial testimonies were reviewed from abstracts written by Freeman Dana Dewey, first settler of Waupaca Falls who published a story called *Indian Child*; *The Lost Child* by F.B. Plimpton; *History of Winnebago County* by Richard Harney © 1880 Chapter entitled "Town of Vinland"

OSHKOSH'S FIRST PHARMACIST

Drug Stores – The Early Years

It was a warm, muggy summer day in 2015 when my cousin, Lee Ziebell, who lives next door to us during the summer months, came walking across the yard and called out to me. "Hey Randy, you're into local history…take a look at this!" he exclaimed. I turned my attention from watering our flowers, dropping the hose as I walked over to meet him.

In his hand appeared to be a stick of sort, and when we got closer to each other he extended it out for me to examine. It was an old yardstick, the kind you might get at the local hardware store or even the county fair as a "give away" item. Many businesses would print their name on it and use it as an economical promotional item for their business.

"I found it in the corner of my garage," he explained. Their cottage was previously owned by my late uncle Neil Ziebell since the mid-1950s. Neil owned a "filling station" for many years…Schneider and Ziebell Standard on the corner of 8th and Ohio Streets in Oshkosh. Uncle Neil was a "pack rat" of sorts and usually threw nothing away. Somewhere along the way he acquired this old yardstick.

As I looked closely at it, I was first amazed that it was in such good condition. It was usually my uncle's modus operandi to use anything within reach to stir paint, stake a tomato plant or shim up a sagging window sill. But the yardstick was in excellent condition, especially for its age having escaped the escapades of my do-it-yourself handyman uncle.

I carefully wiped my hand across it to remove decades of accumulated filmy dirt and dust and discovered the words "*For Drugs, Stationary, Perfumes, Fishing Tackle, Cameras and Photo Supplies, Go to*

N.C. Werbke – Corner of 8th and Oregon Street" along with a phone number. "What do you think this was?" my cousin asked. As I was not aware of a business named Werbke, I took my best guess. "Maybe it was a hardware store or something years ago".

Lee said, "Well, it's yours now," as he turned and walked away. So, I took my new-found treasure and headed back to the house. As I walked, my curiosity grew. "I should be able to find out more about this mysterious yardstick," I thought to myself. So, I set out to do just that.

It didn't take very long before I had my answer. Norbert Werbke was a druggist. Not just any ordinary druggist, NC Werbke is credited as being Oshkosh's first pharmacist.[3]

Drug stores in the early years were small, independent, locally owned operations. The ones from my childhood memories include Mueller-Potter (3 locations-10th and Oregon St., Main St., and Oshkosh Ave), Coe Drug (2 locations-Main and Oregon Streets), Propson's (Jackson St.) and Osco (Main St.). As the supermarkets emerged, they would offer an aisle within the store of what they called HBC (Health, Beauty and Cosmetics) that carried many of the items you would normally go to the drug store for. These were the days before the big box retailers came to town. Much like the grocery store era where "Mom & Pops" were run out of business by Supermarkets, corner drug stores were pushed from existence by mega drug retailers like Walmart, Walgreens and CVS. Unable to compete with these mass merchandising giants with national buying power, one by one the small independents eventually disappeared.

Norbert C. Werbke was born in Manitowoc, Wisconsin on July 2, 1866. Werbke was interested in a career in medicine. He fueled that ambition by working as an apprentice at Barnstein's Drug Store in Manitowoc before attending Pharmacy School in Madison, graduating in 1888.[1]

After graduation, Werbke moved to Oshkosh and gained employment with George Bauman, who owned a drug store on the corner of Main and Algoma at 131 Main Street. The J. Bauman & Co. store was a dealer in drugs, medicines, toilet and fancy articles, surgical instruments, fine domestic and imported cigars, imported perfumes and soap and druggist's sundries of all types.

By1892, Werbke was ready to go into business for himself. He purchased a drug store located on the southwest corner of Oregon and 8th Streets owned by Charles Horn. This location was previously owned by PA Griffith who came to this area around 1850 before Oshkosh was even incorporated, and he is thought to have been one of the first druggists in Oshkosh. [1] Griffith originally operated a drug store on South Main Street but moved his business to this location on Oregon St. in the early 1880s. He sold it to Horn who in turn sold it to Werbke in 1892.

In 1893, Norbert Werbke married Miss Caroline (Lena) Rahr, daughter of Charles Rahr, owner of Rahr Brewing Company in Oshkosh. Initially they resided in the same building as their business on Oregon Street, but shortly after 1900 purchased a home on Washington Avenue. Norbert was very active in the community and held the position of School Commissioner in 1905 and also was the Vice President of the Oshkosh Trunk Company and a member of the Board for the South Side Exchange Bank.

Werbke's drug store was a "Deutsch" Apothecary, serving the large number of German immigrants who recently settled here from their native land.

It was here in 1892 that two paths would cross that would cement a legacy in the Oshkosh drug store business. Werbke hired a young Oshkosh man named F. William Mueller to work in his store.

At the age of fourteen, Mueller went to work for E.A. Horn at the Horn Pharmacy located on Main Street. (Mueller would eventually own his own business in this same location as Mueller-Potter Drugs). After a few years, Mueller went to work for Charles Horn on 8th and Oregon. From there he went to school in Madison to earn a degree in pharmacy. Upon graduation, Mueller returned to the 8th and Oregon store, only to find his former employer, Charles Horn, had sold the business to Norbert Werbke. Werbke hired FW Mueller as a druggist, and he would work there for 16 years before leaving in April 1908 to form his own drug business on the corner of 10th and Oregon.

In 1916, tragedy struck the Mueller Drug Store. Destroyed by fire, the undeterred Mueller rebuilt his store, this time it was constructed using brick (it is the structure that still stands there today).

In 1918, FW Mueller was joined by a partner – Alfred E. Potter. Potter started working for Mueller in 1908 and within two years became assistant pharmacist. The new company name would become Mueller-Potter Drug Company. Over the years, Mueller-Potter would expand their business to three locations and become the predominant drug stores in Oshkosh.[5]

In a 1937 *Oshkosh Daily Northwestern* article, Mueller explained that druggists in those early years worked very long hours. If someone needed medicine after the store was closed, people would call or even knock on the front door (many business owners and managers lived above the same buildings in which they did business).[4]

F. William Mueller died on March 22, 1946. Partner A.E. Potter was a pall bearer. [6] Alfred E. Potter died on September 13, 1957.[7] Mueller and Potter are both laid to rest in Riverside Cemetery.

NC Werbke operated his drug store for 50 years. He retired in 1932 due to failing health and sold the business to Frederick J. Baumgartner.

Norbert C. Werbke died at his Washington Avenue home at 8:25am on July 5, 1940. He was 74 years old. His wife Lena lived to be 100 and passed away on February 16, 1968. Norbert and Lena are buried in Oshkosh's Riverside Cemetery.

That yardstick that started this journey for me has finally found its rightful home. It has been donated to the Oshkosh Public Museum and has been added to their collection of artifacts.

Sources: (1) *Oshkosh Daily Northwestern*, July 5,1940; (2) Oshkosh City Directory 1888-89 pg 94; (3) *Oshkosh Daily Northwestern*, February 17, 1968, Lena Werbke obit; (4) *Oshkosh Daily Northwestern*, October 28, 1937; (5) Oshkosh Public Museum, Oshkosh.PastPerfectonline.com, FW Mueller; (6) *Oshkosh Daily Northwestern*, March 23, 1946; (7) *Oshkosh Daily Northwestern*, September 14, 1957;

THE MOB – JUST PASSING THROUGH TOWN

A uthors note: The following story is written exactly as it appeared in the County Fare, a quarterly newsletter published by the Winnebago County Historical & Archaeological Society in 2002. The only correction is the spelling of the name "Thom".

Back in the 1920's, the Thom Auto Company in Oshkosh was located at Merritt and Jefferson Streets. It was two stories high with a full basement and could store 125 cars for people during the winter months. Since Oshkosh did not have street plowing until 1922, many people stored their cars during the winter.

Thom's building was 200 x 150 feet and the business employed six or seven mechanics. Tome sold Pierce-Arrow and Studebaker automobiles. The building was sold to Sears in 1945 and later became the home of WG&R Furniture.

One Sunday, Dick Thom was sitting near his office window on Jefferson Street smoking a cigar. He heard a car chugging up the street and stopping outside his window of the auto company. It was a Pierce-Arrow limousine. Four men, one short and stocky with a big hat and a scar on his left cheek, one tall redhead, and two "gorillas" got out of the car.

Dick Thom went out and asked if he could help get the car going. They said they needed to get to Eagle River by nightfall. Dick said he would have a mechanic there in five minutes. The car was fixed ten minutes later and they were ready to go.

The redhead, Murray "the Camel" Humphrey (who was second in command), brought three $100 bills to Dick – two for the mechanic and one for him and told him, "Al Capone will not forget this favor", and away they went.

From then on, every spring Al Capone bought a new Pierce-Arrow from Thom Auto until he entered prison in 1931.

(This is a first-hand account of an incident told by Dick Thom to his good friend Tom MacNichol, many years ago. Tom is a native of Oshkosh, is 94 years young and is a member of the Society) (2002)

Source: Winnebago County Historical & Archaeological Society, County Fare newsletter, Second Quarter, 2002

FOUR MILES NORTH

Mental illness has been a social problem for centuries. The struggle to deal with diagnosis and treatment has evolved through the ages and has led us through some dark times and sometimes barbaric methods of trying to cure the disease.

Here in Oshkosh during the mid-19th century, several institutions, both county and state operated, existed just a few miles north of the city…four miles north to be exact.

In this chapter, I write about each one and the history behind them. The research required to gather the history was extensive and exhaustive. It involved many people who previously worked inside the asylums and institutions or had previously done research of their own to uncover facts and stories, some of which you may have never before known. As you read about the development in the treatment of mental illness, keep in mind that techniques and patient treatments were in their infancy. What may seem archaic or inappropriate compared to today's modern science, methods, and technology, was the best applicable practice known in those times. Not unlike today, medical advancement improves with trial and error.

The four institutions included are:

The Northern State Hospital for the Insane
The Winnebago County Asylum
The Sunnyview Sanatorium
The Poor House/Poor Farm

To some extent, State and Federal laws still protect the confidentiality of those who passed through those doors, adding an element of secrecy and mystery to what all happened there. As you join me on this journey, one cannot help but think...if only those walls could talk.

Definition According to Webster's Dictionary
a-sy-lum, n. place of refuge, institution for the insane, blind, etc.

The Northern State Hospital for the Insane

Photo courtesy Julaine Farrow Museum

The year was 1873. Only 20 years earlier Oshkosh became a city and the area was fast becoming noted for its rapid growth in industry and commerce. Oshkosh had survived the first two great fires (1859 and 1866); rebuilding undeterred after each one. Steamships and paddle wheelers cruised along the Fox River and surrounding waters of Lakes Winnebago and Butte des Morts. Rafts of logs from the northern woodlands were fed downstream to Oshkosh and the waiting sawmills, where workers labored feverishly to meet the high demands for lumber and building materials. Dirt streets were the travel routes for horse drawn carriages, and wooden sidewalks were used by those who traveled on foot. Wisconsin was on the edge of wilderness and this city now boasted a population of 12,663 in 1870, doubling the numbers from the previous census in 1860.

Because of this rapid growth, favorable geographic location and numerous other reasons, it was decided the Oshkosh area would be best suited for the State of Wisconsin to build a mental institution. The State would build only two mental health facilities, the first in Mendota near Madison in 1860.

This new asylum on Oshkosh's near north side would be named the Northern State Hospital for the Insane. Erecting the asylum would not be an easy task as early obstacles threatened its very existence. Wisconsin Governor Lucius Fairchild initially refused to approve the site because of potential high-water issues on much of the property. Another roadblock included a law that required an institution must be within two miles of a railroad station, as railroads were the main form of transportation, especially for long distances. No railroad station was present near the propose site, although the General Manager of the Chicago & Northwestern railroad gave assurance that one would be ready. It was then decided that if 40 more acres of land could be purchased, and if the railroad station could be erected, then the site would be accepted. As promised, in early 1872, the Chicago & Northwestern railroad built a train depot slightly to the north and west of the institution near Sunnyview Road (now County Road Y).

The hospital would see a couple of name changes over the years. In 1935 it became the Winnebago State Hospital and in 1973 the final name chosen was Winnebago Mental Health Institute. An interesting fact, I should point out, is that many locals today still refer to the institution as "The Northern". Recently, I was speaking to a man who mentioned to his 84-year old mother that I was writing about the Winnebago Mental Health Institute. She looked at him and replied "Four miles north...that's what we used to say if someone acted odd. He belongs four miles north!"

Located on the scenic shore of beautiful Lake Winnebago about 4 miles north of the Oshkosh city limits (1870), the institution was built on 338 acres of land purchased for $26,000 ($76 per acre). About one-third of this land was in timber. The land was purchased from four families that included Gottfried Wiedeman, Carl Melicke, Jefferson Eaton, and LM Miller. Later in 1872, an additional twenty acres of land was purchased north of the hospital grounds for $2,000. The owner was asking $200/acre for the wild land without improvements while well-tilled farms with fine buildings and good fences that immediately adjoin could be purchased for $100/acre. The Commissioners recommended that immediate steps be taken to condemn the land for state purposes and only pay its real value.

In February 1871, the first construction contracts were signed and shortly after, work began to construct the new asylum. Two years later,

The Northern State Hospital for the Insane accepted its first patient on April 23, 1873.

The original hospital was built according to the Kirkbride Plan, a 19th century design developed by Dr. Thomas Story Kirkbride, superintendent of The Institute of the Pennsylvania Hospital. Dr. Kirkbride's plan featured a central section devoted to the hospital administration and in some cases even housed the superintendent and his family. This section was also the location for other amenities such as a library, chapel, auditorium, kitchens, etc. From this section, wings were constructed that housed the patients. The buildings were designed to provide the maximum amount of daylight and ventilation which was determined to be vital to patient treatments. Patients deemed to be noisy or uncontrollable were usually placed at the far end of these wards to distance themselves from the administrative area. Opposing wings also allowed separation between male and female patients.

By October, the north wings were fully enclosed and the plaster, plumbing, gas piping, painting, glazing and steam heat were almost completed. At the building's rear, the kitchen, storerooms, laundry, boilers, engine room and apartments for domestics and other employees were completed. Also completed was the slate roof.

Subterranean air ducts were installed and a large brick sewer was laid carrying sewage discharge from the building to the lake. This was a common practice throughout the area back then as proper sewage handling and treatment had not yet been developed. Needless to say, conditions in Lake Winnebago were abominable. Sewage lines were installed at a grade of one-foot fall for every 100 feet of length to allow proper flow. It was only a short time before a problem became evident. Lake Winnebago levels fluctuate throughout the year and when water levels dropped, sewage was discharged directly onto the beach. Additionally, the low lake levels prevented the end of the sewer discharge pipe from being submerged, allowing winds to force the gasses back into the building. The pipe was then extended to alleviate the problem.

Underground conduits carried rainwater from the roof to large cisterns. This water was mainly used for laundry production and making of steam for heat. Rooms in the hospital were heated by indirect radiation with bathroom heat supplied by direct radiation. Gas lights were installed to light the institution with gas manufactured from Naphtha. But during the winter of 1873, a considerable amount of difficulty occurred with the gas lighting system. Naphtha gas was causing the pipes to deteriorate and the attendants were forced to use candles for lighting. The hospital was without gas almost half the time, forcing the asylum staff to seek out alternative source for gas lighting. Equipment was purchased that manufactured gas from coal and once the changes were made, the system functioned satisfactorily.

The need to provide a fresh water supply was solved by drilling an artesian well. Drillers were surprised that they were required to drill 520 feet before finding a vein of cold, transparent water free from any disagreeable taste as they were located right on the edge of Lake Winnebago. Unfortunately, the production at this level only measured about 1,000 gallons an hour, which failed to meet the requirements. A temporary water supply was achieved by placing a pump engine on the shore of Lake Winnebago which delivered water through a pipe leading to a reservoir that had been dug adjacent to the hospital. Eventually the wells were dug to a depth of 961 feet, but to no avail, the added depth brought no benefit.

Another problem arose in obtaining enough bricks suitable for the exterior walls of the central building. The recent fires in Chicago and Peshtigo in 1871 created an extraordinary demand on bricks as both cities were looking to rebuild after the fire. Nearly all available bricks in the market area had been absorbed at above market prices. Priority of where bricks were shipped was awarded to Chicago first, then Peshtigo. The Northern was third on that list which created unanticipated delays in construction.

The hospital was furnished with substantially heavy furniture, strong enough to withstand heavy usage. The bedrooms all contained substantial "cottage" bedsteads upon which there was a woven wire mattress, or a straw tick and a 28-pound horse hair mattress. Each bed was provided with sheets and one or two pair of blankets and a coverlet.

Truman Farrow was the hospital's first upholsterer whose main job was making mattresses and pillows. Two kinds of mattresses were made. One of the tasks included separating the horse hair and fluff used to make mattresses. The horse hair came in bales by train and stored in the old water tower until needed. Mr. Farrow had other jobs too. He assisted with the butchering of swine and beef and worked in the butcher shop and shoe shop.

State Hospital Volunteer Firefighters
Photo courtesy of Julaine Farrow Museum

The institution was becoming like a city within its own. The staff now included a Chief Engineer, a carpenter and a mason. According to local historians Paul Janty and Linda Schueler, the hospital had a volunteer fire department from when it opened in 1873 until 1949. The volunteers were comprised of asylum employees and nearby residents on Butler and Sheridan Avenues.

When the hospital opened, it was staffed with 18 aides or attendants, as they were called. This staff of 18 provided care to the initial 205 patients, working 12 to 15-hour shifts. The aides lived on the same wards where patients were housed in special rooms allotted to them. Room and board was provided as part of their pay.

The original building was completed on November 11, 1875 with a 500-bed capacity. But within two years, the patient capacity exceeded the designed maximum with 560 patients on residence and the wards became overcrowded. The State eventually approved appropriations to fund county-based asylums for the chronically ill which eased the overcrowding situation at both Oshkosh and Mendota.

In 1879, State Statutes regarding committing patients to insane asylums were revised. The new laws stated "…every patient committed to a mental hospital must be committed through application to a judge in the county they resided." It also required examination by two competent physicians prior to admission and the patient's right to a trial, if desired.

Near the end of the 19th century, improvements were made to the sewer system at the asylum. A catch basin was built near the lake catching all the solid material and allowing the liquid to pass through into Lake Winnebago. The discharge pipe was moved further north away from the intake pipe. The benefit derived from this decision found the hospital to be entirely free of typhoid fever for over 14 months. It had been years since the hospital had been entirely free from typhoid. The water from Lake Winnebago was oftentimes muddy and full of organic matter, especially on windy days, making it unfit for use for bathing and laundry purposes. In the late 1890s, a filter was purchased for $900 and added to the intake system. The solid materials were collected and spread across the farmland as fertilizer. In 1906 a septic tank was added to filter the liquid waste before it was pumped into the lake.

The staff at the "Northern" also included a shoemaker. Anton Kromchinski was the first hired in 1894 and remained in that position for 32 years. Others that held the job of shoemaker after Kromchinski included:

Otto Schuster	1926–1937
Harvey England	1937–1941
Edward Kuster	1941–1961
Michael Nie	1961–1981

Employees of the shoe shop were responsible for leather and canvas maintenance as well as a complete shoe service for patients. In a 1968 article in the *Oshkosh Daily Northwestern*, Mike Nie told the reporter he estimated he repaired between 4,000-10,000 pairs of shoes in his first seven years at the Institute. Nie went on to say "Some of the shoes that come into the shop are so bad that people living in the community who owned them would throw them away, but the patients must have them repaired because often it is the only pair of shoes they have."

In 1911, State Laws decided that the criminally insane should not be cared for at the Northern Hospital. Legislation provided for the erection of buildings at the Hospital for the Criminally Insane at Waupun. Criminally insane cases continued to be cared for at "The Northern" during the construction of the

Waupun facility until it was completed.

In July 1935, the name of the Northern State Hospital for the Insane was changed to Winnebago State Hospital, named after the nearby lake and county in which it resided.

A nursing school was established in the hospital, largely due to the efforts of Dr. Byron Hughes who continued the effort of his predecessors to have a nursing school within the asylum. The Professional Nurse Affiliate School in Neuro-Psychiatric Nursing was started on September 1, 1941. The first year, 16 students were enrolled. This new program was three months in duration with 64 hours of class and rotating clinical service. At the end of the first year, 70 students had completed their affiliation. The purpose of the course was threefold: to teach factors which caused mental illness, and the best methods of prevention; to teach the application of mental hygiene to the person's own life and personal problems; to teach the intelligent treatment of the mentally ill patient and the integration of the whole person in all nursing care.

Psychiatric Nursing was important as it was reported in the *Wisconsin Welfare Bulletin* published in March 1944. "...it was estimated that about 50% of the hospital beds in the country were occupied by psychiatric patients, and yet only about 2% of the members registered in the American Nurses Associations were employed by state hospitals." The author of the article went on to say "If we are going to make our state hospitals function as hospitals (not crazy houses or asylums), where our patients (not inmates) can expect to receive skilled, trained handling and equipment, this situation must be remedied."

During the early years of the 20th century there began a shift in popular treatment methods for the insane as hospitals moved toward smaller and more segregated styles of asylum construction.

On May 19, 1951, a new $3 million treatment hospital was dedicated as Kempster Hall, named after the asylum's first Superintendent Dr. Walter Kempster. Along with the new facility came improved services and amenities. The new building was erected with cement brick and had Tennessee Marble in the central lobby. Four elevators were installed to eliminate climbing the countless stairs by hospital staff.

Improved heating systems, a two-chair dental office, a beauty salon and barber shop, and numerous therapy and recreational rooms for both men and women were provided. New rooms for specialized treatment included operating rooms, x-ray and laboratory facilities for electro-encephalography, electro-cardio-graph, clinical and chemical laboratory, bacterial and tissue laboratory and a nursery were included in the new facility. The new hospital had all of the facilities of a modern general hospital, plus the specialized psychiatric facilities needed for diagnosis, treatment and rehabilitation of the patient.

Additionally, in 1951 a new well was dug replacing the original well drilled in 1872. In the past, well water was used for drinking and food preparation while lake water was used for laundry and sanitary purposes. The new well would provide a single water source to the facility. A second well was dug in 1953 and an overhead water tower with 100,000-gallon capacity was erected in 1954. The original water tower built in 1889 was torn down. Finally, in the mid-1990s, the wells would be capped and no longer used as the hospital, along with the homes in the village of Winnebago, would connect to the City of Oshkosh water system.

A canteen was located in the hospital and sold such articles as candy, tobacco, cigarettes, cosmetics, stationary and notions. Profits from the canteen were used to fund various events. The Fourth of July Picnic allowed patients to go outdoors and participate in the carnival, races and dancing. Fireworks were also part of the celebration. The Labor Day event featured a picnic and a parade that featured the Oshkosh Indians Drum and Bugle Corp, followed by floats prepared by the patients.

Great progress was being made with Dr. Hughes as Superintendent the past 14 years. Then Dr. Hughes died unexpectedly on January 10, 1952.

During the early years, there had been a real class distinction in the area of dining. There were three menus each day: one for hospital officers and medical staff, another for employees and a third for patients. In 1955, all that changed. Food was prepared in one kitchen and served in the dining rooms with one menu. The only exception was special diet foods for specific patients that had been prescribed by a doctor.

During the 1950s, new buildings were erected replacing the original Kirkbride facilities. Hughes Hall was completed in November

1959 and featured an underground tunnel that connected it to Kempster Hall.

In 1958, Winnebago State Hospital lost its accreditation following an inspection by the Joint Commission on Hospital Accreditation in October of that year. This was a serious blow to the hospital. Measures were immediately taken to correct the shortcomings, but the fact remained they were dealing with an old building and a shortage of medical staff. In spite of numerous efforts on the part of Superintendent Dr. John Petersik, the requests fell on deaf ears regarding the need to replace the old buildings and their outdated medical facilities. Dr. Petersik resigned in frustration on June 1, 1959, his decision influenced by the difficulty in obtaining medical staff members at the hospital.

Winnebago was re-accredited provisionally on October 12, 1962, for two one-year terms. Accreditation was granted because of the new Gordon Hall being built and a staff increase of physicians.

By the mid-1950s, the hospital property consisted of 800 acres: 640 acres devoted to farming and operated by the Wisconsin State Prison as a prison farm, and 75 acres of gardens and orchards that were operated by the hospital staff. Part of the 800 acres included the Pickett Plat, west of the hospital which several past superintendents requested to be purchased.

Petersik's successor would be Dr. Charles Hayden Belcher who would pick up things where Petersik left off...pushing hard to have the old buildings replaced with new, more modern facilities. On August 15, 1961, part of the old main building was demolished and construction a new 200-bed infirmary began (Gordon Hall).

Over the next few years, facility improvements continued under the direction of Dr. Treffert who succeeded Dr. Belcher in 1964:

- The next 220-bed building (Sherman Hall) began construction on May 25, 1965. It was completed in 1967 and was the first building on site with air conditioning
- Alcohol Treatment Program – October 1965
- Construction of an on-grounds permanent campsite on the hospital Picnic Point area – 1966
- Children's Consultation Service – July, 1967

**Razing the 'Old Main',
1969**

Photo courtesy of Julaine
Farrow Museum

The last patients from the old main building were transferred to Sherman Hall in March of 1967, signaling the end of the functional use of the old Kirkbride buildings built in the late 1800s. The final phase of the hospital renovation came in May 1967 when Dr. Treffert announced officially that approval was received for the erection of an $800,000, three-story administration building which would replace the remainder of the "Old Main". Razing the "Old Main" would begin immediately upon completion of the new building scheduled for 1969. The new building was completed by early January 1969 and demolition on the "Old Main" commenced on April 7. On April 18, the big white dome that sat atop the "Old Main", symbolizing the history of the asylum, came crashing down, signaling the end of an era.

The barber shop and beauty salon were deemed to have been important amenities to patient's well-being and overall feeling of self-worth, never at a cost to the patient, but provided as a whole to hospitalization. It was believed that a patient who "looks good-feels good!" A report published in 1958 stated that the barber had given 1,970 shaves (thanks to the recent acquisition of electric shavers in 1958), and 4,011 haircuts. This did not include the many thousands of shaves given in the ward by attendants with electric shavers. Later that year it was reported the barbers discontinued shaves and spent all his time on haircuts and repairing electric shavers.

Licensed beauticians were on staff to provide professional haircuts, shampoos, permanents, and sets to female patients. Color rinsing, tinting or bleaching was not provided for in the early years, however by 1970 some of those services were done for patients who had been used to having that care before entering the hospital. The supply list for the beauty shop included: 250 gallons of shampoo (6-month supply), 25-30 gallons of special treatment shampoo, ten gross of permanent wave lotion and bobby pins were ordered in 50-pound quantities.

The Winnebago State Hospital underwent their final name change on September 6, 1973...the Winnebago Mental Health Institute.

In 1974, Wisconsin Governor Patrick Lucy proposed the closing of WMHI as part of the biennial budgeting process. Lucy's goal was to present a "no-tax increase" budget for the two-year period of 1975-1977. The plan would call for patients being transferred back to their home communities or to the Mendota facility in Madison. Senator Gary Goyke from Oshkosh launched a petition drive in January 1975 to block the proposed closing. The proposal received a huge outcry from various factions and on March 16 of that year, 16 buses carrying 600 individuals made the trip to Madison to organize a rally on the steps of the State Capitol.

On April 24, 1975, the Legislature's Joint Finance Committee voted 8-5 to close WMHI. Then on May 22, the Wisconsin Assembly approved three more amendments to the state budget bill. One of those amendments included keeping WMHI open.

On July 2, 1977 a fifteen-day strike and work stoppage was held by state employees against the State of Wisconsin. Approximately 150 patients were transferred to either their homes or other facilities. Nearly 100 members of the Wisconsin National Guard were assigned duties at the hospital during this strike.

I was one of them.

I was assigned to WMHI with a few fellow comrades while the majority of my National Guard unit, the 1157 Transportation Company, was dispatched to Waupun State Prison.

My assignment at WMHI was primarily one of security within the hospital, watching over daily activities and stepping in to aid a worker or physician when needed. Most of the National Guard support here involved the 32nd MP Company from Milwaukee.

One of our recreational therapy activities involved taking patients to a Milwaukee Brewer game. It was a day game and we were transported there and back by bus.

By the end of the decade, some significant changes took place regarding patient care. In *An Asylum's Journey,* authors Farrow and Janty report:

As a part of the 1979-1981 budget bill, the Legislature approved a remodeling project for Hughes Hall. Using some of the concepts from the Bayside Correctional Institution planning, the Wisconsin Legislature and the Governor approved the creation of the Wisconsin Resource Center. The facility was to house prison inmates with mental health problems from the Department of Corrections but the facility would be managed and operated by the Department of health and Social Services. The operating rules for the facility would be based on the Department of Corrections' administrative rules but the day-to-day management would be by the Department of Health and Social Services.

The initial proposal would convert Hughes Hall from a psychiatric hospital to a medium security male prison. The conversion called for the installation of a gatehouse and a double security fence with perimeter lighting. The Wisconsin Resource Center opened on January 5, 1983.

In the mid-1980s, a secure inpatient program for chemically dependent adolescent men and women was established. The initial size of the unit included only ten beds. It was considered a "secure unit", that is, significant security measures were in place versus a locked unit.

Personal computers were introduced into the WMHI system in 1992.

In late 1996, a new building would be completed and was named Petersik Hall after former Superintendent Dr. John Petersik. Patients were all removed from Kempster Hall and that facility was turned over to the Department of Corrections for use as the Drug and Alcohol Correction Center (DACC).

The Superintendents

Dr. Walter S. Kempster was appointed as the first superintendent on December 12, 1872. His annual salary was $2,000. The title of superintendent was used in the asylum at the very beginning, as it represented the leader as a medical professional. This term would be used until 1980 when it was decided that the hospital administrator needed to have organizational business skills more than medical expertise. To accommodate this change of thinking, the title was then changed from superintendent to director.

Dr. Kempster was born in London in 1841and moved to America when he was seven years old. At age 20, he enlisted in the 12th New York Volunteers and fought in the Civil War. He was commissioned as a 1st

Lieutenant but resigned from service after being injured in a mine run and entered medical school, graduating in June 1864. He reenlisted in the army and served as acting assistant surgeon until the end of the war. During the years of 1866 to 1873, Dr. Kempster was medical assistant and assistant physician at the state asylum for the feeble-minded at Syracuse, New York and the State Lunatic Asylum at Utica, NY. There he and a colleague developed a system for photographing and projecting slides on a screen. They were believed to be the first in the US to show microscopic pictures of the brain.

An assistant physician was appointed to work with Dr. Kempster. Dr. William Gordon was appointed on February 11, 1873. Dr. Gordon worked alongside Dr. Kempster only one year and was then replaced by Dr. James H. McBride. A second assistant was hired in 1875 when Dr. William Hancker joined the staff.

Dr. Kempster put patient care and comfort high on his list of priorities. Religious services were conducted each Sunday with sermons, music and singing provided by the staff. By 1890, local clergy from Oshkosh began performing the services each Sunday. An employee from the hospital would drive into town by carriage or sleigh, pick up the clergyman, and then return him home following the service. Clergy received a small stipend from the State for their services.

Kempster also felt it important to provide recreation for hospitalized patients. Twice each week they provided dances and regular activities including cards, checkers, chess, dominoes and billiards. There was even a bowling alley in the basement level.

A library was also established for patient use. Newspapers from across the state sent their publications to the two State mental institutions. Patients were delighted and anxious to get news from their home town and passed the papers around to each other until they were literally worn out.

The deep compassion of Dr. Kempster is illustrated in the following:

Who can think of the number of unfortunate beings now confined in the receptacles of the different counties of this state, and realize in the most degree, the sorrowing hearts their misfortunes have created; of the hopes once bright now dashed; of the ambitions which lured beyond strength; of life's work begun but left unfinished; of affections ripened only to be blasted – who can consider these calamities of our fellow mortals, rendered insane perhaps not by an act of their own, unwittingly thrown upon the charity of the state, bound by the unyielding fetters of a terrible disease, not knowing how soon it may be our turn to take our place among these pitiable creatures; who can think of these things, of the measureless calamity of insanity, and turn idly away, closing eye and hand, withholding that which is known to be required to making life comfortable? We can conceive of no argument, economical or humanitarian, that can be adduced to show why aid should be postponed; why the sufferer must be compelled to suffer on.

-Dr. Walter S. Kempster, 9/30/1875
(**Source:** "An Asylum's Journey-Healing through the
Centuries" by Julaine Farrow and Paul F. Janty)

In 1882 after eleven years of service, Dr. Kempster resigned his position at the Northern State Hospital for the Insane.

On July 1, 1884, Dr. R.M. Wigginton was named the new Superintendent at the asylum. The medical staff that assisted Dr. Kempster resigned along with him and Dr. Wigginton hired his own staff of physicians and assistants.

Dr. Wigginton, shared Dr. Kempster's beliefs regarding the value of leisure activities for the patient's well-being. So, in addition to the current curriculum of activities, he added steamboat rides on Lake Winnebago. The cost for this was not covered by the state but charged to the patient's families and friends. He also believed that exercise provided additional benefits by improving the patient's overall well-being. "Occupation gave exercise for the brain and body; it stimulated the body to healthy secretion and excretion; an appetite was created; food was digested and assimilated; the blood was properly aerated; and the diseased brain received a healthy stimulus."

In July 1887, Dr. Wigginton resigned his position at the hospital and Dr. Walter Kempster returned, giving up a large consultation practice in Washington DC to the delight of many who remembered and worked with him here during the early years. Oddly enough, Dr. Kempster's return would be short-lived. A few months after resuming his position here, he resigned again. This time stating the reason as being, "I have discovered riches beyond calculations in the Maryland Hills close to the historic Potomac. My confidence in the gold mine is so great that I am unhesitatingly willing to surrender my official position in the state institution to devote my whole time and attention to my mining interests." It is reported the mine was a huge success, making Dr. Kempster a millionaire. He went on to marry Mrs. Francis Frazer, widow of Civil War Confederate Major General Frazer. It was the second marriage for both.

One of Dr. Kempster's professional accolades includes his service as a leading witness in the trial of Charles J. Guiteau, the assassin of President James A. Garfield. His report is recorded in *The American Journal of Insanity – Vol 38, 1881-1882.*

He was also the personal physician to Senator Philetus Sawyer of Oshkosh.

Dr. Walter Kempster died on August 21, 1918 at the age of 77. He is buried in Arlington National Cemetery.

Dr. Charles E. Booth, M.D. was next to be appointed as the new superintendent and assumed his duties on January 2, 1888. Dr. Booth continued to expand the offerings of exercise and amusement for the patients by adding swings, croquet and tennis grounds for female patients, and for the men, a baseball field, swings and a half-mile walking track.

Three years later, Dr. William F. Wegge became the new superintendent and resided there until 1894. His reasons for leaving were concerns over health conditions during the winter months here. He would seek a more temperate climate by traveling to Germany in 1895 to continue his studies of nervous and mental disorders at universities in Europe. Later, he returned to Oshkosh in a private practice before moving to Milwaukee where he became a professor at Milwaukee Medical College.

Dr. Wegge was followed by Dr. Gilbert Hathaway who became superintendent in October 1894, but his tenure was brief and lasted only about 9 months. Due to his brief term, there is no formal record on the reason for his departure or what became of him after leaving here.

Dr. William A. Gordon returned after his departure in 1874, succeeding Dr. Hathaway. Dr. Gordon's passion for patient care equaled that of his predecessor, Dr. Kempster, whom he served as an

Dr. William Gordon

Photo courtesy Julaine Farrow Museum

assistant in 1873. Gordon would be the sixth superintendent (counting two terms for Kempster) in the first twenty years of the institution's existence. It seems unusual that the turnover of superintendents in these early years was so erratic. One must ask if it was the burden and complexity associated with dealing with the mentally ill? Effective treatments were virtually untested, mostly ineffective and at the very least unknown.

Many policy and procedural advancements are credited to Dr. Gordon during his administration including the improvement of bathing patients. Turkish baths were installed in both the male and female wards. Dr. Gordon felt Turkish baths were unquestionably a positive advance in the "therapeutics of insanity" and was nationally recognized as a necessity in progressive institutions. Also, the process of bathing of patients underwent a significant change. The unsanitary bathtubs in which patients had been dipped once a week, using the same water for all patients, had been removed and all patients were washed at least twice a week in running water. This alone is said to have reduced the number of illnesses and patient deaths over time.

Under his supervision, Gordon also installed the first barber shop in the basement where a professional barber was employed. Previously, shaving and hair cutting had been done in the ward. Night service was improved with the addition of gas ranges installed at each end of the hospital so that patients who were feeble or had sleeping disorders could have hot milk during the night. Eight employees were staffed during the evening hours and passed each sleeping room every ten minutes. An electric time detector recorded any neglect on the part of the employee.

Two rooms were appointed for massage purposes, one for men and one for women. A professional masseur performed therapeutic massages under the direction of physicians. Treatments included the use of oil or lard which was said to improve patients experiencing circulatory problems.

Dr. Gordon's other improvements include a school for patients, the fitting of spectacles for patients, and proper transport of patients, which eliminated needless handcuffing, shackling and restraints during transfer.

Almost every superintendent and director at the asylum struggled with maintaining staff. During the first thirty years the hospital was open, over 3,000 employees were on the payroll. The position of 'attendant' was not considered a desirable occupation due to long hours, low pay, and little prospect for advancement. The average tenure for attendants in the early 1900s was about four months. The job could be exasperating dealing with patients who frequently made insulting verbal assaults or vicious physical attacks on personnel. Equally dangerous, injuries from violent patients included broken bones, teeth knocked out, hair pulled out, black eyes, and skin abrasions from being bitten or clawed. Dr. Gordon once stated in his annual report, "The trials of women attendants are especially laborious and exasperating. It is a wonder that we are able to obtain women to do this work." It should be noted that women attendants were also paid less the male attendants... an issue we are still dealing with today.

Dr. Gordon's family consisted of his wife, Helen Jackson Gordon, his daughter, Kate and his son, William Jr. Mrs. Gordon was considered "prominent and highly esteemed" in the Oshkosh area. Her father was Joseph Jackson, one of the first settlers of Oshkosh and it's second Mayor.

In 1909, Dr. Gordon's health started to fail. He underwent an operation in the Northern State Hospital for a bladder ailment with a team of Oshkosh physicians performing the surgery. Initially, he showed signs of improvement but things took a turn for the worse as he finally succumbed on October 11, 1909 in a Chicago Hospital. His age at the time of his death was 63.

Succeeding Gordon was Dr. Adin Sherman who had worked as first assistant physician to Dr. Gordon. Sherman was superintendent for 20 years and worked to within ten days of his death. During his tenure, Dr. Sherman gained the reputation as a proponent for patient treatment and care. Seen as a man of wisdom and compassion, Dr. Sherman was remembered by his colleagues:

His sympathetic understanding, his tenderness of heart, his vision, his foresight and sterling moral qualities made him an inspiration to follow as a physician and a man. In his departure, the thousands to whom he administered, lost a true and devoted friend...

Dr. Adin Sherman died on March 31, 1930 at Mercy Hospital in Oshkosh. He was 63 years old and remembered as a "cultured man, kindly and considerate, a great reader and student." Dr. Sherman was buried at the Forest Home Cemetery in Milwaukee.

Dr. Sherman was succeeded by Dr. Peter Bell in 1930. Bell resigned after the death of a patient resulted from mistreatment by attendants at the asylum. Bell was not found negligent but resigned feeling he was not diligent in his duties that resulted in the unfortunate death. Dr. Bell is credited with setting up the 1951 Sex Crimes Law and establishing treatment for deviates. His work was his life. It is noted he seldom took vacation and worked nights and weekends. He never married. He worked until he no longer could walk and died on the first day of his planned retirement.

The succession of Superintendents and Directors that followed were:

Dr. William Lorenz (interim)	1934
Dr. Gilbert E. Seaman	1934–1938
Dr. Byron Hughes	1938–1952
Dr. John Petersik	1952–1959
Dr. Charles Hayden Belcher	1959–1964
Dr. Darold Treffert	1964–1979
Dr. Richard Stafford (interim/acting)	1979
Dr. E.C. Ping (interim/acting)	1979–1980
Mr. William T. Beorum (Director)	1980–1981
H. David Goers	1981–1990
Stanley York	1990–1996
Joann O'Connor	1996–2007
Robert Kneepkens	2007–2010
Thomas Speech	2010–current (2018)

Dr. Darold Treffert was appointed Superintendent on October 1, 1964. Dr. Treffert was one of the first Superintendents who chose not to live on the grounds, but at his home in Fond du Lac whereas of this writing, he still lives today. Much of his focus during his fifteen years was on youth addiction to drugs and alcohol. One of Dr. Treffert's interests, which he initially started at WMHI, was the study of savant syndrome. He is now regarded one of the world's foremost authorities on the subject. He served as a consultant to the movie *Rain Man* and often appears on television programs featuring stories on savant syndrome. One of his experiences involves a man with savant syndrome named Leslie Lemke.

Lemke was born prematurely in 1952, with retinal problems that quickly advanced to glaucoma. In the early months after his birth, his eyes were surgically removed. Leslie also experienced brain damage and was very ill when given up for adoption. His adoptive mother nursed him to teach him how to eat and taped his legs to hers to teach him how to walk. He learned to sing but only the songs he heard from his mother.

One evening, when Leslie was about age 14, the family watched and listened to a movie on television. Later, in the early morning hours, his mother heard music. She thought her husband had left the TV on. When she went to turn it off she found Leslie, playing flawlessly from beginning to end, having heard it but once, Tchaikovsky's Piano Concerto No. 1, which was the theme song for the movie they had viewed earlier that evening. Lemke's story has been featured on numerous programs including *60 Minutes, The Today Show* and others. My sources tell me the Lemke's moved into a house on Butler Ave, just a short distance from WMHI for a short time so they could be close to Dr. Treffert.

Mr. Boerum was the first non-medical director since the opening of the facility in 1873. He was appointed to the position of director, not superintendent on December 21, 1980. Within a few months, Mr. Boerum was arrested on deviant sexual assault charges in Lyons, Illinois. It was later discovered that Mr. Boerum was actually Raymond Matzker and was wanted in New York on an arrest warrant. Matzker had assumed the identity of a classmate of his along with that individual's educational credentials. Matzker was convicted and sentenced to prison in Wisconsin. Ironically, he served a portion of his sentence at WMHI in the Wisconsin Resource Center (formerly Hughes Hall). He was diagnosed with cancer, refused treatment and died while in custody of the Department of Health and Family Services.

Treatment

The state hospital treated not only the mentally ill but also those with drug and alcohol addictions, malaria and other diseases. Some treatments in the early years were cruel by today's standards and included convulsive therapy, insulin shock therapy, sterilization (1941-1944) and prefrontal lobotomies. Many primitive surgical instruments, medicine bottles and other artifacts from that era are on exhibit in the Julaine Farrow Museum which is located on the grounds of WMHI.

The first known research done at the facility happened in 1875. Drs. Kempster and McBride had been using the drug Amyl nitrate on a large number of epileptic patients. The treatment proved effective in treating the symptoms according to Dr. McBride who published his findings in the *Chicago Journal of Mental and Nervous Disorders.*

It is also a known fact that various types of liquor were used extensively in medical treatment. Wine, ale, and beer were used as tonics and whiskey and brandy were used as specific treatments for certain types of illnesses.

Patients would arrive here from county and state poor houses or jails with little to no personal information. Many were listed as John or Jane Doe, with no reference to the illness or condition of the patient.

Diagnosis in the early years was of course made without the benefit of modern science or today's sophisticated technology. In one of his cases, Dr. Kempster writes about an interesting case of a male patient who was transferred with no information other than he was arrested as "an insane vagrant, having epileptic seizures." Due to the seizures, he was classified as epileptic. After his death, an autopsy was performed and revealed a brain tumor. In another similar case, an epileptic patient was found to have only one-half of the brain developed, the other half being a miniature representation.

In the early years, patient physical restraint was avoided. But by the mid-1880s, it was considered acceptable to use restraint, but only from a medical standpoint. Three types of restraint were used ... medical, manual and mechanical. The goal of restraint usage was for the benefit and protection of the patient and the protection of others and property. Management discarded the use of physical restraints except in extreme cases. An 1888 report states, "Nothing like cruelty toward patients is tolerated, whatever may be said to the contrary by persons ill-informed or viciously inclined, or by discharged patients whose utterances are still controlled by old delusions."

Mental illness was not the only condition that hospital physicians and staff had to deal with. There was a sizeable population in the asylum which made it susceptible to various diseases such as tuberculosis, typhoid, small pox, diphtheria, dysentery, scarlet fever, measles, erysipelas, influenza, etc. Occasionally an illness would reach epidemic proportions which required the hospital to close their doors to outside visitors. In fact, during a national influenza outbreak in 1918-1919, the hospital was closed during the entire winter to visitors and non-essential personnel. Many of the deaths that occurred at the Northern Hospital for the Insane over the years were the result of these diseases.

In 1931, the Northern State Hospital for the Insane suffered unfavorable scrutiny when patient abuse by attendants was reported. For years, several Directors pointed out a problem with some employees being abusive or disrespectful to patients. It was a concern that was difficult to deal with. Some attendants became disgruntled and sometimes their attitudes became "jaded" with the circumstances of dealing with the insane.

On January 31, 1934, the State Legislature ordered an investigation on the treatment of patients in State Institutions and ordered the findings reported to the Governor. The investigation was precipitated by newspaper reports that a patient had died as the result of mistreatment by attendants at the Northern Hospital for the Insane.

A series of meetings were held in Oshkosh for more than a week at the Hotel Raulf in February of that year. The committee investigating the incidents reported their findings, which recommended the suspension and discharge of 19 employees at the Northern Hospital with charges of "malfeasance and misfeasance" in the conduct of their duties. A hearing was held a few weeks later at the Northern Hospital and nine employees appeared on their own behalf. Two were exonerated and seven were discharged.

Dr. Peter Bell, the Superintendent during this time, by his own request was granted a leave of absence. He then resigned on his own volition on February 26, 1934.

In 1941 the Wisconsin Legislature passed a "sterilization law", believing that sterilization would prevent patients with mental disorders from passing their disposition on to their children. Between 1941 and 1944, 24 patients, all women, were sterilized. This heinous and disturbing practice was discontinued after 1944.

In December of 1943, the first prefrontal lobotomy was performed at Winnebago State Hospital. A lobotomy is a surgical procedure in which the nerve pathways in a lobe or lobes of the brain are severed from those in other areas. The concept, which emerged in the 1880s, was intended for the surgical manipulation of the brain which allegedly could calm patients, and was used mainly with cases of schizophrenia. As early science continued to develop through trial and error, the process of how a lobotomy was administered changed. In 1935 a Portuguese physician named Antonio E. Moniz, used a process which involved drilling two holes in the front of the head and injecting pure ethyl alcohol. It was believed this process disrupted the neuronal tracks in the brain, which reduced the symptoms of anxiety and paranoia in mentally ill patients. Dr. Moniz was awarded a Nobel Prize in 1949 for his advancements in treatment. Other developments included the use of a spatula during surgery. By the mid-1940s, the prefrontal lobotomy was replaced with the trans orbital lobotomy, in which a pick-like instrument was inserted through the back of the eye sockets to pierce the thin bone that separates the eye sockets from the frontal lobes. The pick's point was then inserted into the frontal lobe and used to sever connections in the brain. In his report five years later, Dr. Hughes stated that 100 cases had been conducted. The results were as follows: individuals who underwent a lobotomy was "freed from anxiety, lost feelings of inferiority, had less morbid interest in himself." Of those first 100 patients, eight had died, but only one death was attributed to surgical procedure. Eleven persons showed very little change while nineteen showed slight improvement and no longer required protective restraint. Twenty-three showed significant improvement, enough to adjust to a quieter production ward and twenty-four improved significantly enough to adjust to a County Hospital and devote time to productive activities. Fifteen patients improved significantly enough to return to their homes.

According to Dr. William Weber, Medical Director at Parkview Health Center, "Lobotomies were performed to make a patient become more docile. Sometimes patients would lose many of their cognitive skills and experience memory loss for days, weeks, months, or sometimes forever." Lobotomies were performed on a wide scale during the 1940s. The practice gradually fell out of favor beginning in the mid-1950s, when antipsychotics, antidepressants, and other medications were found to be much more effective in treating and alleviating the distress of mentally disturbed patients.

According to the writings within *An Asylum's Journey – Healing Through the Centuries,* by Julaine Farrow:

The 1936-56 period proved an important era to the hospital because it was during that time period when somatic or the so-called drastic psychiatric treatments were started. In April 1937 the use of insulin shock therapy was instituted. Its use was continued at the hospital until 1962. The same year convulsive therapy for treatment of schizophrenia was given trial, the convulsions being introduced by intravenous injections of Metrazol. The drug's use was supplanted in 1939 when the electro-shock machine made its introduction. New treatments were introduced for the care of syphilitic patients, then on the increase. These included Malaria therapy and later, the use of a hypertherm machine.

Shock therapy was believed to be effective in treating certain psychotic disorders. The process involved using drugs or electric shock to induce shock in the patient. Insulin shock treatments were commonly used at the asylum to treat schizophrenia. Large doses of insulin would be injected into the patient, reducing the sugar content in the blood, putting the patient into a coma. Electric shock therapy involved a technique where alternating current passed through the head between two electrodes placed over the temples. The passage of the current caused an immediate loss of consciousness and induced a convulsive seizure. Use of both of these treatments drastically diminished with the onset of tranquilizer medications.

Penicillin was used for the first time in 1947. One of the first patients to receive the new "wonder drug" was critically ill with no hope for recovery. He was given huge doses of penicillin after surgery and made a remarkable recovery.

By the mid-1950s, advancements in the fields of antibiotics, chemotherapy, surgery, drug development, and a greater understanding of the treatment of mental disease increased patient life spans and shortening the length of stay in the asylum. From 1953-1956, the length of stay had been reduced significantly. Also impacting this trend were an increased number of clinics available and improved early detection methods.

Another form of treatment was hydrotherapy. This treatment was administered by trained hydro-therapists and performed on patients suffering manic depressive psychosis: manic phase, agitated depressions and psychoneurosis cases. Neutral baths, cold and hot packs, needle sprays, massage and salt rubs were the treatments of choice.

Intravenous injections of Amytal Sodium were administered to those who exhibited excited manic or agitated depression symptoms. Barbiturates such as this would depress the sensory cortex, decrease motor activity, alter cerebella function, and produce drowsiness, sedation and hypnosis. Many admissions that reacted poorly to hydrotherapy treatments would have progressed to complete maniacal exhaustion without this form of treatment.

It was also the belief of most of the Superintendents that idle time was bad and exercise, interaction, and engagement were good. Idleness, it was determined, perpetuated the mind reflecting on the woes and misery of life while activity helped patients forget their problems, even if for a brief period of time. Dr. Sherman, during his tenure as Superintendent, believed that engagement of the body and mind was paramount to recovery. Work was to be found on the farm, garden, greenhouse, laundry, barns, kitchen, dining rooms, sewing room, on the wards, etc. and patients were employed as much as possible around the hospital and grounds. One of the early indications that a patient was heading toward recovery was hearing a patient express interest in being employed. It was noted that patients who were the most industrious with physical activity showed the greatest improvement toward recovery.

The Farm

Since the very beginning, the need to become as self-sustainable as possible was critical. Not unlike today, budgets were limited. The creation of a farm not only provided fresh food for the patients and staff at the Northern State Hospital for the Insane, but also the therapeutic exercise and learned skills of operating a farm served patients well.

Dr. Kempster reported in his first year that, "The land, good in itself, had not been properly tilled for several years and was overrun with weeds with few fences." To make the land suitable for agriculture, extreme measures needed to be taken. This prompted action and the first step taken was to erect 377 rods of rail fences around the plowed land. Also, some of the unused land was leased back to local farmers and the asylum farm needed fencing to contain their livestock from eating those leased crops or wandering onto the nearby railroad tracks. The land surrounding the hospital was cleared of trees and brush which allowed the staff and a segment of the patient population to begin growing vegetables.

The front of the institution needed to be presentable and representative of the professional services provided within. The appearance of the grounds along the road in front of the hospital was enhanced with 950 feet of picket fence. A more suitable five-board fence was built along the northern boundary of the farm.

The soil here was quite rich and productive. An orchard was started with 500 apple trees, their varieties selected for hardiness to the cold winters and short growing season in Wisconsin. The orchard was located south and east of the hospital buildings. Twenty-five cherry trees and twenty-five plum trees were also planted. Additionally, an asparagus bed was established with 500 root starts and 50 rhubarb plants were placed along with 1,000 strawberry plants.

During this first year, about 100 acres was plowed land with the rest being wooded. Patients worked to clear the underbrush and thin trees near the rear of the building. On a nearby bluff, lovely shaded areas were created to be used by patients and staff for walking or picnicking. An icehouse was constructed on the shore of Lake Winnebago, capable of storing 300 tons of ice. Next to the icehouse, a slaughterhouse and meat processing room were built to process sufficient quantities of protein to accommodate the number of staff and patients. Beginning in the 1880s, the hospital began a hog raising operation, so adjacent to the slaughterhouse a pigsty was built that measured 30 by 100 feet in size. Other accommodations included a four-ton platform scale used for weighing livestock and produce. A 30 x 50-foot vegetable cellar with eight-foot walls that measured two-feet thick was built from stones plowed up on the land.

The harvests on the farm were magnificent. The canning of fruits, vegetables and meat was the important job of the matron Mrs. Butler. In 1906 the Matron's Report to the Superintendent stated 494 quarts of fruit and 5,900 quarts of vegetables had been preserved. 162 glasses of jelly, 200 quarts of sweet pickles and 1,577 gallons of relish and regular pickles were canned.

Greenhouses and gardens not only supplied food, but provided physical activity to help nourish patients well-being

Photo courtesy of Julaine Farrow Museum

The gardens were well cared for and produced abundantly. In fact, vegetables from the asylum were placed on exhibition at the State Fair in Milwaukee in 1876 and received twelve first-place ribbons.

Over the coming years, more land would be purchased as the farm continued to expand. During 1876, four more acres of land had been cleared of stumps, drained and prepared for garden use. In 1877 a new barn was erected as the farm amenities expanded. Makeshift greenhouses were built from field stones and glass. Large forcing beds were used for early starting vegetables and keeping the hospital well supplied with flowering plants.

The largest share of the food consumed at the hospital was produced on the grounds including meats, fruits, vegetables, and dairy products. Other needs such as flour, tea, coffee, sugar, spices, and fish were purchased from outside sources. In reviewing a list of outside purchases, one thing stands out as a bit unusual. More than 200 cans of oysters were purchased one year. Upon further investigation it was discovered that it was an annual tradition to serve oyster stew on the first day of the New Year at the hospital… a tradition that was carried on for many years.

In 1910 the barn from the nearby Neville farm was moved onto hospital property. A remodel was done to add accommodations of rooms, steam heat, electric lights and bath for 30 men – mostly farm hands and patients that worked on the farm. The building was known as the Farm Cottage and was used until 1966.

In 1913, two more farms were acquired. The Rich estate of 124 acres and the Hoehler farm (80 acres) was tillable land located about a mile west of the hospital, bringing the total acreage of the hospital to 596 acres.

In 1916, the cattle herd was tested for tuberculosis. Fifteen cows tested positive and had to be destroyed.

Records show the farm was a profitable venture. In 1918, net revenues after expenses equaled $14, 808.57. This revenue is in addition to the hospital having an abundant supply of fresh eggs, milk, meat, and fresh vegetables from the gardens. These foods were a valuable source to the diets of the patients and would have been had at an exorbitant price had they needed to have been purchased on the open market.

The Creamery, built and equipped in 1921, was a wonderful addition to processing dairy products which included bottling of milk and the manufacturing of ice cream and butter. The butter, heavily used at the hospital and previously a purchased item, was now made on the premises. Excess dairy products were sold on the local open market. The Creamery building still stands proudly today.

A new apple orchard was planted in 1930. 1,708 trees of various varieties were planted. And in 1936 the dairy herd at the asylum numbered 213 head and was reported to produce 2,245,270 pounds of milk over a two-year period. In the same period, the swine raising part of the farm produced 86,375 pounds of fresh pork while the poultry side of things produced 5,877 pounds of chicken, 2,727 pounds of duck and 1,794 pounds of goose. Additionally, 315 pounds of rabbit were raised for consumption in the hospital.

The dairy herd at Winnebago was considered one of the better herds in the country. The Holstein herd known as the "Burke Herd at Winnebago State Farm" was a registered family with the original sire being "Home of Marathon Best Burke" who was bred and raised in the 1930s. An outstanding daughter of this sire was "Winnebago 87 Canary". The entire herd related back to her. One of the best milk producing cows, "Winnebago Ideal Celia Bonnie", was nationally known and won numerous blue ribbons at Wisconsin State Fairs. During her lifetime, Celia Bonnie produced 178,606 pounds of milk and 6,503 pounds of butterfat. In comparison, the 1954 average herd output was 384 pounds of butterfat. She was a true champion!

Although care of the grounds, gardening, the greenhouse operation and the orchard continued to be a vital part of the hospital's existence, the chores of running the farm were becoming unmanageable. Patient help became less available as modern treatments were shortening the length of stay for many. It was becoming economically unfeasible to run the farm operations profitably so in April of 1954 the farm was turned over to the Wisconsin State Prison. The hospital continued to run their creamery and purchased raw milk from the Prison.

The beef cattle, hog and poultry operations were discontinued in 1957 when it was realized it was more economical to purchase meat products from an outside source.

The State Hospital Train Depot at Winnebago

The Northwestern Railway was the first railroad to reach Oshkosh in September, 1858. It was quite a sight when that first steam locomotive came into town, as most people here had never seen one before. The railroad came only as far as the southside of the Fox River until 1861, when the tracks were extended to Appleton.

The Chicago & Northwestern Railroad built a depot north and west of the hospital near Sunnyview Road in early 1872. The train depot was one of the key points in locating the asylum here according to State Statutes.

The unincorporated town of Winnebago, as it is known both then and today, is a small geographic area that was sparsely populated in the late 19th century. But the Northern State Hospital for the Insane changed all that with several hundred patients and staff, the area was in need of some additional amenities…such as a post office and grocery store.

So, on June 26, 1876, the Winnebago Post Office was instituted. Originally it was located inside the train depot. The arriving mail was an exciting event as each day at 5:30 pm, "Old 21" would come steaming down the track with mail pouches sailing through the air in catcher pouches. The Winnebago Post Office was a fourth-class office so the Postmaster's pay consisted of commission from the sale of stamps and money orders. Mail was received with hand-stamped cancellations.

William Walker was the first station agent at the train depot, a position he held for 25 years. He was also the first Postmaster. His daughter Eleanor, recalled as a child she would carry the lantern up the railroad tracks for her dad to hang on the tall pole to let the oncoming train know it was all clear to enter the Winnebago station.

Eventually, the post office was moved from the train depot to Mr. Walker's grocery store situated on the south side of Butler Avenue.

Each day, the mail was carried from the train depot to the grocery store where it would be sorted and sent to three institutions…the State Hospital, the County Hospital, and the Poor Farm. When picture postcards first came into use, the Postmaster (Walker) occasionally made the mistake of placing the cancellation on the picture side of the card. On one occasion, Dr. William Gordon received a number of picture postcards from his daughter Kate who was traveling in Europe. It is said Dr. Gordon became very upset that the cancellation was placed on the picture side of the cards and informed the Postmaster in as much of his dismay. In 1916, Albert Brossard succeeded Mr. Walker as Postmaster. . When Mr. Brossard died in 1945, Elmer Ter Horst purchased the grocery store and managed it until 1958 when it was sold to Franklin Priem. The building remains in that same location in 2018.

The Post Office remained in the Priem grocery store until July 1, 1961. A new post office building was constructed by Elmer TerHorst just south and behind the Priem grocery store. The Ter Horst family leased the brick and lannon stone building to the United States Post Office. That building is still used and leased today (2018) as the Winnebago Branch of the US Post office.

In 1877 a new avenue (Butler Ave today) was created by hospital employees that ran from the hospital entrance to the railroad tracks. The road was graded with fine stone harvested from the shores of nearby Lake Winnebago and the boarded sidewalks made the trek from arriving trains to the hospital more manageable. Elm and maple trees were planted along each side of the road in rows and gaslights were installed so persons arriving by train at night could more easily find their way to the hospital. Soon after the new road was constructed,

Priem Delivery Truck

Photo courtesy Randy Priem

Ter Horst Grocery Store

Photo courtesy of Randy Priem

lots were created and sold. Dwellings were erected, mostly by hospital employees wishing to live close to where they worked.

Author's Note: Joseph Butler, the first Steward, and his wife Adelaide Butler, who was the first Matron at the hospital, worked at the asylum from the very beginning until September 1885 when they both declined re-appointment. It is in their honor that the street in Winnebago that ran from the train depot to the front entrance is named "Butler Avenue"

The railroad and depot were very important to the asylum during the early days. Building materials and equipment all were delivered by rail and almost every patient would arrive by train. Those able, would walk the two-block distance to the hospital entrance, regardless of weather. Non-ambulatory patients would be carried by carriage or sleigh. Dr. Kempster requested that a side-track be laid by C&NW from the main line to the rear of the asylum and into the coal house. This greatly improved the process to unload incoming carloads of coal. A Western Union telegraph office was opened in the train depot in 1896. Each depot agent was able to send and receive telegraphs and communications that mostly were directly related to hospital functions.

Once the avenue was constructed, the Chicago & Northwestern Railroad agreed to move the depot to be closer to the new road and hospital entrance.

Soo Line Depot at the State Hospital on Butler Ave

Photo courtesy Dr. William Weber

Between 1880 and 1882, the Wisconsin Central Railroad built a second depot at Winnebago. It existed there until 1909 whereupon Wisconsin Central signed a 99-year lease to the Soo Line Railroad.

Finally, on March 1, 1920, the two depots were consolidated and the Soo Line depot was torn down. The Chicago & Northwestern depot was then repositioned between the two sets of tracks to make way for a new road (County Highway A today). That depot remained in that location until it was torn down in October 1963.

The Petting Zoo

Operating under the belief that occupying one's time was therapeutic, in 1900, the Northern Hospital Zoo was organized for patient entertainment. Specimens included a live Badger (donated by S.M. Eaton of Watertown) and four English pheasants (donated by Clyde Buckstaff). Other animals included a fox, a raccoon, 2 coyotes, 7 elk, a wild pig, 2 Muscovy ducks, 3 dozen wild ducks, a bullfrog, 15 Tumbler pigeons and an eagle. This was one of the first "pet therapy" programs introduced in the State.

Hauntings at the Asylum

I would be remiss to not mention some of the strange things reported in the state asylum over the years. Some people believe that former patients linger here after death. Some think an asylum is an obvious place for restless souls who never found peace during...or after their lives.

One case involves a former patient named Rufus, whom it is said can be seen lurking in the shadows of Sherman Hall, where he hung himself. A former UW-Oshkosh student claimed that, one day while she was working in one of the offices in the basement of Sherman Hall, she got the eerie feeling she was being watched. As she moved around the basement, she sensed she was being followed. Suddenly, she turned quickly and saw what she described as a shadow swiftly hide behind a vestibule and slip around a corner. She investigated further, but never found anyone there. Needless to say, she was disturbed by this and reported the incident to staff members who recorded the incident, then dismissed it. Undeterred, she decided to investigate further. While searching the internet, she discovered there had been previous reports of "a black, shadowy figure" seen roaming the basement of Sherman Hall.

This wasn't the only time strange things were reported in Sherman Hall. A retired employee from WMHI agreed to share some of her experiences with me.

It was only a few years ago that a social worker had one of the most unusual days of her life. It was a weekend and she was there taking care of some business matters and enjoyed working on the weekends when there was little staff on hand...the quiet allowed her to get things done. Her office was located in the basement of Sherman Hall, which has a labyrinth of tunnels connecting the building to other buildings at the institution. She was sitting at her desk when suddenly the papers on her bulletin board started fluttering as though caught by a brisk breeze. She also felt like her hair was lifting, a strange feeling to say the least. This was odd, she thought, as there were no open windows or fans to create this disturbance but thought nothing more of it. Sometime later, she walked down the hallway to use the restroom. As she walked, she heard footsteps behind her. She paused and turned expecting to greet the person following her…but no one was there. When she reached the restroom, she approached door and noticed through the fogged style glass an image behind it, so she stepped back expecting that person to emerge. When no one opened the door, she proceeded to do so from her side, only find, once again, no one there.

Things were starting to become unsettling, but she proceeded with her routine. Next, she went to the stairway that led from the basement to the main floor. While climbing the stairs, she heard the laughter of a little girl. But again, she was alone in the stairwell.

Still, on the same day, she used the elevator to return to basement. After the door closed, the elevator started to descend when she heard a noise from above, followed clearly by the voice of a young boy. She heard him say in a tone sounding hopeful… "Can you see me? Can you see me?"

She reported the incidents to the on-duty supervisor.

Other sightings in Sherman Hall were reported in the children's "Psych Ward". A child was found scared and crying and when approached by staff said he has seen a man standing in the corner. The staff person investigated but could see no one. The incident was recorded, but upon closer examination it was discovered that previous sightings by other children were made over time. The interesting thing…each description of the "man standing in the corner" were the same.

It has also been said the Julaine Farrow Museum, formerly the Superintendent and Director's home, holds some spirits from the past. I interviewed a volunteer, who prefers to remain anonymous, claims there is something bad and sometimes noisy inhabiting the second floor. The second floor is home to some old medical instruments, a body basket, and a few creepy, old mannequins. She was dusting in the upstairs bedroom when she heard a tapping sound coming from the corner of the room. She investigated further and found the only thing there was the heating unit. I asked her if what she heard might have been the heating system working. She looked at me and said firmly, "NO. It was summer and the heating system was not operating." She described a distinctive "clink" like the sound of someone tapping on a pipe. Then it stopped as quickly as it had started.

On another occasion during a tour, the docent was speaking to a small group at the top of the stair landing when all of a sudden, a low growling sound was heard coming from a nearby room. One quick check of the visitors indicated they either hadn't heard it or they simply ignored it. It was enough to send chills down the spine of the docent. On another occasion near this same spot, the strings of guitar standing on display were strummed. No one was near the guitar.

A psychic medium was brought in about twenty years ago to see if they could raise the spirit of the dead. The efforts were deemed unsuccessful and it was declared the old brick home had no spirits haunting its halls...or *ARE there?*

Just recently, another incident occurred that made even the doubters question their own beliefs...

On occasion, a light in one of the third-floor rooms mysteriously comes on. It is controlled by a wall switch and those on duty in the museum will state unequivocally that a thorough check of the building at closing time was made and all lights were turned off. I was told, "It happens from time-to-time".

But this one evening recently was enough to send shivers down your spine.

An employee, a RN, had finished her shift and was leaving her work station one evening. As she crossed the parking lot to her car, she heard the sound of glass breaking. She looked up to see a light on in the Farrow Museum...up on the third floor. Having been employed there for some time, she was familiar with the stories about the third-floor light, so she grabbed her cell phone and took a photo of it, intending to send it to someone who should be notified.

When she downloaded the photo from her phone to a laptop computer, she was shocked! As she enlarged the photo, she found images in the dark, unlit window right below the lighted window. The images were of two faces looking out.

I saw the image and can personally attest to what I just described. Got goosebumps yet?

I asked the staff person on duty the day I was at the museum this question: "Would you spend the night alone in this house?"

She exclaimed, "Not in a million years!"

Obviously, she had heard these stories too!

The Patients

During the first five months from April to September of 1873, the patient count started to build and the hospital was not yet complete, but well enough along to start receiving and treating patients. In this short time, 205 patients were now residents at the Northern State Hospital for the Insane. Of those admitted, 61 men and 56 women had been transferred here from the state asylum in Madison and other locations such as county jails and poor houses. Dr. Kempster stated that 69 of the admissions were cases of chronic mania and 73 of dementia. 127 of them had been insane from 2 to 50 years. Patient ages ranged from 50 to 80 years of age. Cases of advanced pulmonary tuberculosis, blindness, amputated limbs and epilepsy were present. Life events that led to treatment included homicide, suicidal attempts and arson.

In 1878 there were 37 reported deaths among patients. This represented about 5 percent of the total population that year compared to the average mortality rate in the nation's mental institutions was 9 percent. Dr. Kempster attributed this lower rate to the quality of care received at the Northern State Hospital for the Insane.

During that same time, about 60 male patients were allowed to come and go without accompaniment of attendants. These patients were allowed to assist in the farm, gardens, kitchen, and laundry areas, but their amount of work allowed was limited. Many would simply go for walks or sit in the shade and enjoy the lovely view of the nearby lake. Women patients that qualified also followed the same routines as the men. There was the occasional "walk away" but patients were usually promptly returned. It was the policy of the hospital to pay local farmers and residents for the return of "eloping patients" to the hospital grounds. In 1884, $47.75 was paid for that year.

The Director's Report in 1880 indicated there were 141 patient attempted suicides with none being successful. Some of these numbers included attempts before and after admission to the asylum. The first successful suicide at the asylum occurred on December 14, 1884.

During the two-year span of 1890-1892, an unusually high number of deaths occurred at the asylum. Superintendent Booth attributed this to "the number of those who had died during their first month of hospitalization had been largely because a number of patients had arrived in such a state of exhausted condition that they never rallied, in spite of the most strenuous efforts made to prolong life."

Tragedy occurred in the early months of 1952. Herbert DeBehnke, a psychiatric aide and a five-year employee, was killed instantly when he was struck on the head with a heavy object wielded by a male patient. The chronically ill patient told authorities that a "voice" told him that if he killed an attendant he would be promoted.

It goes without saying, that some of the patients there were famous and sometimes rather infamous.

Percy M. Bradt was born in 1866 in nearby Omro, Wisconsin. He grew up in the Omro area where his father held several jobs including working for the St. Paul Railway Company and secretary of the Western Compound Company of Omro. He also was elected as Town Clerk and eventually Village Clerk for Omro, a position he held for thirty years. Mathew G. Bradt was well known and a careful and conservative businessman. Unfortunately, his business and administrative savvy was never passed along to his son Percy.

Percy Bradt in 1895

Percy who was physically weak since childhood, was described as socially awkward, nervous, timid, and introverted with no business faculties like his father. He also had a speech impediment which embarrassed him. At the young age of 11, Percy developed a strong interest in the game of checkers. He worked hard to hone his skills and it wasn't long before he was virtually unbeatable with local opponents. At age seventeen, he played American champion C.F. Barker at a match arranged in Milwaukee. The match continued for three days with the score Barker 5, Bradt 4, and 4 draws. Percy was gaining confidence as each day progressed, but Barker was unexpectedly called back to New York and withdrew before the final day of competition. Speculation soared that given one more day, Bradt would've defeated the American champ and won the match.

Bradt became such an expert at the game that he wrote several books about strategy and learnings from professional matches where he provided analysis of scores and strategy. His books became regarded as standards for the game of checkers.

Percy was a familiar figure in the area and players would make pilgrimages to Omro to play with the master and have bragging rights back home that they played against him. One year, a player from Chicago named Walker, who was considered an expert in the game, came to Oshkosh to play Percy in a match arranged by Captain James Anglim of Hose Company No. 8, stationed at the Phoenix Engine House in Oshkosh. A large crowd gathered for the well-publicized match. Walker's efforts to beat Bradt were futile…then things got interesting. Bradt "upped the ante" and offered to play Walker blindfolded. A blindfold was put in place and Percy was moved across the room where he could not see the board. The opposition's moves were called out to Percy and he responded in kind, in his mind recalling where every piece was positioned on the checkerboard. His opponent finally surrendered admitting defeat.

It was also said that Percy could illustrate complex mathematical equations that were considered uncanny.

While his mind was "peculiarly organized", he was never considered "crazy". When his father died in 1905, Percy moved to New London, Wisconsin but found he did not like it there. He returned to Oshkosh and paid a visit to a friend of his father's, Dr. W.A. Gordon, superintendent at the Northern State Hospital for the Insane. Knowing of Percy's expertise in checkers, Dr. Gordon arranged a match with patient named "Sam" who also enjoyed a spirited game of checkers.

Sam was an African American man, and one of his patient-related tasks at the asylum included fetching the mail each day from the train depot. It's been told that Sam would frequently be teased by local children who live nearby because the neighborhood dogs would follow him to the train depot each and every time he went there. It was later discovered that Sam would have pieces of meat in his pocket and would feed the dogs as he made his travels.

Sam was also known in the asylum as a "first rate checker player." So, Dr. Gordon arranged a match between the two of them. Percy beat him unmercifully. Sam declared it was Percy's beard that "hoodooed" him, but Percy declined to shave and over the next few days continued to beat Sam so bad that Sam eventually gave up and quit playing in exasperation.

Bradt liked it at the institution and remained there for about a month. Dr. Gordon told him if he was to stay he would need to be committed. An application was made to the Winnebago County Court and Percy was voluntarily admitted. It was determined that Bradt was "unfit to cope with the affairs of the world without some form of guardianship." Later, he was made "companion and special attendant" to Senator Kennedy of Appleton where Percy earned 25 cents a day for his services. After Kennedy died, Percy was "bereft of all income" and eventually sent to the Sunnyview county asylum where he spent the remainder of his life.

At age 47, Percy Bradt died on the day after Christmas in 1913. He is buried next to his parents in the village cemetery near Omro.

Ask anyone who John Flammang Shrank is and you will probably get a quizzical look, one eyebrow raised and a blank stare. Not really a household name to most people, but Mr. Shrank was really quite infamous.

On October 14, 1912, the 36-year old unemployed saloonkeeper from New York City attempted to assassinate former President Theodore Roosevelt as he rode in an open top vehicle en route to give a speech in Milwaukee. The bullet hit the former POTUS in the chest, passing through his dense overcoat, his steel-lined eyeglass case and a heavily folded manuscript of his intended speech. It slowed the bullet enough that Roosevelt continued his speech before going to the hospital 90 minutes later. The investigator discovered that Shrank had followed the Presidential candidate around on the campaign trail for weeks. The hand-written note found in his pocket indicated his symptoms were that of a paranoid schizophrenic. The note read: "To the people of the United States. In a dream I saw President McKinley sit up in his coffin, pointing at a man in monk's attire in whom I recognized as Theodore Roosevelt. The dead President said – 'This is my murderer – avenge my death.'"

He went on to claim his action were in defense of the two-term tradition for Presidential terms. "I did not intend to kill the citizen Roosevelt, I intended to kill Theodore Roosevelt the third-termer," he stated to authorities.

After his arrest, Shrank was examined by doctors who reported he was suffering from "insane delusions, grandiose in character" and declared insane.

Shrank was never tried for the attempted assassination. Instead he was sent to Oshkosh and was admitted to the Northern State Hospital for the Insane. Later, he was transferred to the Central State Hospital in Waupun, Wisconsin. He was not allowed to receive any visitors or communications from the outside world for the next thirty years.

While incarcerated, Shrank wrote several letters to the doctor he was consulting with at the Northern State Hospital, Dr. Adin Sherman. Original copies of his correspondence are preserved in the Julaine Farrow Museum. The letters are dated 1914-1918 and document the correspondence.

In the coming years, Shrank would sue Roosevelt in an attempt to recover the bullet. The court ruled that since the bullet was lodged inside the former President, it was his to keep.

Shrank died on September 16, 1943 of bronchial pneumonia. His body was donated to the Medical School at Marquette University (now the Medical College of Wisconsin) for anatomical dissection.

Other less famous cases included a patient admitted in the early 1990s. The patient's condition was diagnosed as very mentally and physically ill. One week after admission, he died and an autopsy was performed. During the autopsy they discovered $48 in coins in his lacerated abdomen. In reviewing the results of the post mortem exam, the team of medical professionals recalled the patient saying, "I eat little people," referring to the heads on the coins. The coins are on display at the Julaine Farrow Museum at WMHI.

Another case involves a patient that used a bit of ingenuity for his own personal gain. In the interest of maintaining confidentiality, we'll call this man "Gus". Gus was a smoker and loved smoking but didn't like work. Therefore, he had no money to purchase cigarettes or tobacco. This was during the time when usage of loose tobacco was prevalent. So, Gus came up with a plan. His fee for services rendered were a tobacco tin with a small amount of tobacco left in it. He would take the tin, after clearing the contents, and use it to forge a "key". Unlike today where locks are fairly complex in shape and form, keys back then were simpler in design and skeleton keys could be created that could open most any lock. The skeleton keys made by Gus were crude in the truest sense but made well enough to have a good success rate in that most of the keys Gus made worked! Patients used their keys to unlock doors and escape, access forbidden areas or maybe enjoy a late-night rendezvous with a lady friend in the female ward.

The WMHI Cemetery

Due to the nature of patient care and treatment at the State Hospital, the death of a patient was not an uncommon experience. It was somewhat common for patients at the asylum to not have any family or known contacts, in many cases they basically became wards of the state. If a patient died while under the custody of the State, efforts were made to return the remains to the patient's family. Oftentimes there would be no one available in which to send the remains. Some that were claimed by family had the deceased sent back to their hometown for burial there. Those not claimed were either sent to medical research facilities or universities for study, or they were buried in the asylum cemetery. A morgue was built and situated on the grounds at the rear of the coal shed at the back of the hospital to care and preserve the remains for burial.

The original cemetery was established in June of 1873. It was located north and east of what is now the Drug and Alcohol Treatment Center (Kempster Hall). From November 1933 to March 1934, all the remains of 750 graves were disinterred and relocated to a more desirable location on the southern end of the property near the Picnic Point area. It was a WPA (Works Public Administration) project that employed 80 men. As the remains were relocated, they were moved

Asylum cemetery at the Northern State Hospital for the Insane – 1929

Photo courtesy Julaine Farrow Museum

Concrete markers with numbers coincide with records to identify the burials

Photo courtesy Randy Domer

intact from their previous location. During the transfer of remains, long trenches were dug and each of the remains were placed in the trench side by side. No names were placed on the markers due to the State's position on the confidentiality of patient privacy. Each gravesite is identified with a concrete marker with nothing more than a number placed on each. Only one marker in the entire cemetery bears the name of the person buried there. The Julaine Farrow Museum holds map which shows the cemetery layout along with the original logbook, which lists the patient's names, dates of admission, death, and burial, cause of death if listed, grave location, county of residence, and cost of coffin. The cost of coffins in 1883 was $3, children's coffins were $2. Coffins were simple and made of wood. A wicker basket was used to transport the body to the morgue where the staff would work on the final arrangements.

What is striking about this cemetery becomes obvious the minute you enter the gate. Nothing but expansive green space can be seen by one's eye…no flowers, ornamental markers or headstones. It's Potters Field where burials were made at no great expense to the State or the deceased's family. Some of the burials here even contain the remains of heroes from the Civil War.

Access to the cemetery on WMHI grounds is not permitted unless proof of relationship to someone buried there has been established.

Herein lies the final resting place of 870 people whose lives ended tragically and alone within the walls of a mental institution. Nothing more than a number …and eternal obscurity.

The Julaine Farrow Museum

Directly in front of the Winnebago Mental Health Institute stands an old brick home that, at a first glance, seems oddly out of place. Built in 1922 under the direction of Dr. Adin Sherman, the brick house was once the home of the asylum's Superintendents and Directors. Previous to 1922, the Superintendent and his family lived on the second floor of the "Old Main" building. The "new" home gave the family some much needed space and appreciated privacy. The beautiful three-story home was built for less than $8,000 by carpenters who earned 75 cents an hour.

Julaine E. Farrow, a registered nurse at the institution for 36 years, took a personal interest in recording and preserving the history of the Winnebago Mental Health Institute. She started as a staff nurse in 1938 and lived with her husband, George, on Butler Avenue, the street that today runs east to west from the hospital toward County Road A. Her dream was to build a museum where historical items and artifacts could be stored and displayed for observation by the general public. It was through the work and dedication of Julaine Farrow that a museum was created, highlighting and illustrating the history of the ages old institution. To support the project, Julaine wrote a book titled *Winnebago State Hospital 1873-1973* and donated the proceeds from the sales of the book to help fund the museum project. She became the unofficial hospital historian while she was employed, gathering and storing antiques and artifacts that would someday go on display in the museum. Her efforts were supported with assistance from staff members Diane Meschefske and Brenda Wiley.

Julaine retired in 1974 but stayed active as a volunteer, continuing her work to preserve and record the hospital's rich heritage. She died on May 30, 1991.

The site originally selected for the museum was the old Blacksmith Shop. This tired, old building that survived and witnessed decades of changes at the asylum still stood proudly on the grounds and represented the "buildings of old". The Blacksmith Shop was built in 1897 from bricks that resembled the ones used in the construction of "The Old Main". The bricks were made near High Cliff

The Blacksmith Shop

Photo courtesy Julaine Farrow Museum

State Park and were transported to the site by barge or horse and sleigh across the ice when Lake Winnebago was frozen.

A formal dedication was held on September 28, 1976 with Drs. Darold Treffert (Superintendent of WMHI) and William Studley (Shorewood Hospital, Milwaukee) as speakers.

The museum quickly outgrew its space in the Blacksmith Shop and the search for a new home for the museum was underway. In 1989, it was decided the former Superintendent's home would be a suitable site. The house had been unoccupied since the departure of Dr. Charles Belcher, superintendent from 1959-1964. Since then the building was mainly used to house staff physicians and in later years used for programs and office space. What began as a two room exhibit quickly grew to ten rooms.

Today, the museum is full of the rich history of the asylum's past. Photographs, medical devices and instruments, furniture, uniforms, staged treatment exhibits and more are on display to give the visitor a look back in time of the developmental treatments on mental health patients. The Museum is open to the public seasonally and posts its hours of operation on the sign in front of the museum.

Sources: *An Asylum's Journey – Healing Through The Centuries, The History of Winnebago Mental Health Institute 1873-1998*, written by Julaine Farrow(1973) and edited, revised and expanded by Paul F. Janty(2008); *The State Hospital 1873-1973* by Julaine Farrow; Oshkosh City Directory, 1872 & 1873, Christensen and Harney Publisher; University of Wisconsin – Madison Libraries, http://digital.library.wisc.edu/1711.dl/WI.WinnebagoMHI; http://www.asylumprojects.org/index.php?title=Winnebago_State_Hospital; http://www.asylumprojects.org/index.php?title=Kirkbride_Planned_Institutions; www.britannica.com/topic/lobotomy; (Percy Bradt) - Omro Journal, Jan 1, 1914; *Oshkosh Daily Northwestern*, Dec. 4,1905, Jan. 13,1906, Dec 29,1913,p. 10; (Shrank) – www.history.com; www.nps.gov; personal interviews with Paul Janty, Linda Schueler; Gores, Stan, *The attempted assassination of Teddy Roosevelt*, The State Historical Society of Wisconsin, 1980. Source: wikipedia

The Poor Farm, County Asylum, County Hospital, and Sunnyview Sanatorium

During the mid-1860s, the country was just emerging from the painful aftermath of the Civil War. Here in Wisconsin, one in every ten men saw action in the "war between the states". One in seven of those that served did not return from battle. This created a real hardship as families worked hard to try to return to a sense of normalcy with their lives. The war had taken its toll. It was not unusual to see women, mothers and daughters, working in the fields alongside the men to gather the harvest. There was no money to hire hands to assist with the work so everyone pitched in. Local businesses, civic agencies, and fraternal organizations provided assistance and relief when and where they could, but no formal plan was in place to deal with the problems of pauperism, illness, criminals and insanity. It was not uncommon for all to be housed together in the local jail.

The first jail in Winnebago County was built in 1847 alongside the courthouse and served as a prison, asylum and poor house. It soon burned down and a new jail was built in 1849 with better security measures taken, but it too was short lived. In 1860, a new jail and courthouse were built on the corner of what is Court and Ceape Streets today. The new facility would be two-stories high, made of Milwaukee brick with a basement. It also included the Sheriff's residence and facilities for the guards.

The city of Oshkosh was also dealing with the problem of vagrants, transients and people that simply did not have the means to support themselves. Pauperism was also considered a disease. Some people in desperation turned to begging, stealing or robbing…even murder. Horse thieves became increasingly numerous throughout Wisconsin which in turn led to more lynchings. One thing was certain – poverty could not be ignored.

It was during this time that communities started to act by building institutions to deal with the various social and personal issues. It was in 1860 that the State of Wisconsin opened its first State Hospital for the Insane at Mendota.

An editorial in the *Oshkosh Daily Northwestern* dated April 14, 1864 read:

"The County of Winnebago needs a Poor House and farm where paupers can   receive proper care and be made to contribute to the support of the institution…"

The land purchase began in 1865 and with additional land purchases over the following years, enough land was accumulated to allow for both an asylum and poor farm which were to be built over the next five years.

In 1871, Winnebago County established a Poor Farm on land north of Oshkosh purchased in 1865. On this farm, a Poor House was built and four years later, additional wings would be added to the Poor House for an insane asylum. One building was used to

Poor House circa 1880

Photo courtesy Dr. William Weber

accommodate both the poor and the patients with mental illness. Patients of the asylum that were physically able, provided labor for the farm, producing crops and dairy products that were either consumed by the residents or sold to offset the operating costs of the institutions. The idea behind a poor farm was to put the poor people to work by operating a farm and selling the yield to become self-sustainable. That idea would prove unworthy as you will soon discover.

According to Janet Eiler, President of the Winnebago County Genealogical Society and author of *Poor Farm Cemetery, Winnebago County Wisconsin,* "… the sick, poor, vagrants, tramps, elderly, single pregnant women, abandoned children, criminals, the developmentally disabled and mentally ill… all considered to be poor and were labeled paupers and 'warehoused' together on poor farms." Pauperism was the philosophical reason, most people believed, that indiscriminate charity would only spread the disease.

Previous to the existence of the Poor Farm, local vagrants were housed in a vagrant house located in the city of Oshkosh on Ceape Street near the Peters Block. Vagrants were treated as petty criminals – arrested, jailed, or given a ride to the city limits. Conditions in the jail were deplorable as inmates slept on straw pallets arranged on dirt floors. Restrained with chains, these unfortunates were left to sit in their own filth. Vermin and lice were also a problem.

In 1873 the State of Wisconsin stepped in and built the Northern State Hospital for the Insane, just east of the Poor Farm and County Asylum. Almost as soon as it opened, the State Hospital exceeded its patient capacity as local jails and poor houses around the State transferred their more severe cases to the new Oshkosh facility. To provide balance, an agreement was struck between the State of Wisconsin and Winnebago County that *acute* (short term) insane patients would receive treatment at the state facility and the *chronically* (severe and of longer duration) insane would go to the county institution. When the change was made in 1883 it marked the first time the number of insane surpassed that of the poor.[4]

In 1882, a third level was added to the west wing of the Poor House which provided nine more bedrooms and a sitting room[4]. Janet Eiler explains, "The Poor House would house the poor, defined as those not able to contribute to their own well-being, and included the elderly, infants and single pregnant women." Room, board, and all necessary costs would be covered by the county. To the elderly it was a place where they could live and find peace until their death, not unlike today's nursing homes. The process of caring for the poor and sick back then was the beginning of the social welfare system as we know it today.

In October of 2017, I had the privilege to interview Dr. William Weber, Medical Director at Parkview for the past 27 years. Dr. Weber has a strong interest in the history of Parkview and the State Institution as well. He helped shed a clearer perspective on residents of the Poor House.

He reported that in the early years, one-third of the counties in Wisconsin had such facilities that provided only minimum support. "In 1870, the population in Poor Houses across the State of Wisconsin included 1240 inmates. They comprised of the insane (197), epileptics (40), feeble minded (30), blind (20), deaf and dumb (8), and over 200 children with 15-20 babies born each year," he explained. "The children and babies were mostly the product of unwed mothers who were committed to the institutions to have their babies. When the mothers left, sometimes they took their babies with them...sometimes not," he added. Children left behind then became wards of the county until they could be placed into an orphanage or other form of foster care, which sometimes were farm families.

The Poor Farm was well equipped with buildings that one would find on most farms. In 1940, the farm included a poultry house, horse barn, cow barn, barn for young stock, hay barn, three corn cribs, a hog house, tool shed, slaughter house, granary, six silos, and three cottages to house an engineer, farmhand and herdsman. The farm also included two tractors, seven teams of horses, eight purebred registered bulls, cows and heifers, a boar pig, eleven registered brood sows, twenty-eight fattening pigs, eighty-three spring pigs, forty suckling pigs, thirty-three shoats, two young boars and over thirteen hundred head of assorted poultry including chickens and ducklings.

Profitability of the Poor Farm was paramount to its existence as it was expected to be a profitable venture in order to support the operation of the institutions. This incentivized the Superintendents and their staff to seek ways to become more efficient to save money and generate revenue. One idea reported included the exploration of making silk by planting mulberry trees and importing silkworms. [4]

In 1876, sixty-seven acres were in production with twenty-two acres in wheat, thirteen acres in oats, fourteen in corn, two-and-one half in potatoes, and sixteen in grasses. A two-and-one-half acre vegetable farm produced abundant supplies of onions, turnips, cabbages and squash. An additional thirteen acres were maintained for the four dairy cows and horses. Satisfactory income was derived from the sale of vegetables, hogs, chickens, milk and butter.

On November 13, 1878, the *Oshkosh Daily Northwestern* reported the following harvest at the Poor Farm:

Wheat – 405 bushels	Oats – 413 bushels
Corn – 1800 bushels	Potatoes – 125 bushels
Hay – 30 tons	Tobacco – 450 pounds
Cabbage – 1500 heads	Onions – 20 bushels
Peas – 8 bushels	Beans – 8 bushels
Turnips – 15 bushels	Carrots – 30 bushels
Parsnips – 30 bushels	Pickles – 3 barrels
Beets – 30 bushels	Pork – 500 pounds; Stock Hogs – 17

A power house was used to supply heat for the buildings located in the complex with three large boilers of 125 horsepower each providing steam. Two wells provided water for the complex.

Work on the Poor Farm was mostly done by the insane, as the "poor" were unable to work due to age or physical inability. The Poor Farm could not have existed without the help from the patients of the asylum who tended to the farm crops and animals. One of the jobs performed by the patients included harvesting ice from nearby Lake Winnebago. Teams of horses were used to drag the ice to the Poor Farm where it would be stored in the icehouse.

Elmer and Olphene Manuel were the Superintendent and Matron for the Winnebago County Asylum and Poor House from 1908 until their retirement in 1930. Elmer E. Manuel was born in Vinland Township on June 1, 1861. He married Olphene Olson on February 22, 1886. She was born in nearby Winchester on April 10, 1865. The couple had two daughters: Neita Manuel Grueder and Bessie Manuel Briggs; and a son Bernard. Their daughter Neita and her husband George V. Grueder took over their duties at the Winnebago County Asylum and Poor House in 1930. Olphene died of a heart attack on

December 26, 1930 and Elmer died on January 27, 1938 after a two-month illness.

The typical day on the Poor Farm began at 7am with then Superintendent George V. Grueder having breakfast. Grueder was very actively involved in the farming operations and was known as a hard and diligent worker himself. At 7:30 am, Grueder and his staff served breakfast to the inmates that were physically able to perform and work on the farm. They were not forced to work, but most agreed to it as an alternative to life in the ward which was empty and endless. At noon a lunch was served and patients were allowed the afternoon to relax and walk about the grounds. Dinner was served at 5pm with the county asylum being "locked" at 8pm each evening. "Lights out" was 10 pm with a quick toilet time at 11. The night watchman would make his rounds once an hour looking for potential flight risks and fire. During their time off, attendants and staff would ride the train to Oshkosh for pleasure. Superintendent Grueder was the only person who owned a car...a Plymouth sedan which was provided by the County.

It was in 1893 that the County Board voted to appropriate funds to build a new building just east of the Poor House.[4] William Waters was chosen as the architect of the building that would be the new County Asylum. Joseph Webber was selected as the builder. The new facility would be constructed at the cost of $60,000.

Author's Note: To clarify terminology here, "Poor Farm" referred to the farm itself, the new building was referred to as the "County Asylum" and the old building the "Poor House"

This much needed move would finally segregate the poor from the insane, something that was necessary for understandable reasons.

Until 1902, one superintendent oversaw the operations at all of these county institutions. A separation of roles occurred when the County Board elected one man to assume the role of superintendent of the Poor House only, and the former joint supervisor became the superintendent of the County Asylum.

The relationship between the two institutions was symbiotic; at times it was difficult to distinguish the difference between inmates of both. The idea that the Poor House was simply a place for those without

**County Asylum staff. Elmer and Olphene (center)
with two daughters and son**

Photo courtesy Dr. William Weber

means to provide for themselves was without warrant and explained in a report by Dr. W.A. Gordon, Superintendent:

As long as men are ignorant, dissipated, lazy and improvident, there will be poverty. If everyone was governed by the old New England economy or the German thrift there would be no poverty in America. We have spent enough for tobacco and liquor to enrich the world. There are a hundred well-known preventable causes of poverty, but every man wants to be excused of himself and have his neighbor exercised therein. The poor, for whom you provide for are either infants, invalids, or aged persons, all of whom are physically unable to procure a livelihood by their unaided efforts. The typical pauper, whom we are all too well acquainted, is a trembling old man. He has been harassed by want, buffeted by fate, mocked by fortune, deserted by friends, gnawed by disease, discouraged by many failures...In his helplessness and homelessness he feebly knocks at the Poor House door, asking bread and shelter until he finds 'surcease of sorrow' in the pitying bosom of his mother earth. You ask him not for reason or causes. It matters not why he comes. The bended form and the wrecked life are his passports to our assistance. It is your duty and mine to cheer and comfort him with honest manly sympathy and material aid.

Dr. Gordon's compassion for the poor continues...

There are in the Poor House eight women all of whom are over seventy years of age... They are inmates of the county house through no fault of their own. There is something in the lot of the old women who have been consigned to this place that should enlist our sympathy. To them it seems but yesterday that they were strong, healthy, and independent, the roses were on their cheeks; they were admired and caressed; they lifted to their lips life's enchanted cup; the future was radiant with the brightness that only the dreams of youth can give. Today ambition has fled. They have been deserted by beauty and passion. Those they loved are dead or even worse than dead—indifferent. No children climb their knees the envied kiss to share. The feeble arms are empty. There are no words of tenderness in their ears. Helpless, hapless, homeless, and almost hopeless. The wrinkled hands clasp the bible, the last hope, the only friend. With pathetic patience they are waiting in desperation for the last journey—the little journey to the potters field.

[**Source**: Quote by Dr. W.A. Gordon; *A History of the Winnebago County Poor Farm* by G. Koppelberger]

In 1896 Winnebago County built a workhouse for vagrants. Socially considered criminals, vagrants were previously housed away from the poor and insane. At the workhouse, vagrants worked eight hours a day crushing rock by hand and for their efforts received a small wage. The county, in turn, sold the crushed rock to the highest bidder which provided a source of income for the county government. The workhouse existed until 1928 when it was razed to make way for a new County Highway Department garage.

Fear of fire was the greatest concern on the minds of the Trustees of the Poor Farm and Asylum. The buildings were made of wood and built in close proximity to one another. Lack of access to high pressure water and inadequate fire service added to the anxiety. The risk of fire due to frequent thunderstorms was a continual concern knowing that many of the residents here were old and feeble...some were invalids. On July 30, 1902, a fire destroyed the barn and along with it the 1902 hay crop and a nearby shed. A new barn was built that same year only to be lost to another fire once again in 1903. Only one year later, in 1904, the straw barn burned along with its contents. The last two fires were costly as the buildings were only partially insured. Extensive improvements to the water supply and systems were made but to no avail. On November 19, 1908, fire destroyed the laundry facility resulting in a $1392 loss. It would burn again in 1937. Fire struck again on July 2, 1943 destroying the cow barn, the silos, the hay storage barn and the hog house. This time the total loss was over $15,000.

By 1906, the Poor House was in such deteriorated condition, it was decided a new facility would be built. The old building was scrapped and the salvage credit was applied toward the cost of the new building to house the poor.[4] The new Poor House was completed in 1907.

In 1918, a tornado swept through the area, destroying several Asylum and County Home structures in its path. The damage was covered by an insurance policy and the buildings were reconstructed.

Poor House circa 1906

Photo courtesy Dr. William Weber

On June 18, 1944 tragedy would strike once again. During a storm, the Poor House was hit by lightning. At four o'clock in the afternoon, a lightning bolt struck and shook the Poor Home. Although a careful check of the building was immediately made, a small smoldering fire went undiscovered. Five hours later the smoldering fire became an inferno and quickly engulfed the old building. The manager of the home, George Kitzman, tried fighting the blaze but only had the use of a small fire extinguisher. As the flames abruptly moved to the roof, all that was left was to rescue the seventy-two elderly patients trapped inside. The only phone available, which was installed for such an emergency, was knocked out of service by the storm. It was the only means available to summon the Fire Department.

Superintendent Arnemann jumped in his car and drove to town in the storm to get help, dodging fallen trees and flooded streets along the way. The County Sheriff's Department aided in the rescue of the patients, but the building was a complete loss and could not be saved. Luckily, no deaths or injuries occurred. Displaced patients were spread across various facilities, including the County Asylum, and across the state until a new building could be erected. But that, as it turned out, would take some time.

The threat of smallpox resulted in the creation of an isolation ward at the Poor Farm in 1909. All new inmates were screened by the County Physician prior to acceptance for residency. Also, an unoccupied portion of the Poor House was used as a tuberculosis sanatorium until the construction of Sunny View Tuberculosis Sanatorium (built on the same property of the Poor House and County Asylum) was completed in 1910.[5]

Otherwise known as 'consumption', Tuberculosis was a serious global problem and in 1890 the estimated number of diagnosis nationally exceeded one million or one in every sixty persons were afflicted. According to the website webmd.com :

> *Tuberculosis, commonly known as TB, is a bacterial infection that can spread through the lymph nodes and bloodstream to any organ in your body. It is most often found in the lungs. Most people who are exposed to TB never develop symptoms because the bacteria can live in an inactive form in the body. But if the immune system weakens, such as in people with HIV or elderly adults, TB bacteria can become active. In their active state, TB bacteria cause death of tissue in the organs they infect. Active TB disease can be fatal if left untreated. Because the bacteria that cause tuberculosis are transmitted through the air, the disease can be contagious.*

In the late 19th century, people were more susceptible to disease, in general, due to poor health, lack of widespread vaccinations, and lower immune systems due to poor living conditions.

The new sanatorium was designed by architects Auler and Jensen and the contractor chosen was CR Meyer from Oshkosh. A name was now needed for the new Sanatorium, so a contest was held and the winning submission came from a little girl who won the $10 prize. It would be called Sunny View Sanatorium.

Before this time, patients with tuberculosis were mixed within the general population of the mentally ill. This created problems in both the State and County Asylums, as overcrowding put undue pressure on the medical professionals staffed to treat mental illness. By having a facility dedicated to the treatment of TB much needed relief was brought to the asylums and resulted in better treatment for mental illness patients and tuberculosis patients alike. The same would be true for the Poor Farm, as it segmented patients with like illnesses into their respective care facilities. Additionally, Winnebago County received payment from the state to accept some cases of the insane. The chronic insane went to the county asylum, while the acute insane were admitted to the nearby Northern State Hospital.

In 1913 the County Board changed the name of the County Farm to the Winnebago County Asylum Farm and the Poor House and the five-acres surrounding it was renamed the County Home. The asylum facility would now be called the Winnebago County Asylum for the Chronically Insane.

When the Sunnyview Sanitorium opened, there was a waiting list of fifty-four patients, and staffing the new facility was getting off to a rocky start, as the Physician position became a revolving door. Dr. B.C. Gudden was appointed as the first Physician on June 1, 1915, but he resigned five months later. Succeeding him was Dr. H.H. Bessler who, in turn, resigned one month later. Finally, Dr. J.E. Schein became the third Physician in the first six months of operations. Mrs. Leola Trilkeld was appointed as the first Superintendent on March 16, 1915 but resigned after a few months due to ill health. Her successor, Miss Raddatz, also resigned after a six-month tenure.

Admission of infected patients into the Sanatorium was voluntary; they did not have to stay. However, the existence of two laws made the decision to remain easy for most. One law permitted a person within a community to declare another person a public menace. The patient then had a choice…jail or Sanatorium. Usually they chose the latter.

The other law included cases where children were exposed to someone with an active case of TB. In this instance, the child could be declared neglected and the charged adult taken from their home unless admitted as a patient. Patients that left Sunny View were either discharged or "left against medical advice". "Discharged" meant they were cured, where the latter meant they were still considered a public menace and could infect those in which they came in contact. One patient walked out of Sunny View on three separate occasions against medical advice. On one of his visits home, he infected his six-year old son who, in turn, became a patient at Sunny View in 1953.

A stigma was sometimes attached to being a patient at Sunnyview. Because of the contagious nature of TB, the facility was sometimes looked upon as a modern-day leper colony. Often deceased patient's bodies were not claimed by family members over fears of the infectious disease.

In 1923, the long-awaited Nurses Home was finally built with support of a grant from the will of Col. John Hicks. Previous to this, nurses resided in the sanatorium in space that was not being used for patient care. The Nurses Home was basically a dormitory that housed nurses employed at the Sanatorium.

The stock market crash of 1929 ushered in change to the way relief and assistance to the poor was administered. The creation of Social Security in the 1930s added some stability to folks who prospered one day and found themselves in dire straits the next. Federal, State, County, and City agencies offered various forms of relief, and foster care programs, creating improvements for the way children. Older adult assistance, public welfare, soldier relief funds, etc., some of which became long standing relief programs in the community, helped many through this difficult time.

In 1931, a unit for children was built to allow separation from the adult tuberculosis population. It opened on July 18, 1932 with eighteen children accounted for. Because of the number of children receiving lengthy care in the sanatorium, standard school books were purchased so the children could receive academic credit. It was around this same time that testing for TB was implemented in the public school system. The tuberculin test was done by injecting a small amount of tuberculin into the skin. If a slight swelling or redness appeared, it indicated a 'positive' reaction, meaning the person had been in contact with TB and bacteria had entered the body and was still active. If a person was found to test positive, the next step would include an x-ray to see if TB was present. If detected, the recommendation would be admission to Sunny View. X-rays were partially funded through the sales of Christmas Seals by the Wisconsin Tuberculosis Association. Christmas Seals were stamp-like in appearance and revenues collected in their sales was used to fight TB. Patrons would affix Christmas Seals to the envelopes of holiday greetings to show their support of finding a cure for this terrible disease.

Gravely ill patients knew they were getting worse as their condition deteriorated, slipping into a coma and dying. Some coughed until the cavity in their lungs hit a large blood vessel and they bled to death. When this happened, a "hemorrhage bell" would ring alerting the staff of the medical emergency and the medical team would respond immediately. A former patient recalled that when the bell sounded, everyone knew the gravity of the situation. The next morning, they would see the horse drawn wagon parked up next to the building. Deceased patients were put in a box, loaded onto the wagon, and taken to the Poor Farm Cemetery for burial.

With improved technology and treatment, along with the introduction of new medications, the battle with tuberculosis was won. Noticeable declines of TB took place in the 1950s and 1960s. A positive diagnosis that was once considered a death warrant was now treatable disease. Over 1800 patients died at Sunny View from its opening in 1915 until it closed its doors in 1971.

In November 1973, the County Board voted to raze the main building, boiler plant and other small buildings. The Sunny View Sanatorium came crashing down. Along with it went decades of treating a terrible disease…some results were good…some not.

The following quote is from *A History of Sunny View Sanatorium 1945-1974*, by James P. Coughlin and Linda Wolfe…

Tuberculosis no longer leads to a crushing ending like it did 30 years ago when an 18-year old girl was in her bed at Sunny View, surrounded by her family and a nurse. She had lost her awareness, babbling meaningless phrases every now and then between short periods of restless sleep.

Finally, she opened her eyes, staring straight up with a hypnotic gaze.

"I see Jesus," she said. "Momma, I see Jesus"

That was the last thing she said.

The decision to rebuild the Poor House after the fire of 1944 was handed to the Institutions Committee and discussions turned into debates when it was suggested that a new asylum was also needed. Housing insane patients in the same facility as the poor and aged would be a huge step backwards and was dismissed from consideration. Contemplations to possibly transfer the asylum's insane patients to the State Hospital and convert the County Asylum facility into the County Home were then given. The County Asylum building needed to be renovated but the plan was certainly economical as it avoided building new facilities. Further considerations were given to the recent progress of non-institutional relief available in Winnebago County, helping move the thought process more toward care for the aged.

Preliminary work began with architect Henry Auler, who was commissioned to draw up some sketches. Auler's proposal included the two-facility concept. His plan for an asylum included a facility that would accommodate 300 patients and 30 employees at an estimated cost of $585,000. The County Home facility could support 100 patients at a cost of $280,000.

With this new information in hand, the committee's position moved to one of remodeling the old asylum (at a cost of $25,000) to become the County Home for the aged and build a new asylum for the mentally ill. This plan was best suited, as it turned out since the State was over capacity and could not have accommodated the transfer of the insane patients from the County. Henry Auler was retained as the architect to design the new asylum.

Construction for the new county asylum began in 1950 and was not completed until 1952, which allowed the old asylum to be remodeled and used for housing the poor, aged and retired who were displaced with the fire of 1944.

The site chosen for the new asylum would be 300 feet south of the old asylum. The George A. Fuller Company was awarded the general contractor duties and the Winnebago County Highway Department constructed the roads, sidewalks and parking areas. The new facility was renamed the Winnebago County Hospital and housed both the aged and insane. The terms "Poor House" and "Asylum" would now fade into memory. The new County Hospital was completed in 1953 and on March 9th of that year, the Trustees of the Winnebago County Hospital (now known as the Winnebago County Park View Health Center Rehabilitation Pavillion at 725 Butler Avenue) were granted occupancy of the new facility.

In 1953, the Poor House no longer suited its past functionality. The facility altered its style of care and became the Winnebago County Home for the Retired in May of that year.

Remodeling the old asylum facility began in the fall of 1954 with Robert Wertsch of Oshkosh as architect. The remodel was completed in 1957 with a patient capacity of 125.

The renovated facility was nicely decorated with new upgraded amenities including a beauty salon, barber shop, medical office, kitchenettes, room for reading, television and a bowling alley. The improvements were positive, but it was still a sixty-four-year-old building and time was not on its side.

By the early 1960s the Winnebago County Home for the Retired was now named Pleasant Acres and the aging facility came under the scrutiny of the State Department of Public Welfare. Even though the County Home had undergone extensive renovations, problems with termites, a cracked foundation, and antiquated plumbing caused the State Department of Public Welfare to declare the facility in violation of safety standards. Pleasant Acres was staring in the face of possible condemnation. Realization that patient care now required more infirmary care which the old building design did not afford, became an issue. The County Board was once again faced with the consideration of erecting a new facility. With repair costs soaring, the County Board decided to construct a new building.

The decision was made in 1965 to move forward with building a new four-story facility at a cost of over $2.5 million. Ben B. Ganther was hired and construction of the new home began in 1966.

Pleasant Acres reopened on September 11, 1967. The new facility was a vast improvement over the old Asylum/Poor House it replaced. The building now had four stories. Subsequently, the Winnebago County Hospital, Pleasant Acres Skilled Nursing Home and the Park

View Health and Guidance Center all formally became Park View Health Center in April 1973. One year later, a nine-member board was organized and named the Winnebago Community Mental Health, Developmental Disabilities, Alcohol and Drug Abuse Services Board. A separate board was appointed to handle the Pleasant Acres Nursing Home.

County farming operations concluded in the fall of 1965. Buildings had deteriorated into poor condition. Past benefits to patients were no longer deemed critical, considering the cost to maintain the farming operation was a $52,000 deficit annually. Prior accounting methods were shown to inaccurately illustrate the true cost of operations and the decision was made to terminate the farm. A statement made by Superintendent William Vogel in 1963 claimed, "To justify its (reference to the farm operation) perpetuation on the basis of patient therapy is false". In October 1965, an auction was held liquidating all the equipment and animals from the Poor Farm and most of the farm buildings were razed. Those that were still in good condition were rented out to local farmers. In 1968, the old Asylum/Poor House burned down during demolition. The land it once occupied became the current Winnebago County Community Park. Today, the only buildings that remain are the milk house barn and hog shed.

(Authors Note: Sadly, I understand that it is the county's intention to raze the old dairy barn in 2018. Once used by the county for storage and maintenance, the building has fallen into disrepair, due to neglected continued maintenance. The cost to repurpose this historic old building was deemed not worthy according to Winnebago County Executive Mark Harris)

Today Park View consists of the Rehabilitation Pavilion and Pleasant Acres and serves as the County Nursing Home for individuals with short-term rehabilitation and long-term needs including dementia, Alzheimer's disease, psychiatric diagnoses, and developmentally disabled individuals who required nursing home care.

In 2006/2007, a new building was constructed to replace the aging facilities.

Sources: (1) http://digicoll.library.wisc.edu/; (2) *Poor Farm Cemetery, Winnebago County Wisconsin*, 2010, Janet Eiler, Jean Dunn; (3) *Oshkosh One Hundred Years A City*, Clinton Karsteadt pp. 116-117, 119-120; (4) *A History of the Winnebago County Poor Farm* by. G. Koppelberger; Oshkosh Public Museum – oshkoshmuseum.past perfect-online.com; (5) Park View Health Center Timeline 1875-2013; *A History of Sunny View Sanatorium, 1915-1974*, James Coughlin and Linda Wolfe; http:// digicoll.library.wisc.edu/

The Poor Farm/Sunnyview Cemetery

As was the case at the Northern Hospital for the Insane, the County was required to provide a burial place for deceased patients that were not claimed by family. On a plot of land in the far northwest corner of the county owned property, a 'Potters Field' cemetery was established. The date of establishment is believed to have been around 1871. The cemetery sign at the entrance reads 1888, but later research by local genealogists discovered earlier burials. An article printed in the *Oshkosh Daily Northwestern* on November 28, 1879 reported a meeting was held and a request received to have the "burying ground on the farm enclosed in a fence." According to Janet Eiler, Winnebago County Genealogy President, the first year of any known burials was that of Mrs. Porlis in 1876. "The next burials of record we found happened in1878. The early burials did not have a number assigned to them as it is speculated the numbering system was utilized until later."

Patients were interred here because either they had no family to claim them upon their death, or the families did not have the means to provide a burial on their own. Some families refused to accept the remains of deceased tuberculosis patients, holding false fears that the disease was still communicable. It was a difficult time in those early years and for many, especially immigrants, America was a new world. Not everyone was fortunate enough to be able to tend to their own well-being. Some were real heroes in life and left this world a pauper. Seventeen Civil War Veterans are buried here (one veteran received the Distinguished Service Award), two widows of Civil War Veterans and one man from the Spanish American War.

Approximately 400 souls now rest here from so many different walks of life. Each grave is marked with a small, flat concrete marker and a number…no names. Men, women, fathers, mothers and even babies are among the burials. If a mother who resided at the Poor

House or County Asylum died in childbirth and the baby was still born or died shortly after birth, they were buried together. Often a child who died after the parent was buried in the same grave, but not so deep. As you walk through the cemetery, you will notice many graves sunken, evidenced by slight depressions in the ground. Burials back then were made with minimal expense. No concrete vaults were used. Records indicate pine boxes were built at a cost between $2-$5 and placed directly in the ground. Over time the makeshift coffins have deteriorated creating the depressions.

In 2003, local citizen Vicky Redlin became interested in the cemetery and contacted the Winnebago County Genealogical Society for assistance in researching the cemetery. Society President Janet Eiler along with society members worked feverishly to uncover as much information as possible.

Their work is evidenced by the book they published in 2010 titled *Poor Farm Cemetery, Winnebago County Wisconsin*. Vicky and Janet along with the help of volunteers organized improvements to the cemetery that included erecting a flagpole (erected and paid for by Winnebago County) to honor the veterans buried here. The brick base around the flagpole was made of bricks from the old Nurses dormitory that has since been torn down. They also cleared brush, painted the gate, and placed the statue of an angel (which Vicky paid for on her own) in the center of the grounds. Standing in the corner of the cemetery is a kiosk containing a list they compiled of burials that include name, date of birth and death and grave number.

Today, the cemetery is called the Sunnyview Cemetery as it is located at the north end of Butler Avenue behind the Sunnyview Exposition Center on County Road Y. The unpaved, gravel road travels north off County Road Y about one quarter mile and brings you to the entrance of the cemetery. Inside the entrance is a plot of land, roughly one acre in size that is maintained by the Winnebago County Parks Department. The cemetery seems a bit odd at first, as you will notice the absence of ornate grave markers and monuments; no flowers placed in the memories of loved ones…only a small concrete pad with a number, marking someone's lonely existence – their destiny ending in obscurity. No one comes to visit, save the few who still hold the memories of a time when life was not easy.

If you decide to pay a visit to these cemeteries, walk softly and carefully with respect among the markers. Remove your cap and quietly say a prayer for those who have been forsaken in time.

Sources: *Poor Farm Cemetery, Winnebago County Wisconsin, 2010 Edition*, Janet Eiler and Jean Dunn; *A History of Sunny View Sanatorium 1945-1974*, James P. Coughlin and Linda Wolfe; *Oshkosh One Hundred Years A City*, Clinton Karsteadt pp 116-117, 119-120;

FOUR MILES NORTH...CLOSING THOUGHTS

In my past experiences of researching local history, I have never been more moved as much as I have been in writing this chapter. Although I found it to be informative and educational, it became very emotional for me. My thoughts placed me right there during these extremely difficult times and I could feel the sadness that surrounded the lives of so many people. I found myself lifted at times, reading of the compassion of some of the Directors and Superintendents. I was brought to tears with Dr. Gordon's explanation of the residents of the Poor House and the young girl, dying of TB, who described what she saw in the waning moments of her life. I mourned for the emptiness and obscurity of the cemeteries where mothers, babies, war heroes and the hundreds of less fortunates found their final resting place in a potter's field. I felt the ravages of tuberculosis, the calamity of mental illness, the tragedies of poverty and the struggle of so many that often led to a dismal ending in life. Writing this story has truly been a life-changing experience for me. I now view things in a different light through a better understanding of what it must have been like to persevere through such difficult conditions.

I would like to offer my sincere thanks to the people who helped me research and write this chapter. Personal interviews with Vicky Redlin, Janet Eiler, Paul Janty, Linda Schueler, Kathy Krahulic, and Tom Geske...the writings of Julaine Farrow, James Coughlin, G. Koppelberger and others listed within. A special thank you to Dr. William Weber for his personal and professional insights. Without their first-hand knowledge and experience, telling this story in the context in which it needs to be presented would not have been possible.

EPILOGUE

These stories serve as a reminder of not only *our* past, but also of the days previous to our existence. Learning of the struggles of our ancestors who emigrated to this wilderness in the mid-1800s, help us understand that forging a new life here was no easy task. It required a strong back, an undeterred spirit, and a determined will to not only survive, but succeed in their quest to find a better life.

This same spirit lives on today within ourselves, our parents and grandparents…each generation wanting a better life for their children. It always has been the dream.

It is for this reason that we write these stories and tell the tales left behind by those who bravely ventured forth ahead of us. It is our responsibility to embrace and preserve our past for future generations.

For as we know…

We Shall Never Pass This Way Again

ACKNOWLEDGEMENTS

My sincere thanks and deepest gratitude is extended to those who unselfishly gave their time and shared their wonderful memories and experiences with me. Recalling and preserving local history is a collaborative effort of people who share the passion and understand the significance of recalling and recording our past. A special thank you to my Editors - Heather Rae Connors and Karen Domer. Thanks for smoothing out the bumps!

Paul Janty

Linda Schueler

Vicky Redlin

Janet Eiler

Randy Priem

Alan Repp

Robert Miller

Harriet and Brian Bradley

Dan Radig

Mara Munroe

Neil Starkey

Carol Miller

Stanley Schuster

Ed Tiedje

Bob Volz

Dan Butkiewicz

Lee Reiherzer

Patti Yana

Nathaniel Shuda

Richard Miller

Ginny Gross

Steve Cummings

Elizabeth Cummings

Michael McArthur

OTHER BOOKS BY RANDY DOMER...

Yesterday In Oshkosh...My Hometown

"Domer takes us on a nostalgic journey of living in Oshkosh, Wisconsin in the 1950s and 1960s. His tales take us back to a time when a family night out usually meant eating at a drive-in and going to the Outdoor Theater in our pajamas. His experiences growing up on the city's "west-side" are sure to rekindle memories for everyone who enjoy relating back to those days of old in their own hometown. If you remember corner grocery stores, mile delivered to your door, the downtown movie theaters, pizza parlors and the numerous people who made Oshkosh what it is today, then you will enjoy "Yesterday In Oshkosh...My Hometown"

"What a flash from the past! It really brought back lots of great childhood memories. Thank you Randy!" - Georgia Buttke

"The memories you brought back to us are priceless! Almost each chapter had real meaning for our family...I used to live on Otter Street when growing up and when Billy Hoeft would drive by in his Pontiac convertible we (us very young girls) would drool!" - Carol and Jack Schiessl

"I was so moved by the description of your Uncle Ralph's WWII death that I went to South Park and took photos of the memorial" - James M. Frey

"Very well written 'walk down memory lane'. I cried [reading about your uncle's death] in France." - Grace Sullivan

OSHKOSH: LAND OF LAKEFLIES, BUBBLERS, AND SQUEAKY CHEESE

"*D*omer provides an inside glimpse into the people, places and things that make this area special and unique. He leans on personal experiences, memories and research to unearth things you may have never known about historic Oshkosh. Maybe you remember the days when men earned a living catching frogs and turtles. Or perhaps you can recall the Orphanage on Oshkosh's west side. Possibly you even enjoyed an Alaska Pop or that wonderful Smith Ice Cream. He will introduce you to a few people who rose to prominence, built a submarine, or have become a key part of our local history. Join us now on a journey with a closer look at what made Oshkosh what it is today."

"It is vital to the future of Oshkosh that we embrace and celebrate our rich and diverse heritage. Randy Domer provides us with a wonderful perspective about the people, places and events that have made us who we are today."

-Steve Cummings, Mayor, City of Oshkosh

"We found the book most interesting, and the aviation sections were well done." - Abe and Theda Eckstein (daughter of Leonard Larson)

CPSIA information can be obtained
at www.ICGtesting.com
Printed in the USA
FFHW020138231218
49968997-54642FF